Praise fo[r]

POWERLINES

Words That Sell Brands, Grip Fans, and Sometimes Change History

by Steve Cone

"*Powerlines* is an illuminating, informative, and entertainingly irreverent study of slogans that can sustain or sink a brand. With identity and differentiation increasingly central to corporate success, it is an important book for marketers and senior executives."

John Ridding
CEO, *Financial Times*

"Marketing guru Steve Cone rediscovers the lost art of great slogans, mottos, and taglines. The lesson? Be all that you can be. Shots can still be heard 'round the world. Things go better with inspired taglines. And that's the way it is."

L. Gordon Crovitz
Former publisher, *The Wall Street Journal*

"An important primer. Steve Cone shows how picking the right words often makes the difference between success and failure."

Larry King
Host of CNN's *Larry King Live*

"Steve Cone makes the power of words come to life in a remarkable fashion. He has made an art form of crafting a few words to leave an indelible impression. This book should serve as an invaluable guide for corporate executives and candidates on how to succeed with words."

Jim Gray
Emmy Award-winning sportscaster

POWERLINES

POWERLINES

WORDS THAT SELL BRANDS, GRIP FANS, AND SOMETIMES CHANGE HISTORY

Steve Cone

Viva Books

New Delhi | Mumbai | Chennai | Kolkata | Bangalore | Hyderabad | Kochi | Guwahati

First Indian Edition 2009

VIVA BOOKS PRIVATE LIMITED

- 4737/23 Ansari Road, Daryaganj, New Delhi 110 002
  E-mail: vivadelhi@vivagroupindia.net, Tel. 42242200
- 76, Service Industries, Shirvane, Sector 1, Nerul, Navi Mumbai 400 706
  E-mail: vivamumbai@vivagroupindia.net, Tel. 27721273, 27721274
- Jamals Fazal Chambers, 26 Greams Road, Chennai 600 006
  E-mail: vivachennai@vivagroupindia.net, Tel. 28290304, 28294241
- B-103, Jindal Towers, 21/1A/3 Darga Road, Kolkata 700 017
  E-mail: vivakolkata@vivagroupindia.net, Tel. 22836381, 22816713
- 7, Sovereign Park Apartments, 56-58, K. R. Road, Basavanagudi, Bangalore 560 004
  E-mail: vivabangalore@vivagroupindia.net, Tel. 26607409, 26607410
- 101-102 Mughal Marc Apartments, 3-4-637 to 641, Narayanguda, Hyderabad 500 029
  E-mail: vivahyderabad@vivagroupindia.net, Tel. 27564481, 27564482
- First Floor, Beevi Towers, SRM Road, Kaloor, Kochi 682 018, Kerala
  E-mail: vivakochi@vivagroupindia.net, Tel: 0484-2403055, 2403056
- H. No. 12, P. B. Road, Rehabari, Near Arya Hospital, Guwahati 781 008
  E-mail: vivaguwahati@vivagroupindia.net, Tel: 0361-2735624

www.vivagroupindia.com

Published by arrangement with

Bloomberg Press
731 Lexington Avenue
New York, NY 10022

ISBN-10: 81-309-1126-4
ISBN-13: 978-81-309-1126-7

Published by Vinod Vasishtha for Viva Books Private Limited, 4737/23, Ansari Road, Daryaganj, New Delhi - 110 002.

Printed and bound by Raj Press, R-3, Inderpuri, New Delhi - 110 012.

In memory of Thomas T.D. Donovan, my high-school English master who helped me—and so many others—learn to love our language. His often-repeated powerline in class: "Gentlemen, I am your warmest admirer and severest critic."

Words are loaded pistols.

—JEAN-PAUL SARTRE, "What Is Literature?"

CONTENTS

For bonus chapters, full-color ads, and updates from Steve Cone, visit **www.powerlines.biz.**

ACKNOWLEDGMENTS

THANK YOU FIRST and foremost to Faye my "secret editor in chief" and sounding board from start to finish. And thanks to my friends who gave and give great advice and comment on my prose, particularly Joni Evans, Bob Perkins, and Wendy Snyder. Also thanks to my pals at Bloomberg Press who believe in me and my work, particularly John Crutcher, Andrew Feldman, and my editor Janet Coleman.

MARKETING LINGO

powerline. A written or spoken phrase, line, or expression so artful and so compelling that it becomes the line that comes first to mind when people describe the era when it first appeared. In marketing, a unique brand signature that sells a person, place, product, or service more effectively than the lines used by competitors because the brands and brand promises it defines are unforgettable.

slogan. A memorable phrase expressing an idea, purpose, or claim. From the Scottish Gaelic word *sluagh-ghairm*, pronounced slogorm, the word slogan means "battle cry." A political slogan almost always focuses on a goal or belief, whereas slogans used in commercial advertising claim special qualities for a specific product or service.

tagline. A slogan that is trademarked and exclusive to commercial advertising and promotion. It is a claim about exactly what the branded product or service stands for, as well as a promise of what to expect when experiencing the brand firsthand.

motto. An expression of a guiding principle of a family, club, organization, or government. Often inscribed on a badge, banner, coat of arms, monetary instrument, or license plate. Some slogans and mottos are one and the same and in these cases, the terms are interchangeable.

jingle. An advertising slogan or tagline set to a short melody.

INTRODUCTION

Car 54, Where Are You?

We humans have been speaking to each other for thousands of years, yet how often do any of us stop to think about how powerful the right few words can be? Words, when chosen well, have the power to awe, inspire, motivate, alienate, subjugate, even alter something as significant as the course of history, or as cosmically minute as the buying habits of consumers.

Powerful words—ones that persuade, cajole and compel people to buy—are my business. I am a marketing expert, specifically an expert in writing the words that define brands.

A year ago, I started investigating more deeply why some lines stick in the mind forever and others make no impression at all. The expressions that were memorable, persuasive, and powerful were more than mere slogans and taglines. They were truly *powerlines*—words that sell brands, grip fans, and sometimes change history.

At one level, this book is about an important but neglected part of marketing: the slogans, taglines, and jingles that grab our attention, spark our interest, and compel us to remember and buy products and services.

At another level, it is about the human condition. To understand powerlines is to understand ourselves—what we value and remember and what we discard and forget. Powerlines do more than attract us; they change us. They are supposed to. In marketing, the word *impressions* means "the number of promotional units a person is subjected to." A television ad is one unit; passing a billboard on the road is one unit, and so on. Impressions surround us every day of our lives, from our first breath to our last. Based on a casual estimate, we humans crawl, walk, daydream, and even sleep through billions of impressions during our lifetimes. Seemingly random, the stimuli from continuous sights and sounds have a constant influence.

The Mysteries of Memory

Often the impressions that stick in our minds are those that we see or hear over and over again. The ones that linger longest are those that combine sight, rhythm, and sound to deliver a message.

But even a chance exposure can leave a lasting impression. Sometimes hearing or seeing a line once is all it takes to remember it the rest of our lives. Somehow it finds a place for itself inside all that gray matter and stays. We recall the line days later, years later, decades later. It is a part of us. It adds to our makeup, our outlook on all aspects of life. It becomes part of our personal language with all its nuances and double meanings.

Memory's elusiveness remains a constant—why do we remember this … and not that?

For instance, I can remember word-for-word the opening theme of *Car 54, Where Are You?*, a half-hour sitcom about two bumbling New York City cops, which I haven't seen since childhood.

Here's the theme song: "There's a holdup in the Bronx, Brooklyn's broken out in fights. There's a traffic jam in Harlem that's backed up to Jackson Heights. There's a scout troop short a child. Krushchev's due at Idlewild. Car 54, where are you?"

I can also remember the dialogue from a great scene in Stanley Kubrick's 1966 film *Dr. Strangelove*, a dark comedy that ridicules the notion that global nuclear war is actually winnable.

In the movie, the president of the United States, played by Peter Sellers, invites the Soviet ambassador to the nerve center of our military might, the Pentagon War Room, while the president and his security advisers are attempting to recall a wayward B-52 bomber on its way to nuke Russia.

In the middle of Sellers' attempt to convince the ambassador that everything that can be done will be done to recall or destroy the B-52, dissension breaks out among the military men in the room.

First, the head of the Strategic Air Command, played by George C. Scott, starts shouting. "We can get the Ruskies with their pants down," he says. "We should just launch our entire arsenal right now and destroy them once and for all."

The Russian ambassador loudly takes exception to these remarks, and the screaming match quickly escalates the brink of a brawl. Finally, the president shouts at both men: "Gentlemen, you cannot fight in here. This is the War Room!"

Now that's a great line.

The Forgetting of Things Past

Since the beginning of the Industrial Revolution, taglines have been critical elements in building brands, campaigns, and businesses. Yet over the past fifteen years, very few memorable lines have been produced. In fact, most slogans today mean nothing, do not spell out a unique selling proposition, are dull, and get no traction with the consumer.

Take the auto industry. It's difficult to recall one recent slogan for any car company other than BMW's long-running tagline, "The Ultimate Driving Machine." America once had a tradition of decent automobile taglines, including: "See the U.S.A. in Your Chevrolet" and "Have You Driven a Ford Lately?" But these have vanished and not been replaced. The auto industry has scrambled for years to come up with great lines, to no avail.

What about financial services? No great lines today, just meaningless words that do not tell a compelling story. Fidelity with "Smart Move." Bank of America with "Higher Standards" and "Bank of Opportunity." UBS with "You and Us." All these garner little attention and virtually no retention.

Even political rhetoric has fallen into the valley of slogan death. There hasn't been a memorable presidential campaign slogan since 1984 when Hal Riney, a gifted copywriter and advertising agency founder created "It's Morning Again in America" for Ronald Reagan. Walter Mondale, Reagan's opponent that year, could only dredge up "America Needs a Change." What a snore.

Speaking of putting America to sleep, John Kerry and George W. Bush produced these soporifics in the 2004 campaign: "Let America Be America Again" (Kerry) and "Yes, America Can!" (Bush). Is anyone still awake?

Clearly, we marketers have lost our ability to recognize and create memorable slogans and taglines. We must reclaim the amazing power that a well-crafted line can muster for any business anywhere on the planet.

Back to the Future

Here's the plan. First, I will take you on a journey through the powerline universe: from lines in advertising, literature, movies, politics, and history, to the people famous for creating them, and to the effect these lines have had on cultures through the years. There is much to be learned from the powerlines of the past.

I will analyze slogans and jingles from advertising's early days up to the present and leave you with no doubt that creating powerlines is the most critical part of every marketer's job. Then I will explain why, unlike in earlier decades, it is a lost art today.

Next, I will show how to create powerlines that define your business and allow you to rise above—maybe *far* above—all your worthy competitors.

I promise you do not have to be a marketing junkie to enjoy this book. It's not technical or jargon-laden. Anyone from fourteen to ninety-four should find it entertaining and, dare I say, educational.

I hope you come away with a better understanding of a subject that has been kept on the back burner far too long, a subject that binds all humans together and makes us better for remembering the rich and rewarding impressions that make up the fabric of daily life.

PART ONE

POWERLINES

Getting the Right Few Words to Every Nook and Cranny on the Planet

Powerlines can come from anywhere: literature, politics, military leaders, religion and philosophy, theater, stand-up comics, advertising copywriters, even the neighbor next door.

CHAPTER **1**

Powerlines Defined

Factors Distinguishing Powerlines from 99 Percent of All Written and Spoken Language

THINK OF THE ULTIMATE ONE-LINER: "I love you."

It's universally meaningful. It stands by itself. It creates emotion immediately. It cannot be ignored. It's a powerline.

Much more intensely than a typical phrase, slogan, jingle, or expression, a powerline delivers an electric surge, a current that charges the mind long after the initial message is received.

A powerline is one of the most valuable and powerful tools available to any marketer. Think what "When it rains it pours" (1912) did for Morton salt, "You Deserve a Break Today" (1971) did for McDonald's, or "A Diamond Is Forever" (1948) did for De Beers.

Alas, in this technology-driven twenty-first century, powerlines are rarely used and their strength and simplicity are poorly understood.

Powerlines are different from 99 percent of written and spoken language for three major reasons.

First, they tell a *compelling* story that has lasting impact about an event, person, place, product, or a part of human nature. Sometimes these lines are a few words, sometimes several sentences, and once in a great while, just one word.

Second, powerlines *ring true*. They are genuine reflections of whatever they refer to. Overreaching is the cardinal sin when creating a powerline. A powerline that overpromises does not attract people; it pushes them away.

One of the best-remembered powerlines from the World War II era was a single word spoken in the heat of battle by the American acting commander, General Anthony McAuliffe.

The last major battle of the war in Europe was a particularly nasty one called the Battle of the Bulge. The early days of this conflict had favored the Germans. By December 1944, one critical piece of real estate remained—Bastogne, Belgium, where the American 101st Airborne Division was stranded, surrounded by the enemy.

On December 22, 1944, the German forces called on General McAuliffe to surrender and save his troops from certain starvation, death, and defeat. Instead, McAuliffe sent back this message:

> To the German Commander,
> NUTS!
> The American Commander

"Nuts," indeed. From a purely strategic standpoint, the American general's response was spontaneous folly. Yet his attitude prevailed and won the day. American forces successfully defended Bastogne and thwarted the German advance. The tide of the Bulge Campaign had turned, paving the way for the eventual defeat of Germany.

The General told the whole story with one well-chosen word.

Powerlines ring true: "Nuts!"

Powerlines tell a compelling story: We will not surrender.

The Power of Sound

The third thing powerlines have going for them is sound.

Lines that grab attention and turbocharge people's memory banks are usually spoken aloud with skillful inflection … inflection that evolved for the sole purpose of survival. Back in caveman times, "saber-toothed tiger, heading for you, getting close, getting closer, better run, better run faster," had a sound pattern all its own (different from, say, "Throw another log on the fire"). Those who ignored the shouted warning rarely lived to see another day.

We instinctively pay attention when the message has a cadence, when the words rhyme, or are repeated in the same sequence.

Sound = Instant Recall

As a lucky teenager, I attended a superb boarding school. A stone church with a huge clock tower sits at the highest point on campus. Every night and day of my four-year stay, the tower clock chimed in fifteen-minute intervals from 7 a.m. to 11 p.m. and hourly throughout the night.

Since then, wherever and whenever I hear a church clock chime, I'm transported back to my school days and their host of teenage recollections. This memory surge is automatic, like breathing. Nothing waits for me to say, "Hey brain, remember the school church clock."

Sound = Pure Emotion

Sound is a series of vibrations that equals pure emotion. All animals make noises that their brethren instantly recognize, expressing the whole range of emotions from extreme happiness to utter despair. Humans take this one step further and translate sound into marketing cues that signal what to buy and what to avoid.

Of all the senses, hearing evokes the strongest feelings. Remember your favorite movie. Now imagine watching that movie with the sound off. It would be a very flat experience, hardly worth watching. (Even silent movies had soundtracks: theater owners provided live piano players to add sound and keep viewers in their seats.)

Sound Sells

Sound has impact.

Savvy car manufacturers know that one of the biggest selling features of their autos, particularly luxury models, is the sound of the car door opening and closing. Some smart auto executives have whole teams that focus exclusively on the sounds their cars make, including the doors, windows, knobs, shifts, and even seat cushions.

And, of course, there are car engine sounds. Especially in the sports car and high-end markets, the sound of the engine is not only a major selling feature, but a distinct signature that defines the brand … think Porsche, Ferrari, Bentley, Rolls-Royce. Each has its own "engine sound track" that enthusiasts have come to expect.

Sound also affects eating and shopping. A 1982 study by Ronald E. Millman for the *Journal of Consumer Research* showed that the pace and tempo of background music in stores and restaurants affects sales. Basically, the slower the music tempo, the more people shop and the slower they eat. The slower people eat, the more high-profit beverages they drink.

Another curious example of sound's effect concerns Las Vegas slot machines. Casino owners have experimented with electronic machines where coins are unnecessary. No dice. Patrons want to pull the one-armed bandit and insert coins, hear them drop, and listen to the sound of a payout as coins jingle and cascade into the tray.

Words Are for Speaking Like Fish Are for Swimming

For a combination of words to achieve powerline status, it must be spoken or sung, and repeated as often as possible.

The lines we remember best come to us in the sound of someone's voice either at home, at school, at church, at the movies, on radio, or on TV. The richness of the spoken word trumps print every time. Marshall McLuhan, one of the brightest media minds, said this clearly:

> Many a page of prose and many a narrative have been devoted to expressing what was in effect, a sob, a moan, a laugh, or a piercing scream. The written word spells out in sequence what is quick and implicit in the spoken word.

Civilization started with cries, grunts, groans, chants, and songs. This verbal hash eventually turned into language. Alphabets were devised and people were able to more precisely communicate with each other, even from a distance. Progress, yes. But once the face-to-face element was out of the picture, communication became less aural and more impersonal.

Many marketing professionals do not appreciate the power of the spoken word. They have been mesmerized by the siren song of the Internet and e-mail as dominant forms of communication. Fine, except very little in these two channels is spoken or played back in sound form. And when it is, it often seems disjointed and artificial.

Hear Me, Feel Me

Abraham Lincoln wrote the Gettysburg Address in 1863 on a train traveling from Washington, DC to Pennsylvania so he would have something to say to commemorate what was then and still remains the bloodiest battle in American history.

American schoolchildren memorize and recite Lincoln's short speech to get a better sense of the man and his times. Printed words on a page communicate some of the meaning and power of his message. But to feel the full strength of Lincoln's words, recite the speech out loud. Then you will feel the effect of his words and his delivery on the crowd gathered that day in 1863. Had Lincoln's address been printed in a few newspapers and not declaimed to an audience, I doubt American schoolchildren would be memorizing and reciting it each year.

HISTORICAL SIDELIGHT There are no photographs of Lincoln giving this address. Lincoln finished the speech—seven minutes from start to finish—before the many photographers on-site had set up their equipment. They had assumed that Lincoln, like most orators of the time, would ramble on for at least a half hour!

The Power of Story

We humans first organized our thoughts into narratives thousands of years ago. Our ancestors used stories to pass experiences, customs, procedures, and skills from generation to generation. The most important information was formulated into a short set of instructions and repeated, repeated, and repeated until the elders were convinced the younger set could remember and execute their social responsibilities.

It is not surprising that sayings, jingles, slogans, and lines of all kinds that stick in our minds are often short and to the point.

Powerlines in the Nursery

In the West, nursery rhymes are the first stories most children encounter. Basically jingles that use inflection, rhyme, and repetition, nursery rhymes contain all the building blocks of powerlines.

Some of the most popular nursery rhymes have been with us for centuries. These powerlines survive because it's fun to speak in rhymes to our young children and have them appreciate our language and repeat it back to us. This is just what early humans did to communicate with each other in a meaningful way. The power of reciting, of singing, and of acting, versus silent reading should not be underestimated; it is a key element in the evolution of our species. The spoken word repeated over and over makes all the difference in what humans remember.

Popular nursery rhymes have their origins in European history and often refer to extremely violent events, customs of the day, or military victories and defeats. Here are a few of the most well known, accompanied by their backstories.

Warfare on Land and Sea

"Rain, Rain, Go Away," author unknown, first appeared in print around 1600:

> Rain, rain, go away,
> Come again another day.
> Little Johnny wants to play;
> Rain, rain, go to Spain,
> Never show your face again!

This rhyme is about the defeat of the Spanish armada at the hands of the British in 1588. Queen Elizabeth I bickered constantly with the Spanish, finally incensing them so much that they sent a fleet of 130 ships carrying over twenty thousand sailors to crush the British Navy. The latter at the time was comprised of thirty-four small naval boats and a ragtag collection of armed merchant ships.

Stormy weather came to the aid of the British. The wind and rain made it tough going for the heavy and slower Spanish warships, widely separated in the storm and easily picked off one by one by the more nimble British contingent. The Spanish fleet lost half its soldiers and over one hundred ships. And a British nursery rhyme was born.

"Humpty Dumpty," author unknown, originated around 1659, first published in 1810:

Humpty Dumpty sat on a wall,
Humpty Dumpty had a great fall;
All the King's horses, and all the King's men
Couldn't put Humpty together again!

The name of the hero of this seventeenth-century rhyme comes straight from the fifteenth century when "Humpty Dumpty" connoted a short, obese person.

A number of theories claim to correctly identify Humpty. The most popular says that he was a large cannon mounted on the roof of St. Mary's Church in Colchester during the English Civil War of 1648. At the time the rhyme was set, the Royalists controlled the town, which was under siege by the opposing Parlementarians. Eventually, the Parlementarians blew up the church tower and its cannon, sending Humpty tumbling groundward. Humpty was so heavy that all the King's men couldn't get him back into service. The siege ended shortly thereafter and the Royalists surrendered.

Additional verses support this theory:

In Sixteen Hundred and Forty-Eight
When England suffered the pains of state
The Roundheads lay siege to Colchester town
Where the King's men still fought for the crown
There one-eyed Thompson stood on the wall
A gunner of deadliest aim
From St. Mary's Tower his cannon he fired
Humpty-Dumpty was its name ...

Death and Dismemberment

"Three Blind Mice," author unknown, was composed circa 1600:

Three blind mice, three blind mice,
See how they run, see how they run,
They all ran after the farmer's wife,
Who cut off their tails with a carving knife,
Did you ever see such a sight in your life,
As three blind mice?

This rhyme tells the story of Mary I, a.k.a. the farmer's wife, daughter of Henry VIII, and wife of King Philip of Spain. (Mary and her husband owned vast farming estates.) Mary was a staunch Catholic and very unfriendly to anyone Protestant. Her nickname, Bloody Mary, did not come by accident and lives on today in alcoholic form at your local bar.

The blind mice were three unfortunate Protestant noblemen who were convicted of plotting to have Mary removed from the throne and the planet. They were neither dismembered nor blinded as the nursery rhyme implies, but burned at the stake.

In spite of the historical inaccuracy, this rhyme has been memorized by millions of English-speaking children since Mary's reign—another testament to the power of rhymes!

"Jack and Jill," author unknown, was first published in 1795:

> Jack and Jill went up the hill to fetch a pail of water;
> Jack fell down, and broke his crown,
> And Jill came tumbling after.

This rhyme is a direct reference to the beheading of Louis XVI, followed by that of his mate, Queen Marie Antoinette, whose head "came tumbling after."

At the time, the French were living through the Reign of Terror, with public beheadings a daily occurrence. While commemorating the beheading of a king and his queen, the writer apparently wanted to provide a happy ending so parents could recite this story to their children:

> Up got Jack, and home did trot
> As fast as he could caper;
> He went to bed and bound his head
> With vinegar and brown paper.

Death and Disease

"Ring Around the Rosy," author unknown, was composed around 1300:

Ring around the rosy
A pocketful of posies
"Ashes, ashes"
We all fall down!

Probably the oldest known nursery rhyme, "Ring Around the Rosy," is thought to refer to a bubonic plague epidemic that occurred seven hundred years ago. That particular outbreak killed over seventy-five million people in three years—roughly a third of the population of Europe. Symptoms included a red skin rash in the shape of a ring. It was thought that filling your pockets with sweet smelling herbs (posies) would do the trick and ward off the disease. Physicians at the time thought that bad smells, of which there were many, spread the disease from one person to another. The real culprits, rats and the fleas that bit them, were never fingered as carriers. "Ashes, ashes" refers to the cremation of all the dead bodies that, of course, added to the stench.

The bottom line on nursery rhymes is their amazing longevity, despite the fact that we have scant knowledge of their origins or meaning.

Our Brains on Powerlines

This is a good spot to take a short look at why our human brain is geared to recall lines and phrases.

The answer is: to survive. Our brains have learned to store anything and everything that may come in handy for the future … the next minute, day, week, or year. Throughout our lives, we store and recall seemingly endless sequences of songs, jingles, rhymes, lines, and quotes. Just one note or word or even the announcement that a song is about to be played, given we have enjoyed it in the past, will trigger our internal jukebox to immediately recall the song. We can sing along when the music begins, whether we last heard it three or thirty years ago. If we have heard something before, if we are familiar with the sequence, it will come back to us.

We predict speech patterns every day and millions of times throughout our lives. If we have dinner with family or friends and someone says, "Would you please pass the bread basket," we know what they will likely ask for next. We have figured out the most likely sequences instantaneously and therefore reply "would you like the butter, too?" Our brains use memories to constantly make predictions about what we see, feel, and hear.

Some lines are easy to remember because they fit a pattern already imprinted in our brains. We retain others because they make it easier to survive in a social or business situation. When our brains know for certain that something will occur exactly as intended, there is a cranial sigh of relief.

In marketing terms, any brand promise that offers the hope of making life just a little more predictable becomes a desirable message, lingers in the brain, and acts as a reminder to try out the product or service.

When Federal Express first began their overnight package delivery service in the mid-seventies, their advertising agency at the time, Ally & Gargano, came up with the tagline: "When it absolutely, positively has to be there overnight."

This tagline expressed exactly why they were in business. The line immediately struck a chord with any of us who were frustrated with the lack of punctuality and accuracy of package delivery at the time—in other words, the majority of the market. Our brains immediately got it: "Hey, this is all about survival. This service will improve productivity, increase time to market, and expedite the flow of information, as well as the closing of long-distance business deals ...."

If the tagline instead had been something like "Overnight Package Delivery," it would not have made much of an impression. "Overnight ... well okay. But will we really get it the next day? Will we really get it at all?" We might just forget about the line altogether and mentally move on. Plus, lots of other carriers were claiming speedy delivery.

We retain this powerline, the original Federal Express tagline, because it plays perfectly into the brain's central concern: survival. In this case, Federal Express promises to make life easier so that we absolutely, positively, never have to worry again about a delivery from point A to point B.

Throughout the rest of this book, we will look at example after example of powerlines that make an indelible impression and lines that never have a chance. They all rise or fall on the reason our brains exist in the first place. It really is that fundamental.

CHAPTER 2

Powerlines Take to the Air

Radio, Television, and Powerlines: A Match Made in Heaven

THIS BOOK IS FAR FROM a complete history of radio and television and the advertising and related revenues they foster. The part of the story I tell is how the phrases and expressions beamed into our living rooms by two communication miracles have shaped society and made a deep impression on us all.

Before radio, communication across great distances, or even across the street, was cumbersome and time consuming. The only mass communication channels were newspapers, magazines, and networks of family and friends. In the second half of the nineteenth century, personal and/or urgent messages could be sent by telegraph. But no technology delivered the spoken word directly and instantaneously to every home and workplace on a reliable, published schedule. The concept of mass communication was sheer science fiction in the 1800s. And then the dial turned.

In the early twentieth century, the invention of radio transformed communication and created a wondrous world of spoken expression ultimately broadcast to every nook and cranny of the planet. With daily programming and commercial messages, radio provided the platform for powerlines to reach and quickly gain recognition from mass audiences. Mass recall was afoot and its connection to powerlines was immediately apparent.

A favorite catchall phrase during the first half of the 1930s was the slogan from a highly creative weekly news show brought to life by two well-known commentators, Lowell Thomas and H.V. Kaltenborn.

Airing Friday evenings, *The March of Time* dramatized stories taken from each week's pages of *Time* magazine. The show's unforgettable slogan? "Time marches on."

Not surprisingly, powerlines also had a place in the lives of the first American action heroes. On January 31, 1933, in the middle of the Great Depression, a masked man on a great white horse came galloping out of the city of Detroit into millions of American homes. For the next twenty-one years, he rode from one adventure to another with a hearty "Hi ho, Silver!"

George Trendle, the owner of Michigan's WXYZ radio station, along with station staffers and local writer Fran Striker, created the show—characters, the mask, and the name—and aired the first episode. A musical introduction, Rossini's *William Tell Overture*, became the herald of the great doer of good deeds.

Coast to coast, Americans of all ages became diehard Lone Ranger fans and cries of "Hi ho, Silver!" could be heard whenever and wherever the music was played. The radio program ran until 1954, after which a popular television series was created using all the key elements of the original concept. Who was that masked man? No one knew, but everyone knew the line.

Another action thriller, *The Shadow*, was the best-known show during the Golden Age of Radio (1930–1955). A figure only heard and never seen, the Shadow was the first super hero of the airwaves. Each week, this crime fighter moved through the shadows, defied gravity, and got rid of the bad guys who preyed on the weak and innocent. (Walter Gibson created this series, which went on to spawn a *Shadow* magazine that lasted for eighteen years.)

The radio series began on July 31, 1930. Its final broadcast was on Christmas Day, 1954. I remember asking my father what he and his friends did at home for entertainment before the advent of television. Without hesitation, he repeated the opening lines of *The Shadow,* lines every member of his generation knew as well as their middle names: "Who knows what evil lurks in the hearts of men? The Shadow knows."

Probably not a big surprise, the vast majority of successful radio shows created and produced from 1930 to 1955 wound up as television shows in the mid-1950s. Shows like *Death Valley Days*, *Rin Tin Tin*, *Sherlock Holmes*, *The Ed Sullivan Show*, and, of course, *The Lone Ranger*. (The radio longevity award goes to the New York Metropolitan Opera, which began radio broadcasts in 1931 and continues today.)

HISTORICAL SIDELIGHT Most network shows were controlled by a few large and powerful advertising agencies whose staff wrote much of the content, booked most of the talent, and insured non-stop product plugs delivered by the program's stars.

Radio Heads

In 1931, roughly half of America's thirty million households owned at least one radio. That same year, a magazine devoted exclusively to radio appeared called *Broadcasting*. It was immediately popular as a kind of *TV Guide* for radio listeners.

Despite the raging Depression, radio advertising was strong and growing while the country's newspapers saw a net decline in ad revenues. Why? Radio reached millions of consumers of all ages. Young people, for instance, did not read newspapers, but did listen in ever-increasing numbers to radio shows geared just for them. Millions of housewives had the radio on all day long.

How could a newspaper compete with a voice that spoke directly to the consumer hour after hour, day after day? It was no contest then and no contest now. In 2006, Americans listened to the radio on average two-and-a-half hours a day, compared with a thirty-minute reading of the daily newspapers.

By 1933, the power of that radio voice, which came directly into your living room, was not to be denied. After the dinner hour, families who still didn't own radios would join those who did to listen to the evening's news and entertainment.

In that same year, the newly elected Franklin D. Roosevelt instituted "fireside chats" on air and became known as the radio president. For the first time in history, the president became seemingly accessible to each and every American.

The Power of a Key Word

Eight years later, on December 7, 1941, the Japanese surprise attacked and bombed Pearl Harbor, a U.S. Navy base in Honolulu, Hawaii. Roosevelt shared his reaction to the attack in a speech first given to a joint session of Congress and broadcast to the American people at noon the next day. That speech contained the powerline that was to become the single best-remembered phrase of the World War II era: "a date that will live in infamy."

President Roosevelt dictated the first draft of the speech to his personal secretary, Grace Tully. "Yesterday, December 7, 1941, a date which will live in world history...," the draft began. Had he stayed with this opening line, it is doubtful it would be remembered to this day. *World* and *history* are two ordinary words that provide no special meaning in the context of one of the biggest global events ever. Roosevelt recognized this and replaced *world history* with *infamy*. An unusual and seldom-used word, *infamy* shocks and makes the brain take notice. This was just what Roosevelt wanted—a single word to reinforce that the Japanese attack would forever be known as a major affront to civilization. He picked exactly the right word and, instead of ordinary verbiage, created a powerline.

Key words make all the difference between remembering and forgetting. Our brains don't have the interest or time to store and record ordinary words or sounds. Roosevelt's speaking voice was not plain-Jane either. It was passionate and powerful. He made a special point to increase the volume and slow down the tempo as he delivered the word *infamy*.

Key words are so powerful that the rest of the line is just less important. I asked dozens of older friends and acquaintances who lived through World War II if they remembered Roosevelt's opening line about the attack on Pearl Harbor. Every single person said yes and repeated "A day that will live in infamy." None of them got the line exactly right, but they all could recall it. Powerful delivery. Key word. Remembered for all time.

HISTORICAL SIDELIGHT After Roosevelt read the speech on December 8, the pages were misplaced and went missing for forty-three years. By chance, in 1984, an archivist came upon the original text in a records folder of the U.S. Senate. It is now well cared for in the National Archives Building in Washington, DC.

In Your Car and on the Beach

Two technological advances brought radio to the peak of its power in the 1930s and 1940s. First, millions of Americans spent the extra money to have radios installed in their cars and a whole new category of listeners was created through what we still call "drive-time radio." To increase driver safety, in 1937, Motorola created the ultimate in listening convenience. Instead of turning the dials, we could now just push a button.

Two years later, with 45 million radios in use, came the widespread availability of the first portable radios. We could buy an Emerson portable with the catchy feature of a "five-tube superheterodyne" for $19.95. Or, for slightly more money, a company named Majestic offered a portable that weighed in at a mere four pounds, unbelievably light for its day and perfect for the beach.

A Better Business Model

Radio started out as commercial free, primarily because major broadcasters made all their profit from the sales of the actual radios units. As the 1920s got into full swing, so did the radio industry. By 1922, there were 576 broadcasting stations in the United States and, by 1924, that number nearly tripled to fourteen hundred stations. Americans became radio obsessed and in that same year, families spent about one-third of their furniture budgets on cabinet-style units. This new form of radio furniture immediately became the centerpiece and focal point of the "modern" living room.

But success always has unintended consequences. As radio sales increased, so did the public clamor for more varied and entertaining programming. Prior to the early 1920s, radio focused on basic news, simple background music, and an occasional church service. The major networks, notably RCA, AT&T, and Westinghouse, realized they needed to offer better programming, targeted to different age groups, which would cover interests from sports, commentary, and lively music, to drama, comedy, and self-improvement.

By 1922, this unforeseen additional programming, with its high-priced talent and production costs, tipped the equation. Clearly, radio sales alone could not keep pace with this major new expense.

In that same year, AT&T decided to seek a sponsor for what became the first radio commercial in America. WEAF on Long Island, New York, convinced a local realtor to pay $100 for a ten-minute program about a new housing project in Jackson Heights named Hawthorne

Court. The commercial discussed the benefits of suburban living and the announcer ended with, "Let me close by urging you to hurry to the apartment house near the green fields … the community life and friendly environment that Hawthorne advocates." The first radio commercial was "no sell." No price was mentioned, no number was given to call, no suggestion made to set up an appointment. For a short time thereafter, other stations across the country experimented with no-sell messages. But soon, the networks and their outlets realized that a whole new way of commerce was in the offing. Americans wanted to learn about products and services on the radio and advertisers were happy to oblige them. Everybody won. With more revenue, the networks created better programming and listeners now had more choices and first-rate content.

Powerlines for Profit

As radio commercials increased, corporate America discovered the power of the spoken word through broadcast advertising. With practice, they learned the art of creating audio powerlines, lines that could permeate consumer consciousness and stay there.

Here are a few examples of great lines launched on radio:

Coca-Cola Signature

In 1930, listeners could tune into one of the first coast-to-coast radio broadcasts, *The Coca-Cola Hour*, which aired on NBC at 10:30 p.m. This program combined sports news and interviews with stars, intermingled with symphony music played live by a thirty-one-piece orchestra. The conductor, Leonard Joy, wrote a short musical theme for the show, which consisted of a few bars at the beginning and end of the program. He named this score the "Coca-Cola Signature."

By that time, radio commercials were ubiquitous and suffered from the clutter syndrome we still deal with today. Single advertisers supported entire shows and they used the on-air time to broadcast endlessly repetitive commercials delivered in loud voices.

Coke went in a different direction.

The "Coca-Cola Signature" was such a welcome departure from the usual in-your-face commercials that Coke used this pleasing music on all the radio shows it sponsored. In many instances, the score also served as Coke's sole commercial on any given program. One audience-grabbing variation was The Signature, followed by the sound of a Coke bottle being opened, followed by the announcer saying, "This broadcast is presented by Coca-Cola." The bottle opening sound was a brilliant move to remind listeners to rush to the icebox and open a Coke and hear exactly the same sound.

"The Coca-Cola Signature" sold Coke for the next twenty years.

"Lucky Strike Green Has Gone to War"

Hard to believe in the twenty-first century, but in the 1940s, nearly everyone from thirteen years old to his last day on earth smoked. During World War II, the height of Lucky Strike's popularity, American GIs were issued a standard ration of a carton a week.

In 1942, war brought out a new brand of competitiveness among advertisers, and they vied with one another to show the highest level of patriotism. On Lucky Strike-sponsored radio programs, listeners constantly heard "Lucky Strike Green Has Gone to War." This slogan was a direct reference to the green dye in Lucky's original packaging, the dye that was soon to be diverted for exclusive use by the military. The war forced Lucky Strike to change its distinctive dark green and gold to the now iconic white with red and black.

Lucky Strike's parent, the American Tobacco Company, thought they had hit on a great line all Americans would embrace and consequently demanded that it be used over and over again, particularly on the very popular broadcast *Information Please*. Alas, their blatant and constant breast-beating of how patriotic a cigarette could be wore on radio listeners, who complained in large numbers.

American Tobacco finally relented in 1943 and switched to the tagline that was already on each pack, "L.S./M.F.T.," which the public soon learned translated to "Lucky Strike Means Fine Tobacco." Unusual for a tagline to be a sequence of letters as shorthand for the real message, but it was recited continually in all of Lucky's ads and caught on with consumers. Lucky Strike was the first company to go this route, and L.S./M.F.T. appears on every pack today. Millions of people still know exactly what it stands for.

"More Doctors Smoke Camels Than Any Other Cigarette"

From the 1940s through early 1950, cigarette smoking grew even faster than the radio industry. Its meteoric rise was supported by the medical community, which believed smoking relieved stress, helped digestion, and generally made life more pleasant.

The makers of Camel cigarettes decided to capitalize on this viewpoint and, in 1947, hired independent pollsters to conduct a nationwide survey of more than one hundred thousand physicians to determine their brand preference. Camel basically rolled the dice hoping they would come out on top, and they did. Thus was born a campaign that used the medical community to endorse a cigarette brand at a time when doctors were revered above all other professionals.

Launched that same year on NBC's *Mystery in the Air*, Camel's full slogan was "According to a nationwide survey: More doctors smoke Camels than any other cigarette." In addition to radio, Camel went full throttle with a major print effort and their market share grew substantially over the next few years. The campaign finally faded away in the early 1950s as the medical community became more aware of the true effects of cigarette smoking and gradually went public with this information.

A Jingle for the Ages

For all ages actually. In 1949, the folks at Pepsi finally got their promotional sea legs and came up with a powerline that rivaled Coke's two famous slogans "The Pause That Refreshes" (1929) and "It's the Real Thing" (1942).

Pepsi's agency, Newell-Emmett, created "Pepsi-Cola Hits the Spot," and it became one of the best-known lines ever created. To enhance this tagline's staying power, the agency produced a jingle and played it over three hundred thousand times on more than four hundred radio stations in its first year.

> Pepsi-Cola hits the spot.
> Twelve full ounces, that's a lot!
> Twice as much, for a nickel, too.
> Pepsi-Cola is the drink for you!

During its reign, this jingle was imbedded in the brains of every American over the age of five. It even made the unusual leap to becoming a jukebox favorite. Many advertising historians consider this jingle the most pervasive and effective of all time. It was certainly right for America in the 1950s, a country that enjoyed rooting for the underdog, Pepsi, versus Coke, and liked an upbeat sales pitch that reminded the consumer he got a lot of sugared water for a wee small nickel.

"No Good Will Come of It"

As radio became part of the fabric of American life, it also became an indispensable tool to thrill and chill audiences nationwide. Sports broadcasting made us fans of teams we could never see play in locations far afield. Travel shows, news, social commentary, thrillers, westerns, comedy, and politics were now available at the turn of the dial. We literally had the world at our fingertips. Programs for all ages, sponsored by companies selling anything and everything, made youngsters and adults loyal listeners. Radio gathered America and the world together in a way never imagined. It showed how the power of the spoken word delivered to our home, our place of work, our car, and our pocket was a perfect match between technology and the human quest for verbal community.

And then, just as we settled in and became comfortable with those familiar radio voices, came a medium far more powerful—television.

In 1928, C. P. Scott, editor of the *Manchester Guardian* offered this prediction: "Television? The word is half Greek and half Latin. No good will come of it."

Mr. Scott was right about the word. *Tele* is the Greek word for "far" and *vision* comes from the Latin word visio meaning "vision or sight." But he was wrong about its impact.

No question, the concept of sight and sound in a box in your living room was the stuff of science fiction. Even as movie-theater technology evolved in Hollywood and other parts of the world in the 1920s and 1930s, transformation of the big screen to a personal home screen was thought by many to be a far-off pipe dream.

TV Nation

From the first television station broadcast in 1928 to the astronauts' walk on the Moon forty-one years later, television changed the world for all time and made it possible to not only hear about events as they happened, but to see them live and in living color.

Television is clearly responsible for the pace of life we enjoy and complain about in equal measure. No other form of communication has captivated billions of people since its first wobbly beginnings at the turn of the twentieth century. In 1946, less than half of 1 percent of American homes had a television set. By 1954, that number increased to 55 percent, and by 1962, it reached 90 percent.

Today, television is watched more than ever before. A 2006 Nielsen monitor indicates that the average American home has the set turned on for eight hours every day. Not radio, the Internet, newspapers, magazines, or books come close to the daily hours devoted to television.

Television has shaped every culture it has penetrated by providing the ultimate combination of sound and sight to the living room, den, bedroom, bar, and workplace. A media visionary and scientist, Marshall McLuhan, once dubbed television "the electronic fireplace." We are drawn to it, find comfort in it, and share communication around it in the company of family, friends, or strangers.

Television offers content providers and advertisers alike the ultimate vehicle to shape thought, opinion, and buying habits. It has always been a more targeted medium that many pundits give it credit for. Like radio in its heyday, there is a show for every age group, hobbyist, sports nut, and fan of romance, comedy, tragedy, and news: good, bad, left-leaning, right-leaning, and just plain misleading.

Television is a shared and sometimes addictive experience. Millions of people become ardent followers of particular shows at particular times. Most often, these shows are long-running series that strike a chord, or special-event shows like a major movie, the Oscars, or the Super Bowl.

Advertisers Go Wild

All it took was one thirty-second commercial for ad agencies and their clients to realize that television was the ultimate advertising showcase.

Bulova Watch purportedly created the first television commercial in 1941, which ran on NBC in New York at a cost of nine dollars. Gillette Razor, Firestone Tire, Esso (now Exxon), and Pan American Airways all launched commercials immediately after World War II in 1945.

By the early 1950s, as access to televisions became widespread across America, television advertising was the dominant form of advertising. With annual ad expenditures in excess of $1 billion by 1955, television revenues surpassed those of radio and magazines. Again, as they did in the Golden Age of Radio, companies rushed to sponsor specific shows that research indicated attracted their target market. Spokespeople on these commercials became famous in their own right, including animated characters like Elsie the Cow (1952) and Mr. Clean (1958), who still cleans up a storm today.

"Mr. Clean." This widely recognized U.S. advertising icon was created by Tatham-Laird, Inc., in the 1950s. Mr. Clean is a trademark of Procter & Gamble Company.

Not surprisingly, politicians took to the power of television as quickly as funds allowed. It soon became clear that national elections could be won and lost based on which candidates came across more at ease and natural on the small screen. Of course, this had no more bearing then on their actual qualifications as leaders, thinkers, and doers than it does today.

Manipulate usually has negative connotations. However, it is the best word for what radio advertising and to a higher degree, television advertising, does. Radio is limited to sound. But television, with its added visuals and motion, can literally blow away the competition, as a political commercial produced by the Lyndon Johnson camp did to his presidential rival Barry Goldwater in 1964.

Dubbed "Daisy" and created by Doyle Dane Bernbach, the first ad agency to produce a presidential campaign television spot, this commercial included a voice-over by Johnson, featured the nuclear annihilation of a cute little girl picking daisies in an open field, and implied this catastrophic outcome would be the result of a Goldwater presidency. Johnson won in a landslide (see Chapter 4, pages 72–73).

A decade before, in 1952, Dwight Eisenhower and wife Mamie starred in the first paid televised presidential campaign commercials. They appeared to answer questions posed by ordinary Americans from all walks of life. In fact, these commercials were staged from start to finish and were actually quite brazen in their level of audience manipulation. Although it appeared that a two-way conversation took place between candidate, wife, and "ah shucks" questioners, the Eisenhowers never actually met any of the people posing questions. Both parties were scripted and rehearsed in separate sound studios and then the footage was spliced together to give the appearance of a two-way presence and dialogue.

The alchemy of the television commercial remains part truth, part fiction, part staging, part substance, all to create a heavy dose of image with tremendous impact on the behavior and attitudes of viewers.

Beyond commercials, television land produces lines that settle into the memories of the audience as part of regular programming. Like the nursery rhymes discussed earlier, these lines often live on and become a part of our culture.

The shows best remembered are those in which certain phrases or slogans are repeated day after day, week after week, focused on a person or collection of people who become our television pals.

"Heeeeere's Johnny!"

NBC's *The Tonight Show* first aired September 27, 1954. Jack Paar became host in the summer of 1957 and settled on what became the winning format: a talk show with invited guests from all walks of life, most of whom were famous personalities or up-and-coming comedic talent. Paar was a difficult and edgy personality and walked off the stage in a huff on March 30, 1962. Six months later, on October 1, Johnny Carson greeted America on *The Tonight Show* stage and remained night after night, year after year, until his final goodbye on May 22, 1992.

Johnny Carson introduced to America and the world the captivating power of the right personality on the right show. With his second banana, Ed McMahon, and the able showmanship of bandleader Doc Severinsen, Johnny reigned as the king of late night for an incredible thirty years.

"Heeeeere's Johnny," uttered to perfection by Ed McMahon, became one of the best known introductory lines of all time and a perfect example of why television is such a dominant medium. Television alone has the ability to bring a person into our life and home, someone who looks right at us and gives the illusion of a conversation just between the two of us.

There was no one better at that sense of intimacy than Johnny Carson. His natural grace and poise on camera, quick wit, and infinite charm were the perfect combination to put us to bed. Rumor says the zero population growth movement owes Carson its success at drawing down the global birth rate to what it deems an appropriate level.

For many years running, Johnny and team often did commercials for advertisers. Even when slip-ups occurred or when Johnny frequently made it apparent through words or gestures that hawking products was not exactly his favorite activity, the advertisers were pleased. When asked, in a rare interview midway through his career, what he would like on his tombstone, Johnny said: "I'll be right back." And millions of people worldwide wish that would happen. Johnny Carson died on January 23, 2005, and left behind generations of fans who still take his passing as a personal loss.

PART TWO

THE POWERLINE PERSPECTIVE

Countries, Candidates, Cultures, and Companies Rise or Fall on Powerful Lines, Mottos, and Sayings

The invention of a great slogan is an unappreciated art form today. Most people think that any old combination of words will do the job. After all, in this time of media excess, we're all connected, all the time. What we forget is that it's still essential to stake our product or service claim on a word or a phrase that makes perfect sense, and that in effect is—perfect.

CHAPTER **3**

Uncle Sam Wants You, Your Mind, Your Money

How Governments Win Hearts, Minds, and Paychecks

THE FOLLOWING CHAPTERS describe many marketing battles won and lost and show how marketers create an impression with words, visuals, and sound, that either compels consumers to respond to a product pitch, or to ignore it. The bottom line? Companies, candidates, countries, and cultures can rise or fall on powerful lines, mottos, and sayings.

This chapter focuses on the range of ways, from propaganda to publicity, that governments use powerlines.

A Slippery Slope

When I was six years old, my father signed up the two of us for a YMCA program called Indian Guides. Like the Boy Scouts, the Guides were designed to bring father and son closer together through the study of nature, hiking, camping, and general self-improvement. Also like the Boy Scouts, the Indian Guides uses a motto to communicate its values.

"Be Prepared," the Boy Scouts of America motto, encapsulates one idea of what it takes to be a boy and achieve manhood. The Indian Guides had a different and more intimate approach. Their motto was "Father and Son. Pals Forever."

My dad and I stayed in the Indian Guides movement for a couple of years and then I drifted into Cub Scouts and eventually Boy Scouts. Years went by, I grew up, and had my own son, Clifford. Once Cliff could talk, whenever we were together I made him repeat that Indian Guide slogan,

"Father and Son. Pals Forever." We continue this ritual some twenty-five years later. It seems to work.

The mottos above, and all like them, are: propaganda, n, [Latin *propagare*, to reproduce] 1. the creation of a verbal and/or visual event that is frequently repeated and causes a defined population to form a desired opinion.

Propaganda was first employed in 1622 by Pope Gregory XV, who created an organization called the *Congregatio de Propaganda Fide* to oversee missionary work across Europe as a counter to the Protestant Reformation.

Not to be outdone, Reformation supporters attacked Catholicism at every opportunity with the printing press, their most powerful weapon. From then on, mass media became the vehicle of choice for influencing the opinions of large groups of people.

Propaganda became the domain of politicians and governments in the early twentieth century, and after the First World War, the word acquired the negative connotation it carries today.

Using lines to mold minds can be a slippery slope. Had I abused Cliff on the one hand and made him repeat the Indian Guides motto on the other, I would have been guilty of brainwashing with all its evil intent. But, in fact, I used the motto to remind us of our common lifelong bond and affection—clearly an affirmative act.

Some modern definitions suggest that a message is propaganda when the source of the message stands to benefit more than the receiver. This is a decent definition as far as it goes, but much depends on the outcome and consequences for both sender and receiver.

It may be true that all politicians, whether in democracies or totalitarian regimes, use propaganda to stay in power. But the outcomes for the citizenry couldn't be more starkly different.

Consider political advertising in America. Candidates attempt to move opinion in their direction and away from their opponent, whom they attack either directly or by implication. In a democracy, only one candidate wins on Election Day. During the elected official's prescribed term, the voter, that is, the message receiver, ostensibly gains, as the official wants to provide reasons to be kept in office.

In a totalitarian regime, message receivers stand to gain very little other than longer lives, if they toe the line. Certainly this was the case in Nazi Germany, which many historians cite as the best and worst example of systematic propaganda used to ultimately justify mass murder and subjugation.

Since the invention of the printing press, governments and political leaders have used propaganda to hold sway over the governed. In most cases, this propaganda takes the form of symbols and slogans—slogans that sometimes become powerlines. (When a symbol becomes a concrete representation of an idea or desired action, it reinforces a particular slogan.)

When put into general terms, the recipe for success seems simple enough: Create a shorthand message for the mind and eye, and deliver it through mass communication again and again and again and again.

It's no surprise that propaganda reigns in times of war.

The American Revolution had all manner of slogans and mottos including, for example, "No Taxation Without Representation" and "Don't Tread On Me." The rallying cry of the French Revolution was "Liberty, Equality, and Fraternity," and Lenin based the Russian Revolution on a slogan catering to what Russian peasants considered utopia, "Peace, Bread, and Land."

World War I saw the first use of extensive propaganda by all sides in print, radio, and film.

America entered World War I in 1917 after German subs sank several American ships. But the general population lacked enthusiasm for sending its young men to fight in some far-off European War. In fact, millions of Americans were dead set against any involvement.

Facing this situation, President Woodrow Wilson did what any smart leader would do. He appointed a marketing genius, George Creel, to turn opinion around. Creel did a fantastic job with the nationwide campaign he created around the powerline "The War to End All Wars."

Repeated messages enticing citizens to participate in the task at hand popped up on the radio, in movie theatres, and on posters placed in every town in America.

One of the best-known images of the era is a poster of James Montgomery Flagg's 1917 stern Uncle Sam, with his finger pointed directly at the next potential recruit … you. Over nine million Uncle Sam posters were displayed in the first twelve months of America's involvement in the war.

"I Want You" poster. James Montgomery Flagg (1877–1960). Originally published as the cover for the July 6, 1916, issue of *Leslie's Weekly* with the title "What Are You Doing for Preparedness?" Flagg's depiction of Uncle Sam was later used for the World War I recruitment efforts in 1917. This remains the most enduring image of this cultural symbol.

Howard Chandler Christy depicted a very attractive and suggestive blonde in a naval uniform to encourage men to consider joining the U.S. Navy.

Of course, the war to end all wars was not to be.

Events that led up to World War II included the rise of Nazism, the best orchestration of the principles of propaganda ever conceived. Hitler's evil

"Christy Girl." World War I U.S. Navy recruitment poster by Howard Chandler Christy. Originally entitled "Gee!! I Wish I Were a Man," U.S. artist Christy created the Christy Girl for the Navy Publicity Bureau for World War I recruitment efforts. The poster featured Christy's wife, Nancy Palmer, as the model.

genius was matched in equal measure by that of his propaganda minister, Joseph Goebbels, whose primary focus was "the big lie" theory: the transformation of an outrageous lie into conventional thinking by repetition and the addition of powerful symbols, such as the ever-present Nazi swastika.

The Nazis were deadly serious about pageantry, symbolism, and brainwashing. No detail was too small, as Hitler pursued his quest for total allegiance of the German populace to *der Führer*. The government made sure that every German household had a radio and even provided them at cut-rate prices. It commissioned a brilliant filmmaker, Leni Riefenstahl, to make powerful documentaries about the past glory of Germany and its restoration by the Nazi Party. America and Japan also created patriotic films for the masses, but they were no match for Riefenstahl, who reported directly to Hitler and had unlimited production budgets.

When America entered its second major war of the twentieth century, propaganda was a part of everyday life. A series of slogans immediately appeared on posters and in radio broadcasts. "We Can Do It" accompanied posters showing Rosie the Riveter. Rosie became as well known as Uncle Sam, and launched a massive migration of working-age women from the kitchen to the factory floor. Other popular slogans included "United We Win," "Man the Guns," and "Loose Lips Sink Ships."

War bond drives were big business and an endless array of ads implored Americans to buy them. Many were caricatures. One negatively depicted a laughing Japanese pilot, complete with eyeglasses and oversized teeth. This was a common illustration of the "yellow peril" that must be defeated at all cost.

When all the shooting stopped and World War II ended, the use of propaganda kept right on going. China's Marxist leader, Mao Zedong, came to power by borrowing many of the techniques used by Lenin, Stalin, and Hitler. In his pursuit of power, Mao's No. 1 priority was to condition minds to accept his ideology. He introduced a number of slogans on his rise to godlike status and utilized Chinese proverbs in a modern context to great effect.

Like Hitler, Mao established a propaganda ministry that, among other things, created the mystique behind the Long March and Mao's nine-mile swim in the Yangtze River at the age of seventy-three. The films, radio pronouncements, millions of posters, and little red books promoting Mao's doctrine and distributed to every peasant across China all added up. Mao developed a cult following that allowed him to reign supreme. He established the Cultural Revolution, which prohibited access to Western culture and values, and insured that the only messages to reach a billion people were his and his alone.

From Propaganda to Publicity

During the second half of the twentieth century, propaganda, going by the more benign name "publicity," was used to promote all manner of social causes.

When the military draft ended, the Armed Services were quick to realize they were now a product that needed to be sold. That meant spending money on advertising and public relations. Ad agency N.W. Ayer met the challenge with a brilliant concept: the Army as a place where recruits could both have a great adventure and build a great career—a package a private employer could never match.

The campaign theme "Be All You Can Be" appealed equally to men and women at a time when women were aggressively courted for military careers. Matched with an upbeat jingle and bold type, "Be All You Can Be" remained in force for two decades and achieved distinction as the longest continuously running recruiting effort.

In postwar America, advocates of all major social causes wanted a rallying cry for behavioral change on a massive scale. They worked hard to come up with powerlines that would compel and endure. Call it propaganda, publicity, or just plain persuasion, as the pace of life

"Be All You Can Be." U.S. Army recruitment slogan, 1981–2001. Created by N. W. Ayer & Son. The U.S. Army Recruiting Command launched this campaign in 1981.

quickened and information overload began in earnest, it became imperative to develop great slogans to break through the clutter.

In the 1950s, ad agency Foote, Cone & Belding created Smokey Bear for the U.S. Forest Service with the timeless slogan: "Remember, Only You Can Prevent Forest Fires!"

Smokey Bear. This public service ad campaign for the U.S. Forest Service gave the American public one of its most enduring spokes-characters, Smokey Bear. Created by Foote, Cone & Belding. Included in the Special Collections at the National Agricultural Library: U.S. Forest Service Smokey Bear Collection. The fictional character Smokey Bear is administered by three entities: the United States Forest Service, the National Association of State Foresters, and the Ad Council.

SURGEON GENERAL'S WARNING: Smoking Causes Lung Cancer, Heart Disease, Emphysema, And May Complicate Pregnancy.

Cigarette Warning Label. Since 1966, all cigarette advertising in the United States must include a warning from the Surgeon General concerning the health risks associated with the use of tobacco.

In the 1960s, the Vietnam War tore American views apart. Music, literature, and the youth movement were all heavily influenced by the drug culture. Protesters chanted "Give Peace a Chance" and President Nixon launched the War on Drugs. Even the National Rifle Association got into the act with "Guns don't kill people. People do."

The U.S. government made a half-hearted attempt to make people stop smoking. The dangers of cigarettes were discussed, but at the same time, the government continued to allow them to be advertised—a kind of "dance with the tobacco devil" that goes on even today. Since the 1970s, every pack of cigarettes and every cigarette ad must carry the surgeon general's warning: Those tasty cigarettes will turn your internal organs into jelly and undoubtedly send you to an early grave.

The United States of Tourism

Tourism is the largest business on earth. It employs the most people and is a huge source of revenue for states across America as well as countries worldwide.

In the United States, tourism is the second largest source of income for individual states, after personal and property tax. How better to make the locals happy than to bring in as many outside dollars as possible to relieve the burden of state tax? Each state, therefore, attempts to create a slogan that can bring home the tourist bacon and deliver a compelling message about what awaits visitors who drive, fly, bus, train, bike, or walk into the state. Alas, most states fail miserably to make their case and not a single group of tourism officials has a clue about how to really market themselves effectively.

For starters, which states' slogans come immediately to mind? Only three do for me—New Hampshire, New York, and Virginia—primarily because their slogans have remained in force for many years, an unusual phenomenon in state marketing.

"Live Free or Die" is the long running slogan for New Hampshire and while not exactly a tourist turn-on, it does speak to America's heritage as a British colony and our fight for freedom. It is memorable, distinctive, and begs the question: Who are those people up there in New Hampshire and what are they all about?

New York and Virginia have slogans that were created specifically for tourist consumption, and while they are slightly far-fetched, they make a statement and generate a smile. For New York: "I Love New York." For Virginia: "Virginia is for Lovers." (Curious that the states' respective trademark lawyers haven't battled over who has rights to the word *love.*)

And what is it with the use of the word *life* today? As I repeat throughout this book, a powerline, be it slogan, motto, tagline, expression, must ring true and be a genuine reflection of whatever it refers to. Overreaching is the cardinal sin in the attempt to create a powerline, and the net effect actually does the reverse.

As this book goes to press, Visa has a promotional campaign with the tagline: "Life Takes Visa." American Express currently uses "My Life. My Card." And two states stake their positioning on "life": Iowa with the line "*Life*/Changing" and Utah's proclamation, "Life Elevated." How about "get a life" guys. No one believes that their life revolves around a visit to Iowa or even Utah, where there is at least something to see. Visa and American Express are equally guilty in their pompous pronouncements, but they aren't state tourism marketers and should know better.

For years, New Jersey has attempted to entice potential visitors to believe there is more to see than an ugly turnpike with endless oil refineries or flat, sandy pine barrens. New Jersey calls itself "The Garden State," a motto it has used for years on its license plates. But somehow, New Jersey doesn't believe it either and continues to search for just the right saying.

In 2005, the state government paid a marketing consultant $250,000 for the slogan: "New Jersey: We'll Win You Over." The governor at the time correctly pointed out that this line reminded him of what boys attempt to do when they ask a girl out on a first date. It implies "Try me once, and I think I can win you over." Not exactly a strong come-on for a person or a state.

Rejecting the consultant's best effort, New Jersey then ran a contest among residents and received eight thousand entries. My personal favorite is: "Most of our elected officials have not been indicted." One of five finalists had the love word: "New Jersey: Love at First Sight." The winning entry which is in use today is "New Jersey: Come See for Yourself." Perhaps they should have added the word "please." Need I say more?

Other than the state slogans mentioned above, there are few that are just okay and some that are downright awful. Plus, I have included a winner's circle of the top five. Honorable mention goes to the state of Maryland, which steadfastly refuses to have a slogan. Maybe they are on to something.

The Best of the Bunch

"Live Free or Die"—New Hampshire

"I Love New York"—New York
Also, a catchy jingle.

"Virginia is for Lovers"—Virginia
Virginia, of course.

"Land of Enchantment"—New Mexico
It's actually true.

"The Grand Canyon State"—Arizona
When you have it, flaunt it.

Average, at Best

"Unbridled Spirit"—Kentucky
Okay, horses, I get it.

"It's Like a Whole Other Country"—Texas
It actually is.

"The South's Warmest Welcome"—Mississippi

"Great Potatoes. Tasty Destinations."—Idaho

Idaho, of course.

"The Natural State"—Arkansas

"The Green Mountain State"—Vermont

They experiment with other lines. They should stick with what they've got.

"Travel Montana"—Montana

Nothing fancy.

"Beyond Your Dreams, Within Your Reach"—Alaska

A mouthful and plenty of natural beauty to brag about.

"Georgia on My Mind"—Georgia

Also the song.

"Ohio Means Business"—Ohio

It also means high taxes, but that's another book.

Downright Awful

"How Will You Connect?"—Connecticut

I have no idea and … I don't care.

"Come Fall in Love with Louisiana All Over Again"—Louisiana

First, I have to figure out which of the state's six slogans, this being one, they really mean.

"Life/Changing"—Iowa

Perhaps the worst state slogan of all time.

"It Must Be Maine"—Maine

Yeahhh, I guess it must.

"Make It Yours"—Massachusetts

Say what?

"Wide Open"—Nevada

Let's just leave it at that.

"Legendary"—North Dakota

If you say so ...

"Great Faces. Great Places."—South Dakota

At least it rhymes.

"Smiling Faces. Beautiful Places."—South Carolina

So did the two Souths, Dakota and Carolina, hire the same second-rate copywriter?

"Right Here. Right Now."—Illinois

I beg your pardon?

So there you have it. Billions of tourist dollars up for grabs and very few effective powerlines from the various state capitals and tourist boards. Such a lost opportunity, considering the potential impact of a properly constructed line.

Plus not a single state integrates its slogan though all available touch points, an essential strategy for proper brand building.

Take the underutilization of "I Love New York" as an example. No question, it is used well in travel posters and occasional television and radio ads where it comes alive as an easy-to-remember and upbeat jingle. But that's about it. This catchy line is nowhere to be found on state agency letterhead, at the top of state income tax forms, websites, and the millions of pamphlets and informational brochures produced every year. Imagine if the line appeared at the bottom of every citation and ticket issued by state troopers. Let's not *sort of* love New York. Let's LOVE New York.

The Global Tourism War

Despite the global fight against terrorism to protect the citizens of the civilized world, the battle for international tourism dollars goes on.

Countries and destinations spend serious money—up to $5 billion a year—seeking top-of-mind awareness and eventual bookings by millions of visitors. Australia, New Zealand, Greece, Spain, Bermuda, and Jamaica are some of the most aggressive tourist trollers. But almost every country has a tourist board and a group of paid professionals whose sole job is to increase tourism and its accompanying revenue.

Strange that with all that money at stake, there is such a poor group of slogans. The two countries that seem to try the hardest over the years are Australia and New Zealand. And with good reason. They are far from everywhere, including each other, and depend on tourist dollars as a significant part of total government revenues.

New Zealand has the distinction of having the longest-running tourist slogan. Created by the M&C Saatchi agency in the early 1990s, it is still in use today: "100% Pure New Zealand." Millions of dollars each year are spent to reinforce this line through print and cable TV in Asia, America, and parts of Europe. The word *pure* is very strong and translates well around the world. New Zealand ties the word to what it is all about—pure adventure, pure nature, pure water, and so on. They also throw in pristine whenever possible. Not bad, this pure and pristine strategy.

Pure is a powerful endorsement, but is seldom used. The only other pure that immediately comes to mind is "100% Pure Vermont Maple Syrup."

Australia is very serious about promotion and regularly sends tourist ambassadors on goodwill missions to all parts of the globe. In the early 1980s, Australia launched its first major tourist campaign with a series of television spots extolling the country's natural beauty, peaceful settings, and fun-loving people. In 1984, *Crocodile Dundee* actor Paul Hogan signed on to speak one of the best-known tourist promotional lines: "Throw another shrimp on the barbie." Local Aussie's turned that line into a private joke with the retort: "Throw another kanga' on the barbie!" Kidding aside, the line made its point perfectly about the informal, carefree culture and the "quaint" English that awaited visiting tourists.

After "Shrimp" ran its course (how many times can you barbie shrimp and keep interest up?), Australia experimented with a number of slogans, including "Australia. A different light" and "We can't wait to say g'day." But, so far, the high point is still Hogan speaking about the barbie, yet another example of the power that comes from combining a unique character and a unique slogan. No country before or since has created this kind of magical combination.

Four destinations are worthy of mention for superior lines and positioning: Disneyland, Jamaica, Club Med, and Las Vegas.

Disneyland and DisneyWorld parks in America, France, and parts of Asia bring in millions of visitors a year. One of the earliest Disney lines that lives on is "When You Wish Upon a Star," a sentiment which seems to capture the essence of the Disney experience. Two other successful lines are used periodically: "I'm Going to Walt Disney World!" and "The Happiest Place on Earth."

The Caribbean Islands, Jamaica, and the Caymans are pure (to steal New Zealand's word) tourism, 24 x 7, 365 days a year. Their existence depends on endless streams of sun-seeking visitors. To that end, Jamaica's campaign is particularly noteworthy in its use of a simple, straightforward strategy: their island name, in a distinctive boldface type. Credit goes to Doyle Dane Bernbach, the ad agency that developed this unique approach back in the 1970s. That it is still in use today shows the power a single word can achieve.

In the 1970s, Ammirati & Puris, another ad agency, did a bang-up job for Club Med and its global network of resort locations with the line: "Club Med … the antidote for civilization." Your brain instantly gets the message that there really is a place to relax and get away from it all, where people understand exactly what you need on a vacation. The line is purposely lower case to reinforce the calm destination that awaits, far from the blare and glare of the business world, with a capital *B*.

Jamaica. The campaign created by DDB was the first to effectively use culture to promote vacation travel. The "Jamaica" logo is still in use today, in print and online advertising. Trademark of the Jamaica Tourist Board.

Las Vegas, a completely different vacation venue, actually focuses on its glare, constantly lit to maximum wattage. In 2004, the Las Vegas Convention and Visitors Authority, concerned with a downturn in tourist traffic, launched a sexy suggestive ad campaign with the line: "What Happens Here, Stays Here." So much for the previous attempts to position Las Vegas as a great family destination, every bit as wholesome as Disneyland. Las Vegas is about adults with money who want to escape everyday family life and live a bit on the edge. This positioning seems to work and a destination, like any product or service, needs to be mindful of its genuine distinctiveness and then drive that idea home with a line that tells it like it is.

Most government tourist slogans are every bit as nonmemorable and dull as many of the state slogans. Below are five good, five bad, and five just-plain-dumb lines.

Pretty Good for Government Work

"100% Pure New Zealand"

Slogan has been around for decades. Makes the point clearly. *Pure* is a great word and *100%* gets noticed and remembered easily.

"Spain. Everything Under the Sun."

There is a lot to see. Good climate.

"We Can't Wait to Say G'day."

We be friendly ... and the Aussies really are. Highlighting their personality is distinctive and a good counter to the sometime grouchy Aussie, Russell Crowe.

"The Unexpected Bermuda"

You mean there is more than pink sand and expensive cabs and those noisy scooters?

"Malaysia. Truly Asia."

At least, it rhymes.

Bad, But They Tried

"Cyprus. A Whole World on a Single Island."

Okay, and what world would that be?

"Ireland. Awaken to a Different World."
There's that *world* word again. With all that Ireland has to offer, this is the best they can do?

"Pure. Natural. Unspoiled. Iceland."
At least it's straightforward and basically true. Just no zip, sounds a bit like a laundry list.

"India. Eternally Yours."
Sounds like I'm signing a letter. So much they could say and so little with this line.

"Vietnam: A Destination for the New Millennium"
Millennium just doesn't roll off your tongue. A fascinating country that could use a much better slogan.

Just Plain Dumb

"Sicily. Everything Else Is in the Shade."
So you mean I will broil the whole time I am there?

"Switzerland. Get Natural."
You mean go natural? What do you mean?

"Wales. Big Country."
Compared to Monaco, sure.

"Bangladesh: Come to Bangladesh Before the Tourists."
Thanks, but I'd rather wait for indoor plumbing.

"Austria. You've Arrived."
And all along, I thought this was Hungary …

In the introduction, I mentioned that marketers have lost their way when it comes to the creation of slogans with power and personality that express an impossible-to-ignore universal truth. Many of the examples above indicate how far we have fallen and how steep the climb back appears to be. Certainly, countries with their resources and resident brainpower should be able to create powerlines that appeal to the tourist side of us all. Yet, their marketing teams seem to be on a perpetual holiday. No question, the invention of a great slogan is an art form that just goes unappreciated today. We think any old combination of words will do the job. After all, in this Internet age, we're all connected, all the time. What we forget in this time of media excess, is that it's still essential to stake our product or service claim on a word or a phrase that makes perfect sense, and that in effect is—perfect.

CHAPTER **4**

You Can't Put the Toothpaste Back in the Tube

Why the Candidate with the Best Slogan Wins the Race

America's presidential campaigns and presidencies have promulgated a number of lines that both defined a particular era and became well established in everyday language. One of my favorites, the title of this chapter, was H.R. Haldeman's answer when asked how the Watergate incident evolved from a botched burglary attempt to the imprisonment of countless high government officials to the forced resignation of President Richard Nixon in 1974. Not surprisingly, Haldeman had been a career advertising executive at J. Walter Thompson before becoming Nixon's chief of staff. His penchant for timeless expression neatly summarized one of the darkest affairs in American politics.

This chapter uses powerlines to tell the story of American presidential campaigns. Along the way, the power of the right line to infiuence the outcome on Election Day becomes clear as does why some lines deliver votes while others deliver nothing at all.

A Singular Campaign

The 1840 contest between President Martin Van Buren, a Democrat, and William Henry Harrison, a Whig, spawned a number of lasting expressions. (The Whigs, basically the nineteenth century version of today's Libertarians, were a political force to be reckoned with for the flrst seventy-flve years of American politics.) From that campaign came one of the best-remembered campaign slogans of all time and a couple of favorite American expressions, including the most popular two-letter one.

President Van Buren was born in Kinderhook, New York, a distinction that earned him the nickname "Old Kinderhook." During the 1840 campaign, a radical faction of the Democratic Party in New York City started calling themselves the O.K. Club to show their support for Van Buren. On March 27, 1840, they disrupted a Whig gathering with shouts of: "Down with the Whigs, boys, O.K.!" The Whigs quickly removed the O.K. Club from the premises.

A few days later, the *New York Times* ran the story about the ruckus under a headline that reversed O.K.: "K.O. KICKED OUT." No matter, O.K. was here to stay and went on to become one of the world's best-known expressions.

Not to be outdone in the rallying-cry department, the Whigs concocted one of the best-remembered slogans of all time: "Tippecanoe and Tyler Too." Tippecanoe refers to Harrison's military victory over Shawnee chief Tecumseh in the battle of Tippecanoe in 1811. Tyler refers to John Tyler of Virginia, who became Harrison's running mate. The Whigs used the slogan to great effect, whipping up a frenzy of enthusiasm for Harrison's past military victories. No matter that, by all accounts, Harrison was an accidental and uninspired commander whose performance in the War of 1812 proved to be just passable.

During this campaign, the Whigs were on a roll—literally. They actually rolled huge balls, ten to flfteen feet in diameter, made of string, paper, leather, and different metals from town to town chanting verse:

> What has caused this commotion, motion, motion,
> Our country through?
> It is the ball a-rolling on,
> For Tippecanoe and Tyler too, for Tippecanoe and Tyler too.
> And with them we'll beat little Van, Van, Van;
> Van is a used-up man,
> And with them we'll beat little Van!

And so the expression "keep the ball rolling" was born.

Throughout the campaign, the party used images of log cabins to remind voters of Harrison's "populist upbringing." No matter that Harrison's roots were in fact the Virginia elite. One Harrison supporter in Philadelphia who owned a whiskey distillery did manage to express a truth about his candidate, a man who liked to "tip a few drinks" on a regular basis. The supporter, E.C. Booz, began bottling his product in log-cabin-shaped bottles. Shortly thereafter, "booze" became synonymous with liquor.

Harrison won the popular election by a slim margin: 145,000 votes out of 2.4 million. But the electoral vote tally was no contest: Harrison: 234, Van Buren: 60. Harrison has the unfortunate distinction of serving for only thirty days, the briefest presidential tenure in American history. Apparently, he boozed it up to such a degree at his inauguration that he caught pneumonia a few days later and died shortly thereafter.

A Singular President

Theodore "Teddy" Roosevelt, like Winston Churchill, was gifted with great charm, wit, world-class speaking and writing ability, and a photographic memory that astounded friends and foes alike. This explorer, conservationist, military hero, and twenty-sixth president of the United States, left his country a substantial legacy, including the National Parks Service, a world-class navy, and a collection of great powerlines.

Teddy borrowed his best-remembered powerline from an African proverb. He flrst uttered the words "Speak softly and carry a big stick" on September 2, 1901, at the Minnesota State Fair, twelve days before President William McKinley was assassinated and Teddy assumed the presidency.

President Roosevelt made "Big Stick Diplomacy" a central theme of his administration. With it he sent the rest of the world a clear message: America would project power anywhere it deemed its interests to be at stake, in particular, throughout the Western Hemisphere and Latin America. Roosevelt backed up his words with action, including expanding the U. S. Navy into a full-fiedged armada not to be trified with. To communicate the vastly increased capability of the new fieet, Roosevelt coined another powerline, "White Water Navy." Shortly after his election to president, Roosevelt ordered all U.S. Navy ships to paint their hulls white. "White Water Navy" is still a popular way to describe naval power.

Roosevelt coined another famous powerline—"The Square Deal"—during his second term, won in 1904 in a lopsided election against Alton Parker, a little-known and less-remembered challenger. Roosevelt's Square Deal included the establishment of the National Parks System, which notably set aside millions of acres in the western United States for recreation and conservation.

HISTORICAL SIDELIGHT In 1904, the big population centers were still far from the western shore. At that time, Iowa had more electoral votes than California.

Presidential Slogans Rated

Candidates, like countries and tourist destinations, need to depict their personalities and philosophies in a way that suggests greater value when compared to their opponents. And every politician needs a rallying cry his or her supporters can use to spread the word and maintain campaign momentum for days, weeks, and often months. As with all powerlines, the best ones tell a compelling and believable story that sets the brand, in this case the candidate, apart from competitors and in doing so makes a strong case for public buy-in.

In the rest of this chapter, readers will see firsthand how presidential candidates have managed and mismanaged their images through their choice and use of campaign slogans. What follows is the first rating ever done of slogans used by presidential contenders.

I have grouped presidential slogans into four categories:

- Above Average
- Okay
- No Wonder He Lost—Though Not in Every Case
- Since Reagan—Power*less* Lines

I sorted slogans into the first three categories with no regard to which candidate won which election. As it turned out, the winning candidates, with only one exception, used the above-average slogans. In that one exception, *both* candidates had above-average slogans.

The fourth category, "Since Reagan—Powerless Lines," is my commentary on the presidential slogans used in recent times to basically no effect. Despite all the modern techniques candidates use to market themselves as effectively as possible, they completely fail to create compelling slogans that capture attention and help sway voter thinking.

So are slogans a truly important part of the marketing tool chest of a political campaign? My answer is a resounding yes. Throughout history, campaign slogans have made a difference in the outcome of many contests. What's more, the lack of strong slogans may be a factor in many recent close elections.

Above-Average Presidential Campaign Slogans

"Tippecanoe and Tyler Too," William Henry Harrison, 1840

In the Harrison-Van Buren election (see above), Harrison's Whig Party outmaneuvered the incumbent at every turn. The Harrison team made an all-out effort to cover thousands of towns across America and got the masses to root for their candidate through rallies, parades, picnics, and all manner of public displays. This was marketing, pure and simple, and set a new standard for what was necessary to win a national election.

"54–40 or Fight," James Polk, 1844

In 1844, dark horse James Polk challenged a very popular Whig Party candidate, Henry Clay. The Polk camp championed a cause that resonated with just enough voters—thirty-five thousand in the general election—to give him the win. In the year of the campaign, territorial expansion was the hot-button issue. The United States and Great Britain disagreed over the boundaries of the Oregon Territory, which had been under their joint control since 1818, and a similar confrontation with Mexico over Texas was in the wings.

The Polk slogan/chant "54–40 or Fight" summed up the situation and people's feelings about it perfectly. The numbers 54–40 refer to the northernmost latitude that Polk and others wanted America to claim as sovereign territory. This call to arms probably made the difference in Polk's very narrow win over Clay. After Polk became president, he led the successful effort to admit Texas to the Union following the Mexican War, and the acquisition of California and New Mexico.

Finally, in 1846, rather than go to war with Great Britain, Polk settled the Oregon Territory boundary dispute.

"We Polked You in '44. We Shall Pierce You in '52,"
Franklin Pierce, 1852

Two Mexican War heroes squared off in the campaign of 1852: Democrat Franklin Pierce and the better-known General Winfleld Scott. In the previous decade, President Polk had spearheaded a very popular land grab that dramatically increased the size of America and her territories. The Pierce team played their fellow Democrat's success all the way to another victory.

The Scott camp tried to portray Pierce's Mexican War leadership as an embarrassment compared with Scott's outstanding performance, but no one really cared except Scott and his Whig Party handlers. The Whigs also spotlighted Pierce's love for whiskey, a well-known fact, and injected the phrase "Pierce, a hero of many a well-fought bottle" into the campaign, to no avail.

Pierce trounced Scott with 254 electoral votes to Scott's forty-two; Scott won just four states. This election was also notable as the last time the Whig Party had any bearing on a presidential campaign.

"Don't Swap Horses in the Middle of the Stream,"
Abraham Lincoln, 1864

Despite the esteem Americans hold Lincoln in today, he was by no means a shoo-in for a second term. In 1864, the war ground on day after day with no end in sight and many in the North, including the Democratic Convention that nominated General George B. McClellan to run against Lincoln, were ready to come to an accommodation with the South to end the confiict then and there.

The campaign of 1864 was nasty, pitting a war-weary Lincoln against McClellan and his inner-circle of Lincoln haters. McClellan was the MacArthur of his day: remarkably impressed with himself and convinced the country had no chance of recovery and uniflcation unless he became President. Unlike MacArthur, who was a military genius as well as a world-class egotist, McClellan only brought his ego into battle. Lincoln had sacked McClellan in 1862 after the General squandered the chance for early decisive victories against the South and perhaps a much-abbreviated Civil War. No matter, the McClellan team pinned every failure to end the war on Lincoln and his administration.

The Lincoln haters' no-holds-barred approach included listing Lincoln's traits as seen by McClellan supporters in the September 1864 edition of *Harpers Magazine*: "Filthy Story Teller, Despot, Liar, Thief, Braggart, Buffoon, Robber, Swindler, Tyrant, Fiend, Butcher."

Lincoln's campaign held to higher ground with the "Don't Change Horses ..." slogan, a clear reminder to voters that this was decidedly not the right time to change leaders. Fortunately, in the weeks just prior to election time, Lincoln's ablest generals, Ulysses S. Grant and William T. Sherman, won major victories and so did Lincoln on Election Day. He lost only three states, Kentucky, Delaware, and New Jersey, and won the popular vote by a ten-point margin.

HISTORICAL SIDELIGHT This was the first general election by any country to be held during a major conflict.

"Blaine, Blaine, James G. Blaine, the Continental Liar from the State of Maine," Grover Cleveland, 1884

"Ma, Ma, Where's My Pa?" James Blaine, 1884

These two slogans for the opposing presidential candidates in 1884 stand apart from all others as the nastiest, hands down.

The presidential vote of 1880 elected Republican James Garfleld to offlce. After Garfleld's assassination a few months later, Vice President Chester Arthur served out the rest of Garfleld's term. Arthur was generally considered substandard at best, though some historians believe him to have been a modest man who did a decent job, albeit not at self-promotion. Arthur did not pursue nomination in 1884 with any zeal, primarily due to health reasons that he publicly denied. Two years later, Arthur died of Bright's disease, a rare kidney disorder.

Because of Arthur's reluctance to run, the Republicans turned to their most visible standard bearer, Senator James Blaine of Maine. There was one problem: Blaine and his running mate, John Logan of Illinois, were both suspected of any number of crooked railroad schemes involving kickbacks and other shady dealings.

The Democrats, in a fighting mood having not won an election since 1856, were all over the Blaine railroad issue. They picked the young, straight-arrow governor of New York, Grover Cleveland, as their candidate. Cleveland was known for personal integrity: he had been an effective and scandal-free sheriff and mayor of Buffalo, New York prior to his term as governor. However, shortly after Cleveland's nomination, a reporter at the *Buffalo Evening Telegraph* unearthed a story that as a young man, Cleveland had become intimate with a Buffalo widow, had a son with her, and had supported the widow and son ever since.

Both parties saw blood in the water. The Democrats identified a pair of out-and-out crooks in Blaine and his running mate; the Republicans were absolutely gleeful to point out the "sex scandal" of Governor Cleveland, even though he had not been married at the time of his romance with the widow.

In the end, both political camps decided to go for broke and make it crystal clear what each thought about the other. The Republicans chanted "Ma! Ma! Where's My Pa?" and the Democrats took every opportunity to remind voters that, despite his protests to the contrary, "Blaine, Blaine, James G. Blaine, the Continental Liar from the State of Maine" was a crook through and through.

This bitter back-and-forth ended in a very close election with the outcome decided in New York by a razor-thin margin for Cleveland: 1,149 votes out of about a million cast. (Cleveland won the general election by just 23,000 votes.) Still, a win is a win, and the Democrats hadn't tasted victory for almost twenty years. After the election, Democrats voiced two popular refrains: in response to "Ma! Ma! Where's My Pa?" they replied: "Gone to the White House. Ha! Ha! Ha!" The second refrain referenced also the widow Maria and her son: "Hurray for Maria! Hurray for the kid! I voted for Cleveland and I'm damn glad I did!"

"He Kept Us Out of War," Woodrow Wilson, 1916

In 1916, World War I raged in Europe and Americans hoped to avoid involvement. Even the sinking of the *Lusitania* in May 1915 by a German U-Boat, with 128 Americans killed, was not enough to change either public opinion or the opinion of Democratic President Woodrow Wilson, who was contemplating a second term.

Just prior to the Democratic convention, Wilson decided to concentrate on strengthening the American economy and keeping the country out of war. He wanted Americans to put themselves and their loyalty to America flrst and let their old ties and loyalties to European homelands fade into the distant past.

The peace theme was front and center at the Democratic convention. Wilson's campaign slogan came from a podium speech by the famous orator and former congressman William Jennings Bryan, who declared, "I agree with the American people in thanking God we have a president who has kept—who will keep—us out of war."

Meanwhile, the Republicans bickered among themselves about "peace at any cost" and former president Teddy Roosevelt's opposing view: "America must flght German aggression now and retain its honor and standing on the world stage."

The Republicans nominated Supreme Court justice Charles Hughes—like Roosevelt, a former governor of New York. To placate the Teddy camp, the convention picked Roosevelt's former vice president, Charles Fairbanks, to be Hughes's running mate.

In the end, Hughes never found his footing between the two views of the day: stay out of war at all cost or join the flght for freedom from tyranny now. To his credit, Hughes campaigned vigorously. Wilson, however, adopted the "rose garden" approach, sending the message that his presidential duties were too important for him to spend much time touring the country and shaking hands. Despite his strong antiwar theme and the complete backing of his party, Wilson almost lost the election, as he remained cloistered at his private residence in Long Branch, New Jersey. The flnal tally gave Wilson 49.4 percent of the popular vote with 277 electoral votes, versus 46.2 percent and 254 electoral votes for Hughes.

"He Kept Us Out of War," which was repeated at every opportunity by Wilson's campaign staff and supporters, probably made the difference in this tight race. Hughes had no rallying cry to galvanize public support.

As events would have it, Wilson took the oath of offlce in March 1917 and on April 6, the United States declared war on Germany. So Wilson indeed had kept us out of war, but only for one month into his second term.

HISTORICAL SIDELIGHT Hughes's wife was the first spouse of a presidential candidate to tour the country on her husband's behalf.

"Back to Normalcy" and "Cox and Cocktails,"

Warren Harding, 1920

1920 was not a great year for Wilson. His legacy was in bad shape. Americans were mad: mad at the cost of the war, mad at rising infiation, mad at a generally sour economy, and mad at Wilson's focus on the creation of the League of Nations at the expense of ever-growing domestic problems.

This discontent made its way to the Democratic convention where, flnally, on the forty-fourth ballot, a ballot of Wilson supporters was picked: James Cox, the governor of Ohio and his running mate, Wilson's assistant secretary of the Navy, Franklin D. Roosevelt.

The Republicans were keenly aware of the dissatisfaction across the land with Wilson and the Democrats. On the tenth ballot, the Republicans chose Senator Warren Harding of Ohio to be their presidential candidate. Positioned perfectly for the times, Harding was handsome, popular in a critical state, a product of small-town America, and touted the right message: Let's bring back the good times we all enjoyed before the Wilson years. His running mate, Calvin Coolidge, was the quiet and hard-working governor of Massachusetts.

Harding's slogan, "Back to Normalcy," came about by accident. Not a great orator, he spoke in Boston about the need to get back to *normality*, which was his written text, but he pronounced it as *normalty*. Reporters who covered the speech changed what they heard to normalcy, which in fact was the proper spelling of what Harding tried to convey.

Harding also attacked Cox for opposing Prohibition, the Eighteenth Amendment to the Constitution, enacted in 1919, which outlawed the consumption of alcoholic beverages. Harding deserves some kind of credit for his ability to ignore his personal habits while railing on about Cox and cocktails. Harding's private life was the complete opposite of his public piety and return-to-purer-times message. In no particular order, he loved to drink alcohol, chew tobacco, gamble, and bed as many women as his charm and good looks could deliver.

Harding won with the largest margin of victory since George Washington: over 60 percent of the popular vote, 7 million votes more than Cox, and 404 electoral votes to Cox's 127.

"Keep Cool with Coolidge," Calvin Coolidge, 1924

Calvin "Silent Cal" Coolidge was one of the most popular presidents of all time. Some say Coolidge's popularity was high because he so rarely remarked on anything. In truth, part of his appeal was his complete honesty, straightforward approach, and the fact that he was as normal a person as a president could be.

Coolidge took the helm in 1923 when President Warren Harding died of a sudden heart attack. The Republican Convention of 1924, widely considered the most boring political convention of all time, nominated Coolidge for his own full term. Humorist Will Rogers commented that Cleveland, where the convention was held, should open the city's churches to liven things up a bit.

Meanwhile, the Democratic Convention was in complete disarray. They flnally nominated John W. Davis, a lawyer from New York and a West Virginia native, on the 103rd ballot. The greatest round of applause occurred when Senator Pat Harrison of Mississippi, in a keynote address, called for a new Paul Revere and the assembled delegates thought they heard, "What this country needs is real beer."

Coolidge won in a landslide by over seven million popular votes, just as his predecessor Harding had done.

"A Chicken in Every Pot and a Car in Every Garage," Herbert Hoover, 1928

Herbert Hoover, the Republican candidate who followed the popular Calvin Coolidge, projected the message that he would maintain the prosperity that had been administered so well by his predecessor. With cars affordable for many Americans and the economy in good condition, Hoover's simple slogan was a natural.

The Democratic challenger, Alfred Smith, the four-term governor of New York, really had no chance. Smith was the flrst Catholic to run for president and millions of non-Catholics were convinced that a vote for Smith was a vote for the Pope. The other major issue that dragged Smith down was Prohibition. Living in New York City, he saw flrsthand how the mob-controlled flow of liquor created graft, corruption, and a huge economy for gangsters. Smith wanted Prohibition modified to stamp out the mob's involvement. Hoover maintained the prevailing view that alcohol was sinful and the country should officially be "dry, dry, dry."

The election of 1928 was the first in which both presidential candidates used radio as an integral part of their campaigns. Unfortunately, Smith's heavy working class New York accent did not make him sound presidential, especially in comparison to Hoover, a bland speaker with no accent.

Hoover creamed Smith at election time. The electoral votes tell the story: Smith captured eighty-seven to Hoover's 444. The final blow for Smith was his inability to carry his own state, New York.

"Happy Days Are Here Again," Franklin D. Roosevelt, 1932

In 1932, the country still suffered from the Great Depression sparked by the stock market meltdown of 1929. America was not a happy place and because the catastrophic collapse had occurred on Hoover's watch, he was basically defeated before he even ran for a second term.

The Democrats turned to Franklin Roosevelt, who had a comprehensive political resume including two terms as governor of New York, and a nomination for vice president on the Cox ticket in 1920.

FDR, as Roosevelt came to be known, was the first and last paralyzed American to run for president. This disability (he was a victim of polio) didn't stop him from vigorous campaigning. Immobile from the waist down, he stood at podium after podium with the help of leg braces and a strong upper body. According to many historians, Roosevelt was the best public speaker to ever seek the presidency. His extremely effective use of radio in his "fireside chats" to the nation certainly supports this conclusion. There were other great American orators, of course, including Jefferson, Lincoln, and William Jennings Bryan. But none had radio to extend the reach of their speeches to the entire body politic.

FDR is remembered for a number of powerlines. (Chapter 2 discusses his declaration of war on Japan.) He coined "New Deal" when he accepted the Democrats' nomination for president: "I pledge you, I pledge myself to a new deal for the American people." The press picked up on the term and it has been used ever since as shorthand for Roosevelt's pact with America to get the country back on its feet economically.

Roosevelt had asked the band to play "Anchors Aweigh," a reference to his stint as assistant secretary of the Navy during the Wilson administration, as he closed his acceptance speech at the Democratic Convention. At the last minute, a few close advisers decided to go with a more upbeat popular song of the day: "Happy Days Are Here Again." They were right on the money. "Happy Days" quickly became FDR's campaign song. It struck a cord with a nation yearning for exactly that. Soon millions were singing:

> Happy days are here again!
> The skies above are clear again!
> Let's all sing a song of cheer again—
> Happy days are here again!

Roosevelt is best remembered for a line in his 1933 inaugural address. In an attempt to rally the country from its flnancial depression to a healthy economic recovery, Roosevelt focused on the critical role of attitude and delivered a line based on a phrase written by Henry David Thoreau: "The only thing we have to fear is fear itself." Most of what he said around this famous sentence was average political speak and some of it was downright spurious—for example, his suggestion that too many people lived in the nation's cities. America muddled on in continual economic distress for eight more years, until the beginning of World War II. Among other things, the war was an economic boon that helped put everyone back to work. Roosevelt successfully led America and her allies to victory and his "nothing to fear" line continued to deflne how he and America viewed all the challenges during his record four terms as its elected president.

"Sunflowers Die in November," Franklin D. Roosevelt, 1936

An odd slogan, this phrase referred directly to Roosevelt's second-term challenger, Republican Alf Landon, the former governor of Kansas, a state that's offlcial fiower is the sunfiower. Sunfiowers indeed do not last outdoors through the cold of a Kansas winter and Landon's presidential bid died in the heap of a November landslide. Roosevelt won every state but Maine and Vermont, picking up 523 electoral votes to Landon's eight.

"I'm Just Wild About Harry," Harry S Truman, 1948

Harry Truman, vice president during Franklin Roosevelt's fourth term, landed the presidency after Roosevelt died in offlce shortly before the end of World War II. Many remember Truman for his decision to drop atom bombs on two Japanese cities, an event that ended the war with Japan and began the postwar era known as the Cold War.

Most historians view Truman very favorably, but in 1948, much of the country thought it was time for the Republicans to have a shot at the Oval Offlce. Truman and his opponent, the very popular governor of New York and former prosecutor, Thomas Dewey, were both good campaigners. In many senses, Truman wasn't just running against Dewey. He was also running against the image voters had in their minds of Roosevelt, who had seemed larger than life, gifted as he was with a sharp wit, great poise, charm, and sophistication—truly a rock star in his day. Truman had none of those qualities, which was exactly the reason FDR had picked Truman as his running mate.

Thus, there was some brilliance in Truman's choice of a campaign slogan that had the word "wild" in it, for there was absolutely, positively nothing wild about the man at all. "I'm Just Wild About Harry" is the opening line of Noble Sissle and Eubie Blake's popular song of 1921. Its reappearance as a slogan in 1948 caught on with voters, and the Truman camp used it effectively to counter the image of Truman as a meek and mild man. Nevertheless, up through Election Day, every major pollster was convinced Dewey would win with a comfortable margin. In fact, Truman carried the election by over two million popular votes, and won 303 electoral votes to Dewey's 189.

"I Like Ike," Dwight Eisenhower, 1952

"I Still Like Ike," Dwight Eisenhower, 1956

The Republicans flnally had their revenge after a long dry spell when their candidate, Dwight D. Eisenhower, beat Democrat Adlai Stevenson by a huge margin, not once but twice, in 1952 and 1956.

Eisenhower used the simple slogan "I Like Ike" in his 1952 run. A well-thought-out slogan, this line is simple and easy to remember. It doesn't overpromise and, very important, it is fun to chant, particularly in large crowds in increasing volume: "I Like Ike, I Like Ike, I Like Ike!"

Of course, it helped that Eisenhower, supreme allied commander of the European theater during World War II, had been a daily staple of American war news, where headline writers frequently referred to him by his nickname, Ike. Surely, if a public figure's nickname becomes a household word, he should work to keep it top-of-mind during an election campaign.

In the 1952 presidential race, the best slogan the Stevenson camp could muster was "Stevenson. The Experienced Candidate." Not exactly a jump-up-on-your-chair-and-pump-your-fist-in-the-air expression. Besides, who was kidding whom … Eisenhower and a few others—Roosevelt, Churchill, and Generals Marshal and MacArthur—had just saved the world from tyranny. For all intents and purposes, Stevenson's campaign was dead on arrival. Eisenhower won the election by a huge margin of close to seven million votes and took 442 electoral votes, versus Stevenson's eighty-nine.

Stevenson was a perfectly nice man but no match for a real war hero, and both sides knew the outcome of the 1952 election from the day campaigning began. It didn't help Stevenson's cause that he never really believed he had a chance. What seems a bit odd is why he and the party movers and shakers decided to face certain defeat all over again in 1956.

HISTORICAL SIDELIGHT Stevenson looked and acted like a tenured college professor, as did his inner circle. Plus, he was bald. And so Joseph and Stewart Alsop hatched the term *eggheads* in their regular column in the *New York Herald Tribune* to describe all the head-in-the-clouds Stevenson intellectuals. This term, with all its pejorative connotations, has been in popular use ever since.

"All the Way with LBJ!" Lyndon Johnson, 1964

Every American born on or before 1958 remembers exactly where they were and what they were doing on November 22, 1963, when the news came that President John F. Kennedy had been assassinated in Dallas, Texas. We remember all the images from those next few days, including Vice President Lyndon Johnson taking the oath of office on Air Force One as Kennedy's widow and others looked on.

Johnson and Kennedy had been more rivals than friends. During three years as president, Kennedy had effectively shut out Johnson from his inner circle. Despite a basic mistrust and a lack of caring for each other, after the assassination, Johnson adopted Kennedy's plans to improve America as his own. President Johnson went on to create landmark legislation for civil rights, education, and care for the elderly, greatly exceeding the expectations of Kennedy loyalists.

Johnson's campaign slogan implied, "Folks, we are going to complete what my predecessor started." This was the flrst highly visible sign that Johnson planned to carry on the work Kennedy had started. The vast majority of Americans completely supported Johnson's pledge, a commitment to move ahead in Kennedy's footsteps.

The Republican far right just plain misunderstood or chose to ignore the mood of America while it mourned its young president, killed so tragically. In fact, the Republicans attempted to remind the populace that a vote for Johnson was "an echo, not a choice." Their rallying cry for ultraconservative candidate Barry Goldwater was actually "A choice, not an echo." Turns out, an "echo," or continuation of Kennedy's plans for social change in America, was what the majority wanted.

On Election Day, voters went "All the Way with LBJ." Johnson won the popular vote by over 16 million—a record up to that time. He won 486 electoral votes to Goldwater's flfty-two and carried with him into Congress the largest majority since Roosevelt's huge election sweep in 1936. All the way, indeed.

"Are You Better Off Than You Were Four Years Ago?"

Ronald Reagan, 1980

The 1976 election had been a close one between Democrat Jimmy Carter and Republican Gerald Ford, who had become president in 1974 when Richard Nixon resigned in disgrace over the Watergate mess. Now, four years later, the country was in a different kind of mess. By 1979, infiation was out of control, mortgage rates were sky high, and Carter's ratings were so low that the joke around Washington was that Carter's approval ratings were lower than the prime interest rate. Plus Carter, in televised speeches, constantly reminded America about its "crisis of confldence." To tell a nation whose core value is a strong sense of optimism that it needed a collective self-help session to "flnd itself" was just plain dumb.

Enter the Republican candidate: former Hollywood actor and governor of California, Ronald Reagan.

Reagan was an optimist from head to toe who could not and would not focus on being down and out in mind or spirit. He understood exactly what Carter's weak points were: blaming everybody and everything for the poor health of the economy and the supposed mindset of Americans. For example, Carter answered the problem of high winter heating costs by appearing on nationwide television in a V-neck sweater and rather strongly suggested that Americans turn down their thermostats and "sweater up." Not exactly what the populace wanted to hear from the most powerful leader in the world.

Reagan hit his stride and, in hindsight, knocked Carter out of the race during their single live televised debate on October 28, 1980. The debate centered on two issues: the state of the economy and national security, the major issues debated by candidates ever since.

Reagan used his poise and acting acumen to great effect every time Carter attacked his lack of experience as a world leader or his simplistic views on righting the sickly economy. After each of Carter's verbal assaults, Reagan would simply shake his head a bit and with a chuckle quip: "There you go again!" Millions of Americans had the same exact thought. It was a brilliant powerline and maybe the first political-putdown powerline to capture the fancy of the entire nation.

The knockout blow was Reagan's summation at the end of the debate:

> Are you better off than you were four years ago? Is it easier for you to go and buy things in the stores than it was four years ago? Is there more or less employment in the country than there was four years ago? Is America as respected throughout the world as it was? Do you feel that our security is safe, that we're as strong as we were four years ago?

Reagan went on to say in a deliberate and understated way that if the viewer agreed that America was not as well off as before, Reagan offered a very clear choice in his vision and commitment.

The line "Are you better off than your were four years ago?" was so well received that, immediately after the debate, the Reagan camp adopted it as their slogan for the closing weeks of the campaign.

Reagan won in a landslide that stunned the pundits in both parties, pulling in 489 electoral votes to Carter's forty-nine.

HISTORICAL SIDELIGHT Carter was the first incumbent Democrat to lose a second-term bid since Grover Cleveland in 1888.

"It's Morning Again in America," Ronald Reagan, 1984

Reagan won reelection in a landslide. His opponent, former vice president Walter Mondale, never had a chance. During Reagan's first term, the economy rebounded, interest rates went back to normal, and American pride and military might were on the rise after the dismal self-doubt of the Carter years. Reagan won every state except Mondale's home state of Minnesota, which Mondale only narrowly carried by four thousand votes.

Why mention this election at all? The significance is in the slogan, "It's Morning Again in America." Many political analysts cite it as the best slogan ever in presidential politics and they are probably right. Nothing even remotely as good has been created since.

Hal Riney, a legendary advertising executive and creative director, devised this slogan for the Reagan campaign. Riney clearly understood that the most powerful slogan would exactly mirror the personality and deeply held beliefs of the candidate. This match of personality and proclamation is rare and only appears in three other slogans throughout presidential campaign history: "Keep Cool with Coolidge," FDR's "Happy Days Are Here Again," and Ross Perot's 1992 slogan, "Ross for Boss." In each case, the man and the slogan were one and the same. Coolidge was in fact cool under pressure; Roosevelt was an eternal optimist as evidenced by his ability to not let polio keep him from becoming one of the greatest presidents and world leaders; and Ross Perot was a boss's boss and a self-made billionaire by the force of his natural business personality.

Reagan was basically FDR with a better medical history. He believed in the positive power of mankind, that good would trump evil every time through sheer force of character, commitment, and focus, and that occasional setbacks should never actually set you back.

Ronald Reagan was not just Mr. President; he was Mr. Sunshine. Hal Riney saw that quality the minute he met Reagan and developed the 1984 message, "We are optimistic and we damn well should be. Let's not recede into the malaise of the past, but rather celebrate all the accomplishments of the last four years and for the next term to follow."

Here is the full text of the brilliant television commercial written and narrated by Hal Riney.

> It's morning again in America. Today, more men and women will go to work than ever before in our country's history. With interest rates at about half the record highs of 1980, nearly two thousand families today will buy new homes, more than at any time in the past four years. This afternoon, six thousand five hundred young men and women will be married, and with inflation at less than half of what it was just four years ago, they can look forward with confidence to the future. It's morning again in America, and under the leadership of President Reagan, our country is prouder and stronger and better. Why would we ever want to return to where we were less than four short years ago?

Why indeed. Reagan won by one of the greatest margins of all time.

Just Okay Presidential Campaign Slogans

"Vote Yourself a Farm," Abraham Lincoln, 1860

This campaign was one of splintered confusion mainly because in 1860, the nation was in the same state. Lincoln won from a field of four candidates, in part, because he didn't say all that much during the campaign and managed to avoid alienating one voting block or another. The slogan above referred to a Republican platform promise to give land to farmers who would settle in the West. A longer version, "Vote Yourself a Farm, Vote Yourself a Tariff," added the concept of increasing tariffs on imported goods to strengthen prices and boost factory output in the Northern states.

Lincoln's slogan met a need brought on by the expansion of America's Industrial Revolution: more farms to support non-farm workers. It played well everywhere but the South.

The campaign promise to give Western land to those who settled on it was fulfilled with passage of the Homestead Act of 1862.

"Patriotism, Protection, and Prosperity,"

William McKinley, 1896

Republican McKinley got a lot of campaign momentum from a severe depression, the Panic of 1893, which occurred under Democratic President Grover Cleveland's watch. McKinley's dynamic young Democratic challenger, William Jennings Bryan, gave it his all, but oratory power could not make up for a country that had been devastated by economic disaster just a few years before.

The nation wanted prosperity and McKinley, backed up by his brilliant campaign manager, Mark Hanna, struck exactly the right chord. Hanna, who is credited with inventing many of today's political campaign marketing techniques, urged McKinley to outspend the opponent, which he did by a factor of ten, and distribute millions of pamphlets and handbills across the nation. Prior to this election nothing of this scope had ever been done.

"Four More Years of the Full Dinner Pail,"

William McKinley, 1900

This slogan sums up the election campaign of 1900, which ended in victory again for McKinley by an even wider margin than four years earlier. McKinley had done a good job with the economy and helped move America onto the world stage as a power to be recognized. He had actually used this slogan at times during the previous campaign of 1896. And 1900 was basically the same campaign against the same challenger, William Jennings Bryan. Again, the McKinley camp outspent Bryan. Again the Bryan team did not have a campaign slogan of its own to counter McKinley.

But this time around, McKinley had a "take-no-prisoners" running mate: Teddy Roosevelt. A battle hero, Roosevelt was fresh from the 1898 Spanish American War and had done a credible job as governor of New York. Not known for subtlety, Roosevelt told friends after the election that he expected to be "a dignified nonentity for four years" in his vice president's role.

Six months after the election, a young anarchist assassinated McKinley at an exposition in Buffalo, New York, and Teddy went from "nonentity" to activist president, and in many ways was the first leader to begin creating the America we live in today.

"A Time for Greatness," John Kennedy, 1960

Even though a politician with natural public speaking ability created this slogan, it has little to recommend it. Greatness is an overused word—when isn't it a time for greatness?—and neither this slogan nor the opposition's, "Experience Counts," amounted to much in this historically close election. Kennedy's challenger, Richard Nixon, attempted to portray Kennedy as inexperienced compared to Nixon, who had spent eight years as Eisenhower's vice president. The public didn't buy the argument given Kennedy's long record of public service in the House and the Senate as well as the fact that Kennedy entered Congress the same year as Nixon, 1946.

This election centered on two issues that had no connection to either slogan. On September 26, 70 million Americans watched the flrst televised presidential debate. While no hard data was actually complied, historians believe Kennedy outperformed Nixon. Kennedy was calm and poised and looked directly at the camera and, therefore, at the viewing audience. Nixon looked at Kennedy rather than the camera whenever he answered a question or rebutted a point. It didn't hurt Kennedy either that television enhanced his handsome features, while Nixon's expressions came across as stiff, humorless, and odd looking.

The other issue of the day was religion. Would Kennedy the Catholic really pander to the Pope and the Vatican if elected? An absurd notion in today's America but a real fear of millions of non-Catholics back in the late 1950s. At a campaign dinner in New York, Kennedy told a story to the audience about the infallibility of the Pope, based on Cardinal's Spellman's response to the same question, "I don't know Senator—all I know is he keeps calling me Spillman."

Kennedy won by one hundred thousand popular votes, carrying Texas and Illinois by slim margins.

HISTORICAL SIDELIGHT On January 20, 1961, Kennedy took the oath of office. He was the first Catholic president and the youngest ever elected. He was forty-three.

"Nixon's the One," Richard Nixon, 1968

Even with a boring slogan, Richard Nixon got his revenge in 1968 by narrowly defeating Hubert Humphrey. America suffered through 1968, a year marked by the relentlessness of the Vietnam War and the assassinations of two great Americans—Martin Luther King and Robert Kennedy. The country was in a violent, nasty mood, expressed in riots against the war and the racism of the third-party candidate, George Wallace, and his running mate, retired General Curtis LeMay. In the height of poor taste and mean spirit, anti-Nixon posters featured a very pregnant black woman and Nixon's campaign slogan: "Nixon's the One!"

Nixon prevailed in the face of many vicious attacks and won the presidency by five hundred thousand popular votes. Wallace and LeMay carried five states and more than ten million popular votes, a very good showing for a third-party run at the Oval Office.

No Wonder He Lost—Though Not in Every Case

"Who is James Polk?" Henry Clay, 1844

Henry Clay discovered a great way to give notoriety to an obscure opponent: put the opponent's name front and center in your own campaign slogan. Very effective. And the height of stupidity. Clay's misstep meant Polk had two slogans going for him: his own powerful "54–40 or Fight," (see above) and Clay's, "Who is James Polk?" Clay's misguided slogan created name recognition for the unknown Polk and cost Clay the election. Amazing.

"For President of the People," Zachary Taylor, 1848

Some slogans are so mundane it's hard to imagine why the candidate even bothered. "For President of the People"—versus what? Maybe farm animals or aliens from the ex-planet Pluto? Taylor's claim to fame was his war hero status in the Mexican-American War in which he picked up the nickname "Old Rough and Ready." "Ride into Victory with Old Rough and Ready" would have made a far better slogan. But perhaps Taylor's slogan makes sense given the historic obscurity of the 1848 election. Today, nobody remembers and nobody cares.

Taylor, the Whig candidate, won the election in a three-way race against Democratic Senator Lewis Cass of Michigan and Free-Soil candidate Martin Van Buren. The Free-Soil Party came into existence during this campaign and was dedicated to the prohibition of slavery in all federal territories. The Party's slogan was "Free Soil, Free Speech, Free Labor, and Free Men." Quite a mouthful. It would also reappear as the slogan for another candidate eight years later.

In July 1850, two years into his term as president, Taylor, who was sixty-five, died of acute gastroenteritis. His death paved the way for Vice President Millard Fillmore to continue doing very little to distinguish this four-year term.

"Free Soil, Free Labor, Free Speech, Free Men, and Fremont,"

John C. Fremont, 1856

This slogan wins the okay, okay award as in—I get it—everyone should be free. Freedom was a big issue—and the right issue—in the years leading up to the American Civil War. The problem is the slogan is a mouthful and difficult to say in the right order. It would have been better as "Free Speech, Free Men, Fremont."

Republican Fremont, a well-known explorer, lost in a three-way race to the Democrat James Buchanan. The Republicans were adamant about abolishing slavery. The Democrats were more interested in preserving the Union at any cost. A third party, the American Party, which had its origins as a self-proclaimed secret society formed in New York in 1849, was a factor in this election. It represented the antiforeigner faction, maintaining that aliens should not become citizens until after twenty-one years of residence in America, and that no foreign-born person should be allowed to ever hold any political office.

The American Party picked up a curious nickname: the Know-Nothings. No doubt this nickname still expresses how many Americans feel about their political leaders. Nevertheless, the Know-Nothings earned the name because they directed followers to say, "I don't know" or "I know nothing" whenever a member of the press asked about party activities. And yes, the American Party had a slogan, "Americans Must Rule America," as well as a candidate in the 1856 election—none other than former president Millard Fillmore.

Buchanan won, garnering 45 percent of the popular vote and 174 electoral votes. The Know-Nothings managed to win 25 percent of the popular vote but only one state—Maryland.

"Rejuvenated Republicanism," Benjamin Harrison, 1888

Despite two awkward words slapped together to form one thoroughly awkward campaign slogan, Harrison, a former senator from Indiana, helped bring the Republican Party back to life in his 1888 run for the White House.

Nasty seems to describe many presidential campaigns and this one was no exception. Many Harrison supporters portrayed his opponent, President Grover Cleveland, as an out-and-out drunk who routinely beat his wife in flts of drunken rage. It didn't help matters that the flfty-one-year-old Cleveland was married to his twenty-one-year-old ward, Frances Folsom, whom he had wed when she was eighteen. This sort of age difference did not sit well with many Americans and in fact still doesn't. The allegations of drinking and beatings were complete hog-wash, but still regularly appeared in the mainstream press throughout the campaign period.

On occasion, the Harrison camp trotted out another slogan, "Grandfather's Hat Fits Ben," a reference to Harrison's grandfather, William Henry Harrison, who was elected president in 1840 under the banner "Tippecanoe and Tyler, Too." (See above.) Grandpa Harrison only served for a month before dying of pneumonia, but why let thorny details get in the way?

The real issue of the day boiled down to one word, *tariff*.

President Cleveland, a Democrat, wanted to lower tariffs on foreign goods to create a free-trade environment that many felt would help the U.S. economy.

The Republican leadership wanted exactly the opposite, none more forcefully than Harrison, an all-out protectionist.

The Republicans kicked their campaign into high gear. Harrison made countless speeches denouncing free trade. The campaign distributed millions of handbills and fiyers. Wealthy industrialists, who wanted zero competition from Europe and elsewhere, kicked in millions in campaign gifts. The Republican Party started to call itself the Grand Old Party or G.O.P. This name resonated well with voters, who were nervous about a "new America" in which other countries could compete on a level playing fleld without the barrier of restrictive tariffs.

Meanwhile, the Democrats basically sat on their thumbs because President Cleveland refused to actively campaign.

The results on Election Day proved the power of a sitting President to draw votes despite a lackluster campaign and spotlighted the oddity of the electoral system. Harrison beat Cleveland 233 to 168 in electoral votes, but lost the popular count by one hundred thousand.

HISTORICAL SIDELIGHT Four years later, in 1892, Cleveland came back to challenge now President Harrison. This time Cleveland won by a handy margin in popular and electoral votes. He is the only American president who served two terms separated by one term out of office.

"The Experienced Candidate," Adlai Stevenson, 1952

Compared to what Dwight Eisenhower had to deal with in planning, execution, and people management to win the world war against Germany, Stevenson's campaign claim of more experience was downright laughable. Even Stevenson didn't believe it. To be fair, probably no other candidate, short of FDR returning from the grave, could have prevented Eisenhower's victory.

"For the Future," Richard Nixon, 1960

Let's see. Are we all for the future? A show of hands. The only weaker slogan I can think of is "For the Past." Not that opponent Kennedy's slogan, "A Time for Greatness," was other than deeply mediocre. (See above.) The Republican Party's slogan backing Nixon, "Experience Counts," fell on deaf ears as well, since most Americans thought both men had equal experience. As for the word "experience," its use and overuse in the description of politicians from county sheriff to secretary of state renders it pretty much worthless. Forgettable slogans like these are a harbinger of close elections. It was a narrow defeat for Nixon—by one hundred thousand votes.

"In Your Heart You Know He's Right," Barry Goldwater, 1964

About what exactly? Goldwater was the first and last conservative's conservative to make a run for the White House. The outcome was never in doubt. His opponent Lyndon Johnson, running for his own full term after serving out the remainder of John Kennedy's, was only worried about how much of a landslide he could muster.

Goldwater, in his heart, believed that he was right. Right about the waste and distaste of the "welfare state" the Johnson administration had built. Right about the need for absolute military strength in the face of Soviet expansion. Right about a foreign policy that would make George Bush's look downright friendly.

Yes, Goldwater was an extremist and proud of it. His Republican convention acceptance speech is best remembered for the line "I would remind you that extremism in defense of liberty is no vice."

On the subject of foreign policy he was crystal clear about where he would lead the nation. Simply put: leave the United Nations and never look back, break off all relations with the Soviet Union, and use tactical nuclear bombs to flght communists in Vietnam and other Commie strongholds.

Not surprisingly, many of his proclamations during the campaign were outrageous. He was quoted as saying he'd like to "lob one into the men's room of the Kremlin and make sure I hit it."

Small wonder Johnson's only concern was the extent of the landslide to come. The Democrats quickly seized upon Goldwater's "let's nuke 'em when we have the chance" philosophy and came up with their own unofflcial slogan to counter "In Your Heart You Know He's Right." Their retort: "In Your Guts You Know He's Nuts." It didn't stop there. Bumper stickers appeared with "Goldwater for Halloween" and "Vote for Goldwater and Go to War."

To top it all off, the Johnson advertising team created the famous "Daisy" commercial. It showed a little girl plucking petals from a daisy as a nuclear countdown ends in a huge mushroom cloud explosion. President Johnson's voiceover was, roughly, "vote for me or God help us all."

Daisy became a single-word powerline. The commercial only ran once, on the NBC Saturday Night Movie several months before election night. However, the Goldwater camp complained bitterly. That was their fatal error. The news media picked up on the protest and showed Daisy over and over for weeks to follow. Then, *Time* magazine put Daisy on the front cover. (In this era, *Time* was still a giant among its peers in readership and infiuence.)

Apparently, Goldwater was fun for the press pool and those who traveled with him could generally count on at least one outrageous statement a day. They came up with several tunes to parody their man including this one, sung to the tune of "The Battle Hymn of the Republic":

> Mine eyes have seen Goldwater at a million speaking dates,
> Mine ears have heard him give the lie to liberal candidates,
> And my head has quaked and trembled as he tells us of our fate
> If Lyndon should get in.
> Barry, Barry says he'll save us,
> From A.D.A. which would enslave us,
> The curious crew that would deprave us
> He'll save us all from sin.

How big a landslide for Johnson? Very big. An advantage of 16 million popular votes and over four hundred flfty electoral votes.

HISTORICAL SIDELIGHT So was Goldwater technically nuts? *FACT* magazine polled 12,350 psychiatrists, asking the question "Is Barry Goldwater fit to be president?" Only 2,417 good doctors replied. Of those, 1,189 said, "no, he wasn't fit to be president," 657 said he was, and 571 said, "they would have to examine the patient to give a professional response."

"Not Just Peanuts," Jimmy Carter, 1976

"He's Making Us Proud Again," Gerald Ford, 1976

In a nutshell, this race had two candidates who were about as different from each other as the human species makes possible. Ford, longtime congressman from Michigan, Richard Nixon's vice-president after Spiro Agnew's forced resignation and president after Nixon's resignation, was the consummate Washington insider. Carter was about as far from the Washington crowd as someone could be and still be considered a politician. He was so unknown on the national scene that when he told his mother he planned to run for president she replied, "president of what?" His resume included stints as a naval atomic submarine offlcer, a peanut farmer, and a one-term governor of Georgia.

Carter's slogan is as curious as his resume. "Not Just Peanuts" is hardly a ringing endorsement for president of the United States. Many people thought the slogan was a joke, a put on. It never got much visibility and certainly didn't lend itself to rallying a crowd. Not, not, not—an awful choice for a campaign call to arms.

Ford had his own problems. He was plagued with a stalled economy, rising infiation, and the wrath of many who viewed his pardon of Nixon for his Watergate crimes as, at worst, insider payback for the vice presidential appointment or, at best, a stupid political mistake.

Was Ford "Making Us Proud Again" as his campaign motto announced? Not in the minds of many Americans. Yes, he was a nice guy with a wholesome all-American family of blonde, freckled children and grandchildren. But as America celebrated its bicentennial, it was tired. Tired of the years of Watergate investigations. Tired of the sense of failure brought on by the end of the Vietnam War. Tired of the Establishment that caused these two events. Americans didn't feel proud as a nation and no slogan was going to change that.

Jimmy Carter was in the right place at exactly the right time. Americans did want someone to make them proud, someone from outside the Beltway. If that meant electing a peanut farmer instead of a professional politician, so be it. Carter won by a decent margin of 1.7 million popular votes and carried all the southern states except Virginia—a feat last accomplished by John Kennedy. As it turned out, the Carter presidency failed to make enough Americans proud and paved the way for the Reagan Revolution.

"America Needs a Change," Walter Mondale, 1984

Much like the Johnson-Goldwater contest in 1964, the outcome of the Reagan-Mondale election was never in doubt. Unlike Goldwater, Mondale was not an ultra-fringe candidate. But both men believed America wanted a radical change in leadership, and both men were dead wrong.

Goldwater's "Better Dead than Red" conviction implied that nuclear war with Russia was better than existing under their dominance. "Wrong," said the American people, "we'd like to coexist thank you very much." Mondale believed the Reagan administration was responsible for an ever-increasing gap between the haves and the have-nots. By some measures, Mondale was surely correct. He failed to realize that even have-nots want a shot to break out of poverty without resorting to class warfare.

Mondale needed a better frame of mind and a better slogan. On purely technical grounds, the use of America in a slogan almost always puts Americans to sleep. America this. America that. Standard political yada yada yada that doesn't excite anyone. Reagan's slogan, "It's Morning Again in America," is the exception that proves the rule. This slogan brings the word America alive because it expresses a new thought, a new way to perceive what was happening to this country each and every day of the Reagan presidency.

America didn't need a change and it didn't need Mondale. It needed to get its pride back, its economy on track, and revive its view that better days were still ahead. Reagan's "It's Morning Again in America" embodied these sentiments. An original thought trumps same old same old every time.

Since Reagan—Powerless Lines

Alas, Reagan's 1984 slogan "It's Morning Again in America," was the last campaign slogan worthy of much discussion. Politicians are not the only Americans who have fallen into this verbal void. The art of creating and promoting great lines that deflne a political position, or a memorable brand in the commercial world, has gone into a kind of suspended animation.

I am reminded of Simon and Garfunkel's lyric "Where have you gone Joe DiMaggio? A nation lifts its lonely eyes to you." I would add, "Where have you gone Hal Riney?"—the ad genius behind "It's Morning Again in America."

Most of the slogans produced since then seem fiat and perfunctory, or just plain silly and inconsequential.

I have asked thousands of people in group settings over the last two years to name any presidential campaign slogans they can remember. Not a single person has come up with an offlcial slogan in use after 1984.

I often offer a hundred dollars on the spot to anyone in an audience who can recall the slogans used by either John Kerry or George W. Bush in the 2004 election campaign. There is always dead silence. When I show the slogans on a screen, absolutely no one gives any sign of recognizing any of them.

The indifference of today's political establishment to the value of a line that will stick in the voter's mind and possibly tip the balance between victory and defeat is a curious phenomenon. Perhaps this lack of a headline, of a powerline, to give the campaign a visual and vocal edge is why 70 million eligible voters did not bother to cast their ballots in the last presidential election.

Throughout the past twenty-three years, there have been just two slogans worthy of some acknowledgement for their power to excite the populous. And one wasn't even a slogan endorsed by the candidate.

Ross Perot ran for president in 1992 as the Independent candidate in a three-way race with the first George Bush and the young upstart governor from Arkansas, Bill Clinton. Initially Perot charmed Americans with his candor and fresh views on what was right and wrong with the nation and the world. His slogan, "Ross for Boss," was as unorthodox as Ross was in person, and people liked the little billionaire with the big ears.

Early on in the campaign, Perot actually led in the polls, a first for a third-party candidate. His campaign eventually lost momentum because of his own confusing behavior. He dismissed his well-regarded campaign chairman and close friend Tom Luce. He accused parties unknown of threatening to disrupt his daughter's wedding. He even dropped out of the race for a time and then reappeared with little explanation. Still, Perot managed to pick up almost 20 million votes in the general election, which probably was the reason Clinton won and Bush lost.

Not surprisingly, Bill Clinton's approach to campaign slogans was as frenetic as his legendary twenty-hour days. No one inside or outside of his 1992 campaign was ever really sure what slogan was The Slogan. One he used off and on in the final months of campaigning was "Putting People First." Not exactly a revelation for a politician.

The line many people remember from Clinton's campaign wasn't even an official slogan. Clinton adviser James Carville dreamed up "It's the Economy, Stupid," to keep Team Clinton focused on their strategy for beating George W. Bush come Election Day. In an effort to keep the campaign on message during the final run up to the election, Carville hung a large board inscribed with three points at Clinton headquarters. "It's the Economy, Stupid" shared wall space with:

"Change Versus More of the Same," and
"Don't Forget Health Care."

Just to show how the mind plays tricks, when I mention this line to people they are sure it was Clinton's visible campaign slogan. It was not. The line didn't become public until after Clinton won the election.

Here are pithy comments on the other lines listed under "Since Reagan—Powerless Lines." Each gets a sentence or two and then the return to oblivion it so clearly warrants.

"Kinder, Gentler Nation," George H. W. Bush, 1988

Americans actually don't want to be this kind of nation. We want to be fair-minded, hardworking, kind when we can, but tough on the world stage, especially with known adversaries. Bush's opponent at the time, then governor of Massachusetts Mike Dukakis, was so weak that slogan power hardly mattered. Nevertheless, a line Bush delivered in a 1988 campaign speech mattered a lot. "Read My Lips—No New Taxes" was a promise President Bush did not keep. And four years later, voters did not keep him in the White House for a second term.

"Building a Bridge to the Twenty-First Century,"
Bill Clinton, 1996

Clinton should have adopted "It's the Economy, Stupid," as his slogan for reelection in 1996 and called it a day. Okay, we are headed toward the next century. Are you our president or a mechanical engineer? Hoover was the last engineer-president and everyone knows how well he did running for a second term.

"The Better Man for a Better America," Bob Dole, 1996

Dole lost handily to Clinton in 1996. Hey Bob, Americans don't want the better man for president, they want the right man. A bland slogan for a bland candidate. Not a good combination and certainly not a winning one. Anyone using America in a slogan, beware. The slogan better be drop-dead fantastic or at least a brand-new thought or no one will pay attention.

"Compassionate Conservatism," George W. Bush, 2000

What exactly does this phrase mean? Are normal everyday all-around conservatives void of all compassion? Do they not help the sick, poor, and downtrodden in some way? The whole thought is absurd. Did the Bush campaign actually pay a consultant real money for this ridiculous line?

Plus, people have to actually think about what the line means before concluding that it's meaningless. Don't make voters think about the real or hidden meaning of a slogan. They won't.

"Prosperity and Progress," Al Gore, 2000

Is this the best the self-proclaimed inventor of the Internet and various other modern technical wonders could conjure up to rally the country and defeat the compassionate conservative mentioned above? No wonder the election wound up in the Supreme Court.

Both candidates—guilty of boring and meaningless slogans in the flrst degree.

"Yes, America Can!" George W. Bush, 2004

Here we go again with America. I'm pretty sure he's not referring to the American Can Company, but you never know. Can what? Can grow? Can be stronger? Can go it alone and build ten-foot fences to keep the Canadians and Mexicans out? This slogan makes no sense.

"Let America Be America Again," John Kerry, 2004

Seriously, I couldn't make this stuff up. Three Americas appear in the last two candidates' slogans. I suppose it hardly matters since no American in America or outside of America has the slightest idea these slogans existed about … America.

Final Observations

This chapter traveled back through time to see how candidates spoke about the issues of the day. Some of these men rose above the ordinary political verbiage of their time and changed the course of history for America.

Do great men somehow come together with great powerlines? Franklin Roosevelt and John Kennedy did. Sometimes great lines, like Hal Riney's work for Ronald Reagan, are a happy accident or

Four Steps to the Creation of a Powerful Political Slogan

1. Create a new thought about what's ahead or a clear benefit that will occur if elected.
2. Reinforce the personality of the candidate.
3. Create a slogan that can be sung or chanted; rhyming is always a positive.
4. Use the slogan everywhere, in all media.

the creation of a brilliant marketing mind. Sometimes powerlines show up late to the party the way Carville's line for Clinton, "It's the Economy, Stupid," did. And sometimes the media picks up on a line or creates a term like eggheads, used to describe Adlai Stevenson and his inner circle.

And don't forget that the word "booze," the phrase "keep the ball rolling," and the simple expression "okay" all came from a campaign in 1840 between two men little remembered: William Henry Harrison and Martin Van Buren.

Powerlines outlive the candidates, the issues of the day, the relentless passing of time. They make their mark because they made an impression and cause people to take extra notice. Power to the People. Not a bad line when you come right down to it. Not a bad line at all.

CHAPTER 5

Shots Heard Round the World

How Eloquent Speakers and Writers Make Us Think and Rethink

THE CHALLENGE OF creating great political slogans is that they rarely occur naturally. Instead, a paid consultant or two is tasked with delivering a campaign message so that … there is one. That is why most campaign slogans today are so vapid. In contrast, this chapter shows how powerlines created by naturally gifted speakers and writers from all walks of life can capture attention, inspire, and entertain with memorable, fresh ideas.

All of the citations in this chapter are lines that continue to live on, remembered by many. They are lines that make us think and rethink. And they make us interpret meaning, beyond mere communication. True powerlines.

Powerlines from the Battlefield

Credit for the title of this chapter goes to that great artist, Anonymous. "The shot heard round the world," a reference to the skirmish that ignited the Revolutionary War, was actually an exchange of gunfire between British soldiers and a ragtag band of American colonists on a clear day in April 1775. Both sides took casualties when their accidental encounter on Lexington Green, Massachusetts escalated into a shooting match. The phrase caught on in the press and went on to become one of the most famous lines in history.

This war generated another famous line a few months later, on June 17, 1775, during the battle of Bunker Hill, when one William Prescott yelled out to his American colleagues: "Don't fire until you see the whites of their eyes." Given the accuracy of firearms at the time, it seemed an excellent point to make.

Men in battle are fodder for powerlines. The following are my favorites.

Military Powerlines

"I do not fear an army of lions, if they are led by a lamb. I do fear an army of sheep, if they are led by a lion." Attributed to Alexander the Great (356–323 BC), King of Macedonia.

Hard to argue with a legendary military leader who, at an early age, had conquered most of the known world of his day.

"Alea iacta est." (The die is cast.) Gaius Julius Caesar (100–44 BC), Roman political and military leader.

With these three words, Caesar clearly let his army know that they had reached a point of no return. It was the year 49 BC, and they were about to cross the Rubicon River into Italy and instigate a war with Pompey and the Roman Senate.

"Veni, vidi, vinci." (I came, I saw, I conquered.)

These are the words Caesar chose in 47 BC to make sure the Roman Senate understood his commitment to complete military victory. He wanted the august gathering, most of whom he thought were pompous, fat, and lazy, to know that he meant to continue what he started when he defeated the Pharnaces at Zela.

St. Crispian's Day Speech

And Crispin Crispian shall ne'er go by,
From this day to the ending of the world,
But we in it shall be remembered—
We few, we happy few, we band of brothers;
For he to-day that sheds his blood with me
Shall be my brother, be ne'er so vile,
This day shall gentle his condition;
And gentlemen in England now-a-bed
Shall think themselves accurs'd they were not here,
And hold their manhoods cheap while any speaks
That fought with us upon St. Crispin's day.

Generations of English schoolchildren memorize this passage from Shakespeare's *King Henry V* some of which remains a part of military language, often quoted in abbreviated form:

"We few, ... we band of brothers. For he today that sheds his blood with me shall be my brother ...."

"Put your trust in God, but keep your powder dry." Oliver Cromwell (1599–1658), Lord Protector of England during the 1649–1653 conquest of Ireland.

Another great line from an Englishman. During Shakespeare's lifetime, Cromwell determined who to remove from the world's stage before their time.

"Never interrupt your enemy when he is making a mistake." Napoleon Bonaparte (1769–1821), French general and politician.

Napoleon, the premier military leader of his day, had a pretty fair sense of humor.

"I only regret that I have but one life to lose for my country." Nathan Hale (1755–1776), captain, Continental Army.

These were Hale's last words, spoken as British soldiers marched him to the gallows in 1776. He was the first American spy to be executed.

"I have not yet begun to fight." John Paul Jones (1747-1792), captain, Continental Navy.

Jones yelled this to the British captain, who asked if he wished to surrender. Jones wasn't kidding. He stared into the eyes of defeat and then led his crew to victory in one of the fiercest naval battles of the Revolutionary War. Because his ship, the *Bon Homme Richard*, sank from damage sustained in the battle, Jones transferred his crew to the captured British ship, HMS *Serapis*. On October 3, 1779, on the deck of the *Serapis*, Jones wrote a lengthy report to the U.S. Congress, which contained this famous line:

"I wish to have no connection with any ship that does not sail fast, for I intend to go in harm's way."

"Praise the Lord and pass the ammunition." H. M. Forgy, Chaplain, USS *New Orleans*, Pearl Harbor, December 7, 1941.

Chaplain Forgy reportedly shouted this to the soldiers around him on the deck of the *New Orleans* as he shot at incoming Japanese war planes from a gun turret. The line was incorporated into a song popular throughout the rest of World War II.

"I shall return," General Douglas MacArthur (1880–1964).

In 1942, on orders from President Roosevelt, General MacArthur abandoned the Philippines, leaving behind thousands of troops to surrender to the Japanese and endure the infamous Bataan Death March. Two years later, he kept his promise and liberated the American survivors, including his friend General Jonathan M. Wainright.

Powerlines from the Halls of Power

No less than soldiers, statesmen throughout history have left a legacy of powerlines that ring as true today as when they were first spoken.

Benjamin Franklin (1706–1790)

"Early to bed and early to rise makes a man healthy, wealthy, and wise."

Hard to argue with Mr. Franklin's philosophy of success.

"We must indeed all hang together, or most assuredly we shall all hang separately."

Franklin is credited with saying this, a line that speaks like no other to the heart of the American Revolution, as he and other "rebels" signed the Declaration of Independence in Philadelphia on a hot July day in 1776.

Georges Clemenceau (1841–1929)

"Mr. Wilson bores me with his Fourteen Points! Why, God Almighty has only ten!" Georges Clemenceau, French prime minister.

World War I was absurd on many levels, including the millions of lives lost for what turned out to be a false peace, and the elaborate oratory that took place at the war's end as the Allies tried to outdo each other with detailed rules for the future conduct of world diplomacy. None was better at this task than American President Woodrow Wilson who, after all, had an earlier turn as president of Princeton University. The above is the French prime minister's comment on Wilson's Fourteen Points for Peace.

Franklin Roosevelt (1882–1945)

The stock market crash in October 1929 flattened financial markets and deflated investor hubris around the world.

The day after the crash, a headline in *Variety* proclaimed: "Wall Street Lays an Egg." Many thought the markets would quickly recover. They did not. In America, unemployment soared to 25 percent over the next few years. A lesson hard won—to never put all your money in one account—still reverberates today.

In 1932, Franklin Roosevelt was elected president largely on the basis of his belief that radical change was necessary to get the country back on its feet. In accepting his party's nomination earlier that year, Roosevelt spoke of a new beginning between government and the workingman and workingwoman:

"I pledge you, I pledge myself, to a new deal for the American people."

Later, during his inaugural address to the nation, he fervently rallied the nation to take on the challenges of recovery:

"The only thing we have to fear is fear itself."

Winston Churchill (1874–1965)

One of Roosevelt's most storied contemporaries was the brilliant Winston Churchill: British politician, prime minister during World War II, and winner of the Nobel Prize for Literature in 1953. Churchill could outwrite, outspeak, outsmoke, and outdrink . . . well, everybody.

During one period of the war, Churchill moved into the White House to work more closely with Roosevelt on plotting strategy and the hoped-for Allied victory. Churchill pitter-pattered through the White House corridors in pajamas, which he wore during the day as well as at night. He also liked to soak in hot baths for hours with a cigar and brandy handy, reading communiqués and dictating responses to hovering secretaries.

Many great lines are attributed to Sir Winston, but two are in a class by themselves. Both lines come from speeches Churchill delivered to the British House of Commons in the summer of 1940, a time when many thought saving England was a hopeless cause and defeat was inevitable. Churchill vehemently disagreed. In this passage he rallies his fellow politicians for the long, hard struggle ahead, which included the likelihood of a German invasion:

> Upon this battle depends the survival of Christian civilization. Upon it depends our own British life and the long continuity of our institutions and our empire. The whole fury and might of the enemy must very soon be turned on us now. Hitler knows that he will have to break us in this island or lose the war. If we can stand up to him, all Europe may be free and the life of the world may move forward into broad, sunlit uplands. But if we fail, then the whole world, including the United States, including all that we have known and cared for, will sink into the abyss of a new Dark Age, made more sinister, and perhaps more protracted, by the lights of perverted science. Let us therefore brace ourselves to our duties, and so bear ourselves that, if the British Empire and its Commonwealth last for a thousand years, men will still say, "This was their finest hour."

A few months later, Churchill gave the second speech to honor the Royal Air Force who had, against all odds, outmaneuvered and outlasted the German bombers in months of daily and nightly air attacks on London and other population centers. Eventually, the young RAF fighter pilots inflicted enough damage on their enemy that the air war over England petered out, a major feat and a significant early turning point in the war. Churchill summed it up in one concise sentence:

"Never in the field of human conflict was so much owed by so many to so few."

John F. Kennedy (1917–1963)

Kennedy was the youngest American president ever elected, which gave him a certain natural vitality in a world traditionally governed by "old men." Like Churchill and Roosevelt, he was a superb orator and writer. He was also a natural on camera and embraced television to get his message directly to citizens of America and the world.

Kennedy was a study in contrasts, many of which only came to light after his assassination in November 1963. He was active and vigorous, but also in constant pain, often heavily medicated. His public statements were measured and nuanced; his private ones hard-nosed and, on the subject of Communism and tyranny, rabid. He was reckless in his private life and sometimes in his public one, embracing high-risk ventures like the Bay of Pigs, a failed invasion of Cuba. Yet, he could also step back and come up with creative solutions under pressure as he did during the Berlin and Cuban Missile Crises.

After taking the oath of office on a freezing day in January 1961, Kennedy delivered one of the best speeches ever given on the value of freedom and its obligations:

> My fellow Americans, ask not what your country can do for you, ask what you can do for your country. My fellow citizens of the world, ask not what America will do for you, but what together we can do for the freedom of man.

Martin Luther King Jr. (1929–1968)

On August 28, 1963, in one of the most stirring and impassioned speeches ever delivered, Dr. Martin Luther King Jr. called for the end of discrimination and the realization of the true American dream:

> When we allow freedom to ring, when we let it ring from every village and every hamlet, from every state and every city, we will be able to speed up the day when all God's children, black men and white men, Jews and Gentiles, Protestants and Catholics, will be able to join hands and sing in the words of the old Negro spiritual, "Free at last! Free at last! Thank God Almighty, we are free at last!"

Ronald Reagan (1911–2004)

Freedom is a powerful theme, evoked brilliantly in 1987 by President Reagan. Before a huge crowd at the Brandenberg Gate in the Berlin Wall, Reagan issued this challenge to Michail Gorbachev, the Soviet empire's leader:

"Mr. Gorbachev, open this gate! Mr. Gorbachev, tear down this wall!"

A few years later, Gorbachev did exactly that.

Powerline Poets—Ten of the Very Best

It's nearly impossible to pick a few lines from just ten poets and leave it at that, but here are my favorites with a little commentary.

Andrew Marvell (1621–1678)

Andrew Marvell was basically thrilled to be alive and thought everyone else should be, too. As these passages from "To His Coy Mistress" illustrate, he recognized how brief life could be, especially in the seventeenth century, and believed in living every day to the fullest:

> Had we but world enough, and time,
> This coyness, lady, were no crime.
> We would sit down, and think which way
> To walk, and pass our long love's day.
> ....
> An hundred years should go to praise
> Thine eyes, and on thy forehead gaze;
> Two hundred to adore each breast,
> But thirty thousand to the rest; ....

Without an endless amount of time, to beat around the bush and spend years being civil and socially correct was, to Marvell, a terrible waste of time. He was all for the moment. Clearly, he had no patience with the norms of the day:

> For, lady, you deserve this state,
> Nor would I love at lower rate.
>
> But at my back I always hear
> Time's winged chariot hurrying near; ...

And just to drive the point home ...

> Thy beauty shall no more be found,
> Nor, in thy marble vault shall sound
> My echoing song; then worms shall try
> That long preserved virginity,
> And your quaint honor turn to dust,
> And into ashes all my lust.
> The grave's a fine and private place,
> But none, I think, do there embrace.

William Blake (1757–1827)

Both poet and songwriter, Blake's best remembered hymn is "Jerusalem," sometimes known as "And Did Those Feet," a stirring composition about the struggle with dark forces and the effort it takes to overcome them. Almost two hundred years later, we are still trying. Here's the last stanza:

I will not cease from Mental Flight,
Nor shall my Sword sleep in my hand,
'Til we have built Jerusalem
In England's green and pleasant Land.

Alfred Lord Tennyson (1809–1892)

In "Ulysses," Homer's hero of Trojan War stardom, now an old man, recollects his youth, fame, and vigor. Ulysses despairs about the hopelessness of his fate: to leave his deeds and conquests to his son and then fade from view, a used-up old man.

How dull it is to pause, to make an end,
To rust unburnish'd, not to shine in use!
As tho' to breathe were life! …

Talk about a baby boomer nightmare.

Ulysses, however, refuses to accept the conventional vision of old age: devoid of passion, energy, and lust for life. Rather:

… Life piled on life
Were all too little, and of one to me
Little remains: but every hour is saved
From that eternal silence, something more,
A bringer of new things; and vile it were
For some three suns to store and hoard myself,
And this gray spirit yearning in desire
To follow knowledge like a sinking star,
Beyond the utmost bound of human thought.

The last lines of the poem sum up Ulysses's philosophy: live every day to the fullest, until the last breath, age be damned.

Tho' much is taken, much abides; and tho'
We are not now that strength which in old days
Moved earth and heaven, that which we are, we are;
One equal temper of heroic hearts,
Made weak by time and fate, but strong in will
To strive, to seek, to find, and not to yield.

Often quoted, the last line has been used as a slogan by the outdoor adventure organization, Outward Bound.

Matthew Arnold (1822–1888)

Like *The Thin Red Line*, a 1998 film about Japanese and American soldiers at war in a tropical paradise, Arnold's "Dover Beach" depicts unspeakable beauty as the backdrop to unspeakable horror. This is a classic tale of the stupidity of war in a world of endless natural wonder and beauty, a world indifferent to the violence and aggression of mankind.

Ah, love, let us be true
To one another! For the world, which seems
To lie before us like a land of dreams,
So various, so beautiful, so new,
Hath really neither joy, nor love, nor light,
Nor certitude, nor peace, nor help for pain;
And we here as on a darkling plain
Swept with confused alarms of struggle and flight,
Where ignorant armies clash by night.

Arnold's last line makes you shake your head in total agreement with the futility of it all.

A. E. Housman (1859–1936)

For Housman, the fewer words the better. "To an Athlete Dying Young," his warning that great achievement at an early age is no guarantee of future fame and fulfillment, hits the mark in just twenty-eight lines. The following are two stanzas from this poem.

Smart lad, to slip betimes away
From fields where glory does not stay,
And early though the laurel grows
It withers quicker than the rose.

Now you will not swell the rout
Of lads that wore their honours out,
Runners whom renown outran
And the name died before the man.

Powerlines frequently contain an implied thought that forces us to fill in the blanks. Similarly, Housman's compact writing encourages the reader to make mental leaps to fully appreciate his meaning. His "Stars, I Have Seen Them Fall," a rarely cited poem, is a great example.

Stars, I have seen them fall,
But when they drop and die
No star is lost at all
From all the star-sown sky.
The toil of all that be
Helps not the primal fault;
It rains into the sea,
And still the sea is salt.

Making an even bigger leap, this poem is almost a proxy for Einstein's famous equation, $E = mc^2$. Like Einstein, Housman knows that you can't snuff out what is endless to begin with.

William Butler Yeats (1865–1939)

Some scholars consider Yeats to be one of the outstanding poets of all time. He lived in an era of unprecedented change. Horses and steam engines gave way to automobiles and airplanes. Single-shot muskets and crude cannonballs grew to become massive firepower on ships, tanks, planes, and in the arms of individual soldiers. Candle and gaslight were extinguished by electricity. Telephone, radio, and television filled the airwaves. Appliances were invented at lightning speed. And the list goes on.

As World War I raged on, with its outrageous examples of man's inhumanity to man, Yeats wrote "The Second Coming," one of his most praised poems. A vision of more horror to come, "The Second Coming" fears evildoers—fanatics who grasp the reigns of power while the rest of us look on, refusing to get involved or somehow incapable of doing so—will supersede the behavior of good and reasonable people.

Turning and turning in the widening gyre
The falcon cannot hear the falconer;
Things fall apart; the center cannot hold;
Mere anarchy is loosed upon the world,
The blood-dimmed tide is loosed, and everywhere
The ceremony of innocence is drowned;
The best lack all conviction, while the worst
Are full of passionate intensity.

Is all hope lost? Yeats suggests it is:

Surely some revelation is at hand;
Surely the Second Coming is at hand;
The Second Coming! Hardly are those words out
When a vast image out of Spiritus Mundi
Troubles my sight: somewhere in sands of the desert
A shape with lion body and the head of a man,
A gaze blank and pitiless as the sun,
Is moving its slow thighs, while all about it
Reel shadows of the indignant desert birds.
The darkness drops again; but now I know
That twenty centuries of stony sleep
Were vexed to nightmare by a rocking cradle,
And what rough beast, its hour come round at last,
Slouches towards Bethlehem to be born?

Robert Frost (1874–1963)

Frost is remembered for three poems in particular, often learned by many Americans in school: "Mending Wall," "The Road Not Taken," and "Stopping by Woods on a Snowy Evening."

In "Mending Wall," two New England neighbors rebuild a broken stone wall on their joint property line. One bemoans that the wall is always falling apart for one reason or another.

Something there is that doesn't love a wall,
That sends the frozen-ground-swell under it,
And spills the upper boulders in the sun,
And makes gaps even two can pass abreast.
The work of hunters is another thing:
I have come after them and made repair

He even questions whether they need a wall:

> There where it is we do not need the wall:
> He is all pine and I am apple orchard.
> My apple trees will never get across
> And eat the cones under his pines, I tell him.

The other neighbor insists they must regularly mend the wall, as their fathers did: "He only says, 'Good fences make good neighbors.'" And that is the line we remember.

> "The Road Not Taken"
>
> Two roads diverged in a yellow wood,
> And sorry I could not travel both
> And be one traveler, long I stood

Choices—how often we think about them and wonder in hindsight if we made the right ones. One can opt for the conservative approach or instead, go in a new direction in a burst of liberation as Frost's narrator does:

> Then took the other, as just as fair,
> And having perhaps the better claim,
> Because it was grassy and wanted wear;

But striking out alone and cutting a new path, may not be nirvana. He communicates all this with a pause in the last stanza:

> I shall be telling this with a sigh
> Somewhere ages and ages hence:
> Two roads diverged in a wood, and I—
> I took the one less traveled by,
> And that has made all the difference.

"Stopping By Woods on a Snowy Evening" opens with a solitary evening sleigh ride through a dark forest blanketed with snow. The solitary sleigh rider seems at peace with the quiet and solitude. But then, Frost makes you believe the rider would like to just get lost for a while, maybe permanently:

My little horse must think it queer
To stop without a farmhouse near
Between the woods and frozen lake
The darkest evening of the year.

But as the ending makes clear, it just isn't going to happen. As the last stanza suggests, the rider can't pack it in, not yet, not now:

The woods are lovely, dark and deep
But I have promises to keep,
And miles to go before I sleep,
And miles to go before I sleep.

In a rare interview with the press, Frost once was asked if he thought there was such a thing as hell. Frost replied, "Gentlemen, I have seen hell. Hell is a half-full auditorium."

T. S. Eliot (1888–1965)

Many people believe Eliot was English, perhaps because of his close relationship with Ezra Pound, but in fact he was born and raised in Ohio. Eliot produced several of the most thought-provoking poems of all time, including a number of lines that burn into the memory of even the casual reader.

Three poems that stand out are "The Love Song of J. Alfred Prufrock," "Preludes," and "The Hollow Men."

"Prufrock" is by far the most famous of the three and perhaps the single work Eliot is best known for. The tale is simple: a middle-aged bachelor wants to ask an attractive woman for a date and just can't gather the courage. The poem goes on and on as he torturously muses on a decisive course of action.

In the room the women come and go
Talking of Michelangelo.

The reference is to Michelangelo's naked statue of a perfectly proportioned David—they talk of men, but never of Prufrock.

Later in the poem, Prufrock makes a decision at last, and a pathetic one at that:

I grow old ... I grow old ...
I shall wear the bottoms of my trousers rolled.

Finally, in the last stanza, as he daydreams about walking on a beach with a woman, referred to as a mermaid, it is clear that life will go on but with loneliness as his only real company:

We have lingered in the chambers of the sea
By sea-girls wreathed with seaweed red and brown
Till human voices wake us and we drown.

In the end, it is clear that Prufrock is too timid to ever pop the question. Too bad he didn't have Internet access—online dating was made for guys like Prufrock.

"Preludes" takes place in 1917 London on a cold, raw winter morning. World War I has been raging for three years with no end in sight, and poets like Eliot were generally distraught by the stupidity of it all. Toward the poem's end, Eliot acknowledges that he still has a dim hope that mankind might come to its senses with perhaps a God to intervene:

I am moved by fancies that are curled
Around these images and cling:
The notion of some infinitely gentle
Infinitely suffering thing.

Hopes dashed, Eliot finishes with a famous powerline stanza describing the bleak world as a hopeless case:

Wipe your hand across your mouth, and laugh;
The worlds revolve like ancient women
Gathering fuel in vacant lots.

Eliot's negative outlook goes one step further in "The Hollow Men." Indeed, he believes we stumble about and fail to grasp that our insignificant existence will not make the slightest ripple in the universe. When the world finally ends, absolutely no notice will be taken:

This is the way the world ends
This is the way the world ends
This is the way the world ends
Not with a bang but a whimper.

Dorothy Parker (1893–1967)

The cynical worldview gene was not exclusive to Eliot by any means. A female contemporary, Dorothy Parker, was very much his equal, though with a more humorous approach in her writings and daily life. Her wit was legendary and her view of men was on a par with Eliot's sobering take on mankind.

Below are two of her typically short and pointed poems, one on men, one on the dilemma of suicide. Here is a writer who knew the impact of a powerline.

"Unfortunate Coincidence"

By the time you swear you're his,
Shivering and sighing,
And he vows his passion is
Infinite, undying—
Lady, make a note of this:
One of you is lying.

"Resume"

Razors pain you;
Rivers are damp;
Acids stain you;
And drugs cause cramp.
Guns aren't lawful;
Nooses give;
Gas smells awful;
You might as well live.

E. E. Cummings (1894–1962)

E. E. Cummings, known for his unorthodox style, slammed words together, ignored basic grammar, employed space between words more creatively than anyone else, and rarely used capital letters. It's always fun to spend a few minutes reading his take on life and death. His style is so unique that he inspires partly with just the way the words flow on the page. I reference two of his poems here: "in Just" and "I sing of Olaf glad and big."

"in Just" is about good and evil: the happiness of each new spring with its fresh flowers and children released from the indoor confinement of winter, and the ever-present evil never far from the balloons and hopscotch and innocence of youth. To Cummings, evil can mean disease, physical malformation, untimely death, and even the lurking pedophile, as in this last stanza:

> it's
> spring
> and
>   the
>   goat-footed
> balloonMan   whistles
> far
> and
> wee

"I sing of Olaf glad and big" is a marvelous description of a conscientious objector caught up in the web of the draft. Here are two famous lines:

> I will not kiss your f__ing flag.
>
> there is some s___ I will not eat.

And the last stanza:

> preponderatingly because
> unless statistics lie he was
> more brave than me: more blond than you

Shakespeare's Genius

William Shakespeare has contributed more to literature's treasure trove of powerlines than any other writer. His extraordinary way of turning a phrase makes his words unforgettable reminders of universal truths about human nature. Four hundred and forty-three years after his birth, Shakespeare's work still inspires, angers, and amazes.

Some of the best-known lines in literature come from *Hamlet*. In a modern context, this play would be the perfect daytime drama—lots of intrigue, misplaced passion, jealousy, family problems, and miscommunication. All in all, it's a dark tale where no one is happy and some people wind up dead.

"To be or not to be, that is the question." (*Hamlet*, Act 3, Scene 1, 56)

Hamlet, Prince of Denmark, is having a remarkably bad day. In the famous soliloquy that begins with the line above, he thinks aloud about suicide and revenge. Should he take his own life and end it all, or stay the course and avenge his father, murdered by his mother's new husband?

What makes this line so special is the simple use of the word *be*. It would have been easy for Shakespeare to write "To die or not to die." After all, it is exactly the same thought. But, as mentioned in Chapter 1, a solid powerline uses a keyword or phrase that the brain does not expect, and thus retains for future reference. To be. Or not to be. So simple; I can be here one minute and vanish for all time the very next. It is a dramatic thought.

Of course, Hamlet lives on to avenge his father. In the full speech he says, "Thus conscience does make cowards of us all," meaning that suicide may be a gate to purgatory or hell. Hamlet took those words to heart, decided it was best to stay alive, and sent his dad's murderer to hell instead.

"Get thee to a nunn'ry." (*Hamlet*, Act 3, Scene 1, 121)

Hamlet lashes out at his girlfriend Ophelia with the above. The word *nunn'ry* had a double meaning: the technical definition was a convent, but the common meaning was "go to a whorehouse where you-of-so-little-worth really belong." Ophelia eventually becomes so depressed she kills herself, leaving Hamlet about the only one standing at the end of the play.

"The lady doth protest too much, methinks." (*Hamlet*, Act 3, Scene 2, 239)

Hamlet throws an evening's entertainment, a play, for his mom, Queen Gertrude, and her new husband, whom Hamlet suspects killed his father, the true king. The play is meant to make his mom and stepdad feel real uncomfortable.

It succeeds. Queen Gertrude says the line above as she watches the "queen" in the play continually declare her complete affection and love for her first husband.

"Why, then the world's mine oyster." (*The Merry Wives of Windsor*, Act 2, Scene 2, 3)

Falstaff appears in a number of Shakespeare's plays, always the incorrigible grifter surrounded by bawdy pals, gals, abundant booze, and stolen goods. Falstaff and a petty thief, Pistol, are arguing heatedly. Pistol refuses to help Falstaff seduce and then rob two wealthy wives in Windsor. Falstaff refuses to make a loan to Pistol. Pistol arrogantly says the line above, meaning that he will damn well do what he pleases, and steal and rob at will.

"All the world's a stage." (*As You Like It*, Act 2, Scene 7, 139)

Jacques, a self-proclaimed philosopher, declaims this famous line in a long speech propounding his theory that life is a play written by a higher authority. Shakespeare, an actor first and writer second, always reminded his audiences that they, too, were part of a larger story, not totally removed from the drama they paid to watch.

"Good night, good night! Parting is such sweet sorrow." (*Romeo and Juliet*, Act 2, Scene 2, 185)

The doomed lovers have just exchanged their vows of total love and devotion. They are trying to say goodbye but cannot pry themselves away from each other. At last, they agree that parting is part pain but also part pleasure, and anticipate the hours until they meet again.

THE NEXT THREE POWERLINES are from *King Richard III*, a play about a particularly evil monarch who kills everyone in his path in his relentless quest for power. Physically deformed in the extreme, Richard is in love, well actually in lust, with the beautiful daughter of the king he must murder to ascend the throne. He is one bad dude and doesn't care who knows it.

Some say the real Richard, who was a king but not deformed, is Shakespeare's symbol of the corruption of the crown during the War of the Roses—a particularly dark period in English history. There is endless debate about whether Richard III was guilty of any of the horrors that Shakespeare depicts. Nevertheless, historians agree that Shakespeare's wealthiest patron, King James I of King James Bible fame, intensely disliked Richard's side of the royal family and was quite pleased with Shakespeare's take on family history. It's probably safe to assume a fair amount of hyperbole on Shakespeare's part. Whatever the background intrigue, this play has great lines. Here are several that have been winners since their stage debut.

"Now is the winter of our discontent." (*King Richard III*, Act 1, Scene 1, 1)

Richard opens the play with this line. In the soliloquy that follows, a powerful description of evil intent and doom, Richard introduces himself in all his hateful glory.

"Off with his head." (*King Richard III*, Act 3, Scene 4, 76)

Richard believed that anyone who blocked his path to the throne should be used, abused, and eliminated. So when he suspects Lord Hastings is plotting to destroy him, Richard announces the punishment above. Just normal everyday despot behavior. Unfortunately, Hastings had made the fatal assumption that he and Richard were close pals.

"A horse! A horse! My kingdom for a horse!" (*King Richard III*, Act 5, Scene 4, 7)

Richard is now king, having achieved his goal through ruthless brutality. Our famous playwright had an audience to delight, so the last act sets up Richard to receive payback in battle. His horse is killed and he is left exposed, without steed, on the field. Afoot and surrounded by the good guys, Richard's only thoughts are for another horse, to escape, and exit stage right. No such luck. Lord Richmond runs him through with his sword and goes on to become the new and popular king of England.

"Et tu, Brute?" (*Julius Caesar*, Act 3, Scene 1, 77)

A group of Roman senators assassinate the arrogant Caesar. During the attack, Caesar recognizes Brutus, heretofore one of his closest friends, among the assassins and says the above. The translation of the Latin is particularly poignant: Even you, Brutus? You can feel Caesar's amazement in his last moments as he takes in this ultimate betrayal.

MACBETH'S ENEMIES ARE CLOSING IN. He has just learned that his wife, and accomplice in the murder of the previous king, has killed herself. Macbeth proceeds down the path to his doom and faces his premature "way to dusty death." He recites this stoic soliloquy, shortly before paying the ultimate price:

> Tomorrow, and tomorrow and tomorrow,
> Creeps in this petty pace from day to day,
> To the last syllable of recorded time;
> And all our yesterdays have lighted fools
> The way to dusty death. Out, out, brief candle!
> Life's but a walking shadow; a poor player
> That struts and frets his hour upon the stage,
> And then is heard no more: it is a tale
> Told by an idiot, full of sound and fury,
> Signifying nothing.
>
> (*Macbeth*, Act 5, Scene 5, 19–28)

Talk about a tough line to follow.

CHAPTER 6

There Is Nothing Wrong with Your Television Set

How Writers and Marketers Keep All Eyes Glued to the Screen

FOR LINES TO ACHIEVE maximum power, they must be spoken with a unique delivery that cements the expression firmly in the mind. No better platforms for verbal expression exist than motion pictures and television. This chapter highlights lines that had their potential enhanced and, in most cases, fully realized through powerful delivery on either medium. Once heard, these lines never disappear from the subconscious and can often be recalled in an instant, years or decades later. Why? Read on.

As stated at the beginning of this book, sound shapes people's lives. Human brains are wired for sound almost from the moment of conception. Children learn to speak before they can read or write. No surprise, sound has more impact on the brain's memory function than any of the other senses.

When triggered, sound memory can evoke a single emotion, or several combined, from delight or sorrow, to fear or anger. These emotions can be felt in varying intensities, from low to high, and individuals who hear the same sound or series of sounds at the same time will not always react in the same way.

Two facts go a long way toward explaining the power of sound:

1. *Hearing is the purest sense.*

Human senses have evolved the same way most other species' senses have. Sight, touch, and taste can all mislead. But sounds mean exactly what people think they mean.

Short and harsh sounds are often warnings, such as a dog barking in the middle of the night, a car horn, or a police siren. Other sounds are smoother and longer, like most forms of music, laughter, and even crying.

Response to sound is fundamental to human survival and was honed through thousands of years of reaction and inaction to sounds that could harm or help.

2. *Hearing triggers instant recall.*

Infants and young children are highly receptive to learning sounds. Young brains take in any and all patterns of music and speech and more easily remember whatever comes their way. This is why it is so much easier to learn languages at an early age than later in life. As people age, they forget more, and remembering becomes harder, except when a sound triggers instant recall—that still happens as fast at eighty years of age as at four. Music or verbal phrases with distinctive patterns of tempo and rhythm are more likely than other sounds to trigger instant recall.

Because of sound's purity and ability to trigger instant recall, its role in today's media mix is paramount. By merging images and sounds, television and movies turbocharge the senses beyond what evolution intended or expected.

The Movies

The long road from silent films to the talkies was one worth traveling. Silent films had lots of visual drama, interrupted by written captions, and on better days, an impassioned live piano accompaniment. The talkies were born when synchronized spoken dialog was added to the mix; then Hollywood was really in business. Some of the world's most memorable and cherished powerlines started life as movie dialogue. These unforgettable lines usually shock and shake up conventional wisdom. Three combined factors make them memorable:

1. The speaker's inflection
2. The context and dramatic impact of the scene
3. The use of music or lack thereof

Below are my top ten picks. Each line tells a unique story. What they share is staying power. These lines have struck a chord with our social conscience and live on and on—the true test of any powerline.

Top Ten Movie Powerlines

"Frankly my dear, I don't give a damn."
(*Gone with the Wind*, 1939)

Clark Gable delivers this best-remembered line with just the right amount of disgust and disdain to Vivien Leigh's Scarlett O'Hara in the movie's closing scene. A large part of its impact in 1939 was the use of the profane *damn*, which by today's standards, or lack of, seems ludicrous. But the real power of the line is its summation of the entire story of Rhett, Scarlett, and the events that brought them together, complete with the changing emotions of fear, passion, anger, and finally loathing. There is satisfaction and power in telling a self-absorbed, spoiled beauty, despite her grit and will to survive, that her life ahead means nothing to the man she wants desperately to love and be loved by. An epic love story with a bitter ending.

"There's no place like home." (*The Wizard of Oz*, 1939)

Despite relatively primitive special effects, this story comes to life for every generation with its good-wins-over-evil message. Whatever wonders beckon from over the rainbow, in the end, the genuine friends people make along the way and the family and community they come from are what really matter. Judy Garland's Dorothy convinces every viewer that home is where people all want to be.

"Here's looking at you, kid." (*Casablanca*, 1942)

This is as good as it gets. Onscreen, a love story set in World War II Nazi-occupied French Morocco; offscreen, World War II rages in all corners of the globe. Danger lurks behind the eyes of every German in uniform and on every lonely street in this backwater country where spies and other shadowy figures go bump in the night.

Humphrey Bogart is the perfect love interest for Ingrid Bergman's conflicted beauty. Bogie says, "Here's looking at you, kid" to Bergman four different times in the movie, but the one viewers most remember is the last. Bogie has decided to stay behind in Morocco to deal with some nasty Nazis knowing that his potential soul mate will go off with her sometime husband, out of harm's way, and forever separated from the man she truly loves. "Here's looking at you, kid" is his farewell to Bergman. Got the tissues handy? It's a perfect ending and a perfect line.

"Bond. James Bond." (*Dr. No*, 1962)

The most successful movie franchise ever. In each Bond movie, Agent 007 reveals his name to all manner of bad guys and beautiful women. With this matter-of-fact declaration, Bond makes it crystal clear that the free world's deadliest agent really wants to make sure you know whom you are dealing with—no ifs, ands, or buts. The line is delivered as a warning, as in "Do you have any idea who I am?" What guy wouldn't want to be James Bond for just a moment?

"I want to say one word to you. Just one word. Are you listening? Plastics." (*The Graduate*, 1967)

At every level, this film is about the pull of the World War II generation on their baby boomer children and the boomers' attempts to push back. Wherever college graduate Ben Braddock (superbly played by Dustin Hoffman) turns, he is pressured to grow up, get with the program, and accept the 9-to-5-job-with-respectable-home-and-country-club life that his parents and friends want their children to replicate. Why? Because the adults want exact duplicates of themselves—even if they have adulterous affairs or cheat in business to keep the right car in the driveway while feeding the illusion that they really know how to make a killing financially because they are so, so smart.

Ben's parents and their friends bore him. When one of them corners Ben at his birthday party cookout and delivers the line "Plastics," Ben is ready to check out. Everything about this man with drink in hand screams "We older folk know exactly what's right for your future. Details aren't the least bit necessary. Nor are your interests. Just do as you're told. Go to college—don't argue. Go to Vietnam—don't question. Get a job in plastics—now. Just do as you are told." At the end of the movie, Ben does exactly the opposite. The graduate finally graduates.

"I know what you're thinking: Did he fire six shots or only five? To tell the truth, in all the excitement, I kind of lost track myself. But being this is a .44 Magnum, the most powerful handgun in the world, and would blow your head clean off, you've got to ask yourself one question: Do I feel lucky? Well, do you, punk?" (*Dirty Harry*, 1971)

Harry Callahan, played by Clint Eastwood, is a clean cop with dirty methods. He ignores the policies and procedures of the hapless police establishment, instead acting like a vigilante with a badge and a big gun. One day, Harry's hot-dog-stand lunch is interrupted by a robbery gone bad. Many shots and several dead bodies later, he walks up to a wounded bad guy lying on the pavement with his hand inches away from a sawed-off shotgun. Harry speaks his piece (quote above) while holding his .44 Magnum pistol inches from the robber's head.

The scene delivers a one-time image so powerful that viewers never forget it: a young, vibrant detective towering over a street punk, aiming a huge pistol at the punk's head, and uttering a perfect taunt that, in similar circumstances, most people would love to deliver.

Harry, his methods, and this sequence of sentences summed up the mood of the times: "Crime is out of control, criminals get off because of too much due process, and something must be done." Think swift justice.

These thoughts flooded the minds of viewers in the early seventies and still resonate with audiences today.

"I'm gonna make him an offer he can't refuse."

(*The Godfather*, 1972)

This movie is considered by many critics to be the best adaptation of a book ever brought to the big screen. There are so many great lines that scores of people can rattle off their favorites with little effort. Even many of the throwaway lines are near priceless, such as "In Sicily, women are more dangerous than shotguns."

But it is Michael Corleone's line, "My father made him an offer he couldn't refuse," that is the "godfather line" of the movie. Repeated by the godfather, played by Marlon Brando, to his inner circle of family and paid hit men, the line is pure intimidation backed up by the power to act—the only way to get what you want when you want it. Honor among thieves? But of course. Listen to the godfather. Real power means never using words like "I will kill you." It's far more effective to imply the dark deeds that will happen to whomever attempts to disrupt or impede the family business. Viewers love the understatement of the line and understand exactly what it means every time it is delivered.

"Leave the gun. Take the cannoli." (*The Godfather*, 1972)

Good to know hit men have their priorities straight. This completely unexpected line sticks with a viewer like a sticky cannoli. The godfather's henchman, Clemenza, is ordered to dispose of son-in-law Paulie, who thinks he is clever enough to turn against the family and get away with it. In the sequence leading up to this line, Paulie drives Clemenza and another family hitman on a bogus errand. On a deserted stretch of road, Clemenza tells Paulie to pull over for a minute so he can relieve himself. As Clemenza does his business in the tall reeds, his backseat companion puts three shots into Paulie's head. As the shooter gets out of a car splattered with brains and blood, Clemenza remembers the cannoli still on the backseat. Why leave that for the cops? After all, dessert is important, whereas ratfinks, especially dead ones, aren't worth the slightest thought.

Viewers can't believe what they just saw and heard. Cannoli, 10. Human life, 0. It's a scorecard that makes a powerful impression.

"I'm mad as hell and I'm not going to take it anymore."
(*Network*, 1976)

The line above is embedded in a long, rambling passage delivered with great force by Peter Finch, playing the burned out, burned up network anchorman, Howard Beale. With his nightly news ratings on the decline, Howard is desperate to hold on to his job. He becomes despondent and warns his viewers that the world is "going to hell in a hand basket." While Howard rants and raves to the world, the network's top executive sees an opportunity to increase ratings and, of course, revenue.

The more Howard protests and laments society's lack of values and passion, the more viewers see the hopelessness in his attempts to wake his apathetic audience to the dangers of consumerism. He rails against a society that has sold out to big cars, big oil, big business, and big profits. And indeed, as Howard unhinges on air, the ratings go ever higher, as do the spirits of his network handlers. In the end, when Howard throws in the towel and himself out the window to his death, viewers understand that he's right—and that there's not a thing they are going to do about it.

"I'll have what she's having." (*When Harry Met Sally*, 1989)

Everyone who saw this movie remembers Meg Ryan as Sally and her show-topping performance in a crowded Manhattan coffee shop when she proves to Harry (Billy Crystal) that an orgasm can be faked at anytime. Clearly, the power of sound is front and center, as Harry and all the lunchtime customers watch Sally pant and moan with increasing volume until she finally launches into a huge, blissful, "oh god, oh god, oh god," of contentment. After her "climax," a lone older woman at a nearby table tells her waitress in deadpan fashion, "I'll have what she's having." The director Rob Reiner's mom, Estelle, plays the older woman.

Why Movie Taglines are Important

Movies cost a ton of money to make. Most fail to earn back production and distribution expenses. Some eventually break even and a few occasionally break the bank, thanks to DVD sales and international distribution. But why is it so tough to bring home a moneymaker? Here are four reasons why most attempts at filmmaking just don't add up:

1. The talent demands and gets too much money.
2. Production locations and sets often cost millions.
3. Unions control every aspect of production and require a small army of union members on the set for even the most minor tasks.
4. Marketing costs typically amount to half as much as the total production budget.

A Daunting Picture

Of all the costs, the marketing budget has increased the most throughout the past ten years. It is not uncommon for Hollywood to spend upwards of $50 million to let the public know about an upcoming film. And with good reason: there seems to be a long road between knowing about an upcoming film and deciding to see it.

The movie marketing challenge is to get people to set aside precious leisure time, spend two hours with a bunch of strangers in front of a big screen in a dark theater with sticky floors, and part with a tidy sum for their tickets (not to mention popcorn and other necessities). Given people's demanding work and family schedules, and the added competition of so many media conveniences right in their own homes, the job of getting them to fill movie seats has never been harder.

Selling a movie is much like selling a political candidate: There is a specific window of opportunity to let out all the stops and get the message to as many voters or potential viewers as possible. In politics, the time to ramp up the volume is the last three weeks before Election Day. In movie land, the studio marketing team executes a similar media blitz in the final month before the release date. Politicians win or lose on Election Day. Movies thrive or die on the opening weekend.

For those who market movies and those who market candidates, the keyword is anticipation. People want to know: Will the candidates live up to the hype? Will they work to make a town or state or nation a better place? Will this film move the viewer to laughter, horror, tears, or revelation? Will it be clever, or dull as dishwater? Reviews, previews, and word-of-mouth certainly answer these questions.

But a powerful tagline can be much more convincing and build anticipation for the movie's release.

A movie tagline must make moviegoers want to get the whole story. It should grab attention by saying something provocative or suggestive. It should be the central part of an ad, large enough so that it is easily seen and retained. Ninety-eight percent of commercial taglines are too small to be read. Movie marketers don't make the same mistake. The taglines are big enough. But are they bold enough? Unfortunately, most today are not. I have listed my eleven favorites, all of which are pre-2000, in order of personal preference below:

Eleven Taglines with Punch

"In space no one can hear you scream." (*Alien*, 1979)

Talk about creating anticipation. Sure doesn't sound like a friendly alien. Moviegoers' immediate thought: This movie will be one frightening experience. They were not disappointed.

"Don't go in the water." (*Jaws*, 1975)

A universal fear is being grabbed by something unseen in a large body of water. Add to that fear a visual of a huge shark fin breaking the ocean's surface. Finish with the line above and you have everybody's undivided attention.

"Size does matter." (*Godzilla*, 1998)

How can you not smile at this line? All those male insecurities are sublimated by the image of a huge beast that can whack tall buildings with its pinky finger. Yes, a really, really big reptile is hard to resist. How big? After reading this powerline, moviegoers rushed to see the movie and find out.

"A long time ago in a galaxy far, far away." (*Star Wars*, 1977)

Hard to believe that Luke Skywalker and Darth Vader first appeared three decades ago. This genius line says that this is a fairy tale for all ages. And we all want to see the tale unfold.

"Just when you thought it was safe to go back in the water." (*Jaws 2*, 1978)

Oh, oh. Another great white is back in town and he's looking to snack on more limbs and create more hysteria among the beach-blanket-bingo crowd of teens and their beached whale-like parents. Millions went right back—to the theater.

"A lot can happen in the middle of nowhere." (*Fargo*, 1996)

So how do you describe a tangled tale of intrigue, mayhem, murder, and comedy that takes place in North Dakota, wherever that is? You don't give anything away. You simply imply there is a story here not to be missed. A brilliant use of anticipation, without which the movie might have gone nowhere.

"Earth. It was nice knowing you." (*Independence Day*, 1996)

Fun for the whole family on July 4,1996. Nationwide, families flocked to the theater on opening weekend. After all, who can resist superior aliens trying to do a global human stir-fry with all manner of cool special effects.

"He is afraid. He is alone. He is 3 million miles from home." (*ET, the Extra-Terrestrial*, 1982)

One of the highest-grossing movies in the known universe, ET is a twist on the usual sci-fi tales of evil aliens. Here is a sweet, fragile, outer-space creature who got way off track and misses his mother. Afraid and alone? An alien? Now, that's different. The line was a perfect setup.

"Look closer." (*American Beauty*, 1999)

The poster showed a very pretty young blonde reclined on a bed of red rose petals. But wait. Who knows what evil lurks behind this suggestive come-on? Where do I need to look? That's the point. Come see what is really going on in middle-class, small-town America.

"Love means never having to say you're sorry."
(*Love Story*, 1970)

Insipid, I know. But this line became the rage in the early seventies. *Love Story*, the book, sold millions of copies and was adapted into a movie that every American female twelve years and up saw at least once. Call it the ultimate chick flick. A few guys got dragged along to show proper respect for their dates and to supply endless tissues during the last half hour.

"Die harder." (*Die Hard* 2, 1990)

The original *Die Hard* starred Bruce Willis, playing a broken-down cop who still had what it took (firearms of all descriptions with endless spare clips of ammo) to stop superhuman bad guys in their tracks. The line above for the sequel is like a strong punch to action-craving moviegoers' hardened six-pack abs. It dares them to see if the first movie's nonstop action, with nary a believable plot in sight, can be topped.

Television

In 2006, for the first time, televisions in the average American household actually outnumbered the people in the household. It is estimated that Americans watch between six and eight hours of television a day, more time than they spend on any other activity besides work and school.

What makes television so compelling? As social creatures of the highest order, we have an unrelenting appetite for shared experience, be it social habits, education, occupation, or vacation. Television is a way to connect with each other and participate in a common event.

Humans evolved from packs of nomad hunters and gatherers to create small villages, then towns and cities, and finally nations. The telegraph, telephone, and radio all tapped into our social DNA and allowed us to stay connected. In earlier generations, a telephone and a radio meant one was never alone. As a popular AT&T tagline from the 1970s put it, people could "always reach out and touch someone." Television went one step further, beaming the physical presence of people talking, laughing, singing, crying, killing, and dying right into living rooms, dens, breakfast nooks, and bedrooms. With today's technology, this endless parade of people appears whenever the viewer wants.

When Ed McMahon announced, "Heeeere's Johnny" on *The Tonight Show* five nights a week, Americans welcomed Carson like a beloved older brother to the most intimate hours of their lives. "Heeeere's Johnny" meant exactly that—John is here tonight and everyone feels better for the visit.

Talk about power. No king, president, pope, or other historic ruler has had the power to connect to us like a television personality who "speaks" to people daily. Sure, we can turn on the radio, read a newspaper, or go to CNN online, but nothing beats the connection with our television buddies as we gather around the electronic fireplace—an activity that started around a real fire roughly two million years ago.

An entire book could easily be written on the influence of powerlines that originated on television. Here are a few examples of lines that stand out.

Like many lines that come to define who we are and what we do, the two most powerful words created for television were conjured up purely by accident. The two words were: Super Bowl.

In 1967, the NFL's first commissioner, Pete Rozelle, suggested the game be called "The Big One." Lamar Hunt, who then owned the Kansas City Chiefs, proposed "Super Bowl" as a stopgap name until a better one could be thought up. His thinking: 1) college football championships were called bowl games, a reference to the original Rose Bowl game which was played in a bowl-shaped arena; and 2) his young daughter's favorite toy was called "Super Ball." The other owners could not agree and went with a more literal name for the first two contests in 1967 and 1968: the AFL-NFL World Championship Game. (The two leagues had merged in 1967. The merger agreement stipulated that there be an annual championship game between the best teams in each league.)

Not surprisingly, fans and sportscasters latched on to Hunt's snappier name and started using it. By contest number three in 1969, the name "Super Bowl" became official. The two previously played games were retroactively named *Super Bowls I* and *II*.

The Roman numerals add to the power of the name because they conjure up the image of gladiators in an arena, assembled for a fight to the finish, and all manner of glory for the winner. (The numerals were actually added to make sure there was no confusion over what calendar year each contest represents, since Super Bowl Sunday is always played in January or early February for the previous year's championship.)

The Super Bowl is the most-watched television broadcast each year. Total viewing audiences approach 100 million people and the economic and social effects are numerous—and often humorous. For instance, Super Bowl Sunday is the second-largest food-consumption day in America, topped only by Thanksgiving. And, town water/sewage systems across America are taxed to maximum capacity during commercial breaks in the football action.

As a curious twist to normal viewing habits, this is the one television event each year in which Americans look forward to the advertising as well as the show. Super Bowl Sunday has become the showcase for television commercials that advertisers spend millions to create and pay the networks millions more to air.

The shift from a long literal name to a short snappy one is particularly important on television, a medium where less is truly more. Camera angles constantly shift to keep the eye interested. Long drawn-out dialogue isn't possible.

On television, fewer words produce better results. Viewers have been conditioned to expect a quick pace and rapid delivery. After all, unlike feature-length movies, television shows rarely last more than an hour and roughly half are thirty minutes in length. And these shorter time frames are interrupted by commercials, which occupy 15 to 20 percent of the running time. Today's network evening news consists of just seven minutes of headline news. The rest of the time is devoted to human-interest features and drug commercials, as the average viewer is sixty years of age. The one evening news program with a more leisurely pace airs on the public broadcasting network and is hardly watched at all.

The characters in television shows even refer to each other in shorthand. Take McDreamy and McSteamy, for example: two male "hunks" on the very popular *Grey's Anatomy*, a well-written drama about good-looking doctors and their love lives, on and off the operating table. Comparing these two fine fellows to McDonald's, where billions of burgers are served, is a great form of word play and makes us smile instinctively. These guys are, well, beef on the hoof that any woman would want again and again and again.

Media executives have long understood the natural tendency to shorten speech whenever possible and follow that guiding principle when they create the titles of television shows. Take seven shows that, combined, have held the top-rated spots since the beginning of television: *Bonanza*, *Dallas*, *Friends*, *Frasier*, *Gunsmoke*, *M*A*S*H*, and *Seinfeld*. One thing they have in common is a one-word title.

The simple rule, applied over and over again, is that less is more. Great lines are poetry in motion. Every word counts and the whole line must mean something special—so special it just has to be remembered.

Taglines for the shows themselves are no exception to the rule. Most often, these taglines open the show and become so familiar that they jump into common language and are used for decades to come. Some are even familiar to millions of Americans who weren't even alive or old enough to watch the show when it aired. Occasionally, a show's name and tagline are one and the same. And, news shows often close with a tagline.

Several taglines listed below have jumped from the screen into popular lingo. Many live thirty to forty years after the show's final episode, thanks to their singular staying power and, perhaps, to the TV Land cable channel—on which old shows never die, they just stay black and white and many shades of gray.

As you read below, think about how these three common elements cause a line to draw millions of people into a common bond of understanding:

1. The line is repeated during every show in exactly the same way.
2. The line sets up an expectation and then meets it.
3. The line tells a story that makes the audience root for the main characters' success.

These three elements apply to the business world as well, and should be used by marketers of commercial products and services. Applied on all fronts, they make a line come alive in consumers' minds and, in the process, reinforce positive brand attributes.

Nine Outstanding Television Taglines

"Tonight, we have a really big show."

For twenty-three years, every Sunday evening at 8:00 p.m. on CBS, Ed Sullivan appeared onstage at Studio 50 in New York City and opened his show with the line above. His pronunciation was a bit affected and the word *show* sounded like *shoe.* (The offbeat delivery made it more memorable to viewers.)

For the first eight years (1948–1955) the show was titled *Toast of the Town.* Sullivan was so central to every aspect of this one-hour variety showcase that in 1955, the show became *The Ed Sullivan Show*, the name it kept until its final episode in June 1971.

In a very real sense, Ed Sullivan and his show were the Super Bowl of entertainment, not once a year but every Sunday night. Watching Ed and his array of well-known stars, and up-and-comers who became stars, was a weekly family ritual, hard to imagine in today's fragmented lifestyle.

Two notable appearances broke all viewing records in the 1950s and 1960s, and still hold to this day: the first television appearances of Elvis Presley and The Beatles. On September 9, 1956, Elvis took the stage on *The Ed Sullivan Show*, introduced by guest host Charles Laughton. Eight years later in February 1964, the "British Invasion" known as The Beatles performed on the initial stop of their first tour in America. The Rolling Stones and the Doors followed a few years later.

But it was Elvis and the Beatles that broke the record with more than sixty million viewers—roughly 85 percent of the television audience on those respective nights. What the other 15 percent watched is hard to imagine, given the excitement around these two Sunday night performances.

Interesting to note that during the show's lifespan, Sullivan had to quicken the pace significantly after the first ten years on the air. Time waits for no man, as the saying goes, and neither did television as it matured as the dominant medium during the later years of the 1950s. What had started as a show with six acts had grown to include eleven or twelve during the same one-hour time slot by 1958. But what never changed was Sullivan's appearance on stage at the start of each show with his famous welcoming line.

"Faster than a speeding bullet! More powerful than a locomotive! Able to leap tall buildings in a single bound! Look! Up in the sky! It's a bird. It's a plane! It's Superman! Yes, it's Superman … strange visitor from another planet who came to Earth with powers and abilities far beyond those of mortal men! Superman … who can change the course of mighty rivers, bend steel in his bare hands, and who, disguised as Clark Kent, mild-mannered reporter for a great metropolitan newspaper, fights a never-ending battle for truth, justice, and the American way!"

A mouthful to be sure, but millions of boys and girls who watched the original *Adventures of Superman* from 1952 through the last episode on April 28, 1958, memorized this opening narration.

As every human knows, the only thing that can harm Superman is kryptonite. The Superman story, concocted in the 1940s by two unknown midwestern college students, began as a radio series, and jumped to television in 1952, with George Reeves in the title role. Since the original series ended, Superman has spawned several cartoon shows, as well as other television reincarnations such as *Lois & Clark* and, most recently, *Smallville*. Six feature-length Superman movies have attracted a worldwide audience of millions.

All Superman stories are about rescuing someone in dire straights. When all hope seems lost, Superman beats the clock and appears at the speed of, well, Superman, before it's too late. Perhaps Woody Allen's famous quote, "80 percent of life is just showing up," is really the core reason for Superman's enduring commercial success. Even the mysterious and still unsolved death of George Reeves in 1959 had no effect on the franchise, which continued to delight audiences on the big and small screens in later years.

Clearly the appeal of a superman, a superhuman who can right wrong and beat evil at every turn, is universal. We all wish that someone could save us just in the nick of time.

"Have Gun—Will Travel"

In the 1950s and 1960s, characters from the fabled Western frontier rode into America's homes on evening prime time, as well as afternoon slots, early evening, and Saturday mornings. Westerns were everywhere.

Many, including *Gunsmoke* and *Bonanza*, won top ratings in their peak years. Many others sustained a strong loyal following for years, like *Wanted Dead or Alive*, *The Rifleman*, *The Lone Ranger*, *Wyatt Earp*, *Bat Masterson,* and *The Virginian.*

One of the most unusual Westerns had a tagline that was the same as the show's name: *Have Gun—Will Travel.* This stark message was powerful, because it promised so much more. Its message implied: "I am a hired gun and I am so good that I choose not to say anything more than that." Richard Boone played the professional gunfighter who could be hired by telegraph as each show opening reminded us: "Wire Paladin. San Francisco."

Paladin's large physical presence contrasted with his soft voice, measured gait, and calm demeanor, and reinforced the understated nature of the show in every episode. An edgy persona who eclipsed the good-guys-always-wear-white image, Paladin dressed in black from his hat to his boots. Yes, a real pro not looking for a gunfight, who intimidated all with his presence—no other action required.

For six seasons from 1957 through 1962, Paladin showed up each week to help right the scales of frontier justice. And unlike any other Western before or since, a gun for hire—a professional killer—was actually the biggest "white hat" on the screen.

"Man, woman, birth, death, infinity."

Guess that sums it all up. It did in *Ben Casey*, one of the first breakthrough medical dramas. From 1961 to 1966, every episode opened with a close-up of symbols drawn on a chalkboard, accompanied by actor Sam Jaffe's voiceover description. For the first five seasons, Jaffe played Dr. David Zorba, chief of surgery, and Vince Edwards played Ben Casey, a young, talented, never-smiling neurosurgeon. Ben Casey and the opening line are so memorable because they fit together so perfectly—mostly clinical, with just a hint of personality and very little levity. A far cry from the in-your-face sexual tension, sex and more sex in today's top-rated doctor shows where the operating table plays second fiddle to romance.

"Spanning the globe to bring you the constant variety of sport, the thrill of victory, and the agony of defeat, the human drama of athletic competition—this is ABC's Wide World of Sports!"

Wide World of Sports' debut episode in April 1961 covered the Drake Relays from Drake University in Des Moines, Iowa. Not exactly a major event in sports history, which was part of the charm of this long-running show. The original goal was to cover sports events from around the globe, including many not often seen or mentioned by sports writers, such as curling, hurling, logging competitions, and martial arts.

For most of its existence, Jim McKay hosted the weekly Saturday afternoon broadcast and narrated the standard introduction. Beginning in 1970, the visual sequence of sports action during the narration showed a hair-raising ski jumping accident as McKay intones "... and the agony of defeat." After the first showing of the accident, ABC received thousands of letters expressing alarm that a family show would highlight such a tragedy in the making. Suffice it to say, this spectacular ski crash, shown week after week and year after year, became an enduring icon for exactly what the words say: the agony of defeat. ABC did get the word out that the jumper, Vinko Bogataj, did not suffer any serious injury. Later, in the 1990s, the network added an Indy 500 multiple car crash, which also resulted in no injury to the participants.

The point these images make is that sports are about winning and losing. Ties are few and far between. Defeat is often handed to a contestant in a fraction of a second, after months and years of training. Agony? Drama? Thrilling? You bet. We love to watch others succeed and fail in sports competition. Nothing is better than that ringside seat. "The thrill of victory and the agony of defeat" sums up all sports competition in a simple, powerful, elegant phrase that deserves its powerline status as the best remembered line in sports commentary.

"There is nothing wrong with your television set."

Back in the 1960s, this statement got attention since, frequently, there was in fact something wrong with the family television. Color sets were brand new, and adjusting the color to look natural was often beyond the ability of even the techno geek home on vacation from MIT or Cal Tech. Black-and-white sets were also far from perfect, needed frequent vertical/horizontal tuning, and often lost the picture to an onslaught of wavy lines.

The line above opened a long voiceover that began each episode of *Outer Limits*, a dark and scary sci-fi thriller that originally ran for three seasons on ABC from 1963 to 1965. The message, a reminder that not everything was under one's control, sparked hidden fears in its viewers, whose only recourse was to admit their lack of courage and turn off the set. Its scare-the-family cousin, *The Twilight Zone,* had a similar opening monologue that promised menace and mayhem.

After 1965, the show disappeared for decades, only to reemerge in 1995 and run for 154 episodes—far longer than the original series—on Showtime and the Sci-Fi Channel. A master of the space drama and ardent follower of the original show, Gene Roddenberry, hired a number of the *Outer Limits* professional crew for his hugely successful *Star Trek* series.

Here's the opening narration of *Outer Limits*, 1963–1965, in its entirety:

> There is nothing wrong with your television set. Do not attempt to adjust the picture. We are controlling transmission. If we wish to make it louder, we will bring up the volume. If we wish to make it softer, we will tune it to a whisper. We can reduce the focus to a soft blur, or sharpen it to crystal clarity. We will control the horizontal. We will control the vertical. For the next hour, sit quietly and we will control all that you see and hear. You are about to experience the awe and mystery, which reaches from the inner mind to the Outer Limits.

"To boldly go where no man has gone before"

Gene Roddenberry created the original *Star Trek* series, which ran on NBC for three seasons from 1966 through 1969. William Shatner, who played James T. Kirk, captain of the starship *Enterprise*, delivered the voiceover that began each episode.

Although *Star Trek* ran on NBC for only three seasons, it spawned an impressive number of spin-offs: five additional television series and eleven feature-length movies. It also became popular in syndication and continues to be a rerun staple. Captain Kirk and six other main characters achieved household recognition status and are still familiar almost forty years later. In order of popularity they are: Spock, science officer and second-in-command; Leonard McCoy, chief medical officer; Scotty, chief engineer; Uhura, communications officer and the sole female on the bridge; Sulu, senior helmsman; and Chekov, senior navigator.

The show's enduring appeal came from its depiction of a future where all races, human and alien, were embraced. Earth was a peaceful planet and part of a Federation that helped other societies across the galaxies without imposing any particular form of government. Given the tension of the Cold War during the 1960s, *Star Trek* was a feel-good fantasy about an idealized future in which the human race survived in harmony with members of other planets and even helped them to face their own wars and social challenges.

Roddenberry believed science fiction was more than monsters and space aliens intent on the destruction of Mother Earth. He brought to life the secret wish of many to put all the gifts of planet Earth to good use and help others throughout the galaxy as we continue to reach for the stars. *Star Trek* is all about the ultimate challenge, as the complete narration states:

> Space: the final frontier. These are the voyages of the starship *Enterprise*. Its five-year mission: to explore strange new worlds, to seek out new life and new civilizations, to boldly go where no man has gone before.

How can you not want Kirk and crew to succeed? If success is measured in popularity, *Star Trek* is in no danger of being "lost in space." Generations to come will be rooting for the *Enterprise* and its crew.

"Yada Yada Yada"

When sitcom shorthand for "you know what I mean" becomes part of everyday language, a television show has had an impact on society. For trivia buffs, the *Seinfeld* episode entitled "The Yada Yada" was the 153rd show, which ran in season eight of the nine seasons *Seinfeld* aired on NBC. The date was April 24, 1997.

Seinfeld, a weekly half-hour comedy show, depicted the lives of four Upper West Side, thirty-something New Yorkers—Jerry, George, Elaine, and Kramer. It was a show about nothing in particular and pictured life as a series of small events that can get in the way of just enjoying life.

The four characters endlessly debate the ups and downs of their friends, their dates, their parents, their jobs (which don't seem all that important), and their observations about one another. *Seinfeld* showed that life as a single in New York City can be pretty funny as one tries to navigate with street smarts through neighbors, landlords, bosses, small-shop owners, present, past, and future girlfriends, boyfriends, and all manner of everyday interactions at restaurants, movie theaters, office buildings, and ballparks.

In this episode, the core "yada yada" exchange begins with George's complaint that his current girlfriend always says "yada yada yada" instead of saying what exactly is on her mind. Elaine and Jerry weigh in:

> GEORGE: You don't think she would yada yada sex?
>
> ELAINE: I've yada yada-ed sex. I met this lawyer, we went to dinner. I had the lobster bisque, we went back to my apartment, yada yada yada, I never heard from him again.
>
> JERRY: But you yada yada-ed over the best part!
>
> ELAINE: No, I mentioned the bisque.

The world has been yada yada-ing ever since that day in 1997, and most likely will continue to do so when stating the facts seems so beside the point.

"... And that's the way it is."

The signoff line used by Walter Cronkite, anchor of the *CBS Evening News* from 1962 through 1981, is a fitting line to end this chapter.

Cronkite began as a newspaper reporter in 1935, and then changed paths to become a radio announcer a year later. Like many reporters of his generation, Cronkite's big chance for visibility came during World War II, and he rose to the top of his profession covering the war in North Africa and Europe. He went on to report on the Nuremberg trials, and then did a stint for the United Press in Moscow for several years.

In 1950, legendary newsman Edward R. Morrow recruited him for CBS. During his nineteen-year reign as the one America looked to first for straightforward news reporting, Cronkite covered many of the remarkable news stories of the day, including the Cuban Missile Crisis, the Kennedy assassination, the Vietnam War, the Moon landing, and the Watergate affair.

At the end of nearly every evening newscast, he delivered the line above, followed by the date. (If he finished the broadcast with editorial opinion, he would omit this closing.)

As of this writing, Walter Cronkite is alive and well and in his early nineties. He is still an American icon and continues to be held in the highest esteem. And that's the way it is.

The power of a tagline or expression with an expectation that rings true can have long-lasting resonance when millions share the same experience in the theater or watch a favorite television program. It often becomes part of the fabric of social interaction, and can outlast the first run of the particular movie it promotes, or the number of years a television show stays at the top of the charts.

The mind is the ultimate media mixer. It sees and hears billions of impressions. Yet, it retains only those impressions, those powerlines, that thrill and chill and inspire the thought, "I couldn't have said that better myself."

Screenwriters live to entertain with lines delivered through the big or small screen. The talented ones create standout lines that our minds are very receptive to, especially with repetition and a unique inflection in delivery.

The bombardment of advertising, particularly on radio and television, that repeatedly interrupts enjoyable entertainment is another matter altogether. The challenge for advertisers is to make viewers retain their brand promise in spite of the strong inclination to ignore their intrusion. This is a task made even harder by a general inability of marketers to recognize both the hurdles they face and the techniques they must use to get consumers to willingly pay attention.

The remainder of this book describes how and why commercial taglines become powerlines, and why so many fail. There is no reason for this widespread failure other than sheer inattention to well-defined "rules of the road," and lack of appreciation for what a single line can do to make a brand all-powerful for all time.

PART THREE

PUT A POWERLINE IN YOUR TANK

Putting Powerlines to Work in a Marketing Campaign

So far, twenty-first century marketers haven't created much in the way of lines that make us think, smile, or are easy to remember. Perhaps this century needs a good tagline. The good news is there is still plenty of time.

CHAPTER 7

When It Rains It Pours

Getting the Brand Promise Through—Whether Customers Want to Hear It or Not

TODAY, MOST MARKETERS seem to have forgotten that great taglines—powerlines—all have the same six basic elements. Without each of these elements, the brain simply will not retain the line. When an actor wants to learn a part, he or she rehearses over and over to commit the lines to memory. Powerlines make a similar mark, but with a slightly different method.

Here's what it takes to make a line that makes a mark:

1. ***The tagline must convey a genuine truth or depict an experience, real or imaginary.*** At its best, a tagline crystallizes the primary feature of the brand that sets it apart from the competition. For example, "M&M's, melts in your mouth, not in your hands."
2. ***The line must be built to last. It should rarely, if ever, be changed.*** Part of its magic is its ability to speak to different age groups and generations. For example, Winchester's "The gun that won the West."
3. The line must do at least one of the following:
   - ***Convey a product benefit.*** For example, Morton's "When it rains it pours."
   - ***Show how the product will improve customers' lives.*** For example, FedEx's "When it absolutely, positively has to be there overnight."
   - ***Recommend specific action.*** For example, Hallmark's "When you care enough to send the very best."
   - ***Offer specific satisfaction.*** For example, Coke's "The pause that refreshes."

Often, a powerline can deliver more than one of the above.

4. ***Make no mistake—setting a line to music and rhyme makes it much easier to remember.*** So does constant repetition during the early weeks of a campaign.
5. ***On television and the Internet, the line should move on the screen***—what marketers call a pneumonic.
6. Hey, twenty-first-century marketers—focus heavily on this next point. ***The line must play a central role in all visual touch points with the consumer.*** Meaning, it must be LARGE enough to see and often should be the headline on all advertising and promotion materials.

Point six should be taken to heart. It is easy to do correctly, but is usually done incorrectly. This error translates into billions—yes, billions—of wasted marketing dollars. For example, in 2006, the new AT&T, created through mergers with BellSouth and Cingular, launched an ad campaign. They spent countless millions of dollars in the creation of ads like the one you see here.

"Your World. Delivered." Trademark of AT&T. Multimedia campaign, in print (major newspapers and magazines), TV, Internet, and outdoor media. Created by GSD&M Advertising, 2005.

Or not. You literally cannot see the body copy no matter how hard you try. Where is the tagline? Why, it's in very small white reverse type somewhere out of sight at the bottom of the ad. If you can find it, this line attempts to convey an improvement to our lives. Alas, we have no idea what that improvement might be and therefore couldn't care less. The markeing team for this high-tech force in communications should be lined up and handed their severance checks.

Fortunately, marketers haven't always done such a bad job with taglines. There are many great lines from the past that illustrate what makes a powerline. After several decades of service, more than a few of these are still as crystal clear and powerful as they were the first day they appeared. This chapter is about understanding the special place they hold in our memories, and why.

One of the very first commercial slogans was for castor oil, a particularly nasty-tasting cure-all for children's minor ailments. The line made famous at that time (the late 1800s) was "Children cry for it." Clearly the purveyors of this syrup had a warped sense of humor, since the last thing on earth most children wanted was to be held down while some parent or other large adult administered this awful-tasting potion.

From this humble beginning, taglines took center stage in building product awareness and brand loyalty and marketers have been at it ever since. Today, roughly 85 percent of all products have an associated tagline.

Following are my picks for the ten best commercial powerlines.

Top Ten Commercial Powerlines

"A Diamond Is Forever"—De Beers

Agency: N. W. Ayer & Son, 1948

Is there a better way to say I love you? A better way to remind men and women what the gift of a diamond conveys? Copywriter Frances Gerety of N. W. Ayer & Son penned this tagline for De Beers in 1948. It perfectly captures the romance and allure of the diamond and turns it into a symbol of eternal love.

Those four words are a simple statement of a fact that plays perfectly against the reality of life—everything changes, runs out, or wears down. Everything, except a diamond. Like a diamond, this powerline is timeless and will be around as long as people express their love for each other.

"Come to Marlboro Country"—Philip Morris
Agency: Leo Burnett Co., 1955

The story of Marlboro cigarettes is one of the greatest product transformations in the history of advertising. In 1948, Philip Morris bought the failing female cigarette brand from a British tobacco company and began advertising it in America in similar fashion—as a cigarette for women smokers only. Note the ad below from 1950 with the headline: "Before you scold me, Mom … maybe you'd better light up a Marlboro."

Marlboro Cigarettes. "Before you scold me, Mom … maybe you'd better light up a Marlboro." Published as a half-page ad in the *Saturday Evening Post*, 1950.

Marlboro continued to flounder in the United States until 1955 when the legendary Leo Burnett and a group of his top lieutenants decided to change strategy. They came up with a handsome cowboy to depict the real pleasure of smoking. Almost immediately, the universal appeal of the American cowboy made Marlboro the cigarette of choice for women and men, first in America, then worldwide. Marlboro has remained the No. 1 cigarette brand ever since.

The Marlboro Man. Trademark of Philip Morris, Inc. Created by the Leo Burnett Company, 1955.

The meaning of the cowboy ad above can be summed up in one word: *independence*. The experience imagined is this: "I as a smoker can do what I want when I want. I can feel free like a cowboy on the range. Free to think for myself, move at my own pace, be an individual and yet, at the same time, recognize there are others like me who feel exactly the same way." Thus the lines: "Come to where the flavor is. Come to Marlboro Country."

After several years, these two lines became so well known that the agency was able to shorten it to simply "Come to Marlboro Country."

Recognizing the universal appeal of a rugged, handsome cowboy to both sexes was a stroke of brilliance. Moreover, this allure extends to all economic levels and all age groups. Everybody loves the cowboy. Everybody can feel the attraction of a breathtaking mountain range somewhere out there, where cowboys and horses operate with the peace of mind that the rest of us envy. We know it is a complete fantasy and yet we still want to believe in it. We say to ourselves, "You know, maybe someday I really will come to Marlboro Country."

Over the years, Marlboro used other images, including men fishing off ocean jetties and racecar drivers taking a break from the action on the track, but nothing ever topped the cowboy. Sometimes alone, sometimes on a horse, sometimes herding other horses, he is always comfortable just being in the great outdoors enjoying a smoke.

Every image ever used in over fifty years of advertising this product has reinforced the idea that Marlboro Country is a special place, a dream partially realized with the purchase and enjoyment of a cigarette. Part of the line's power is the constant reminder that people are welcome to join the others who enjoy freedom. It's instructive to note that no competing brand issues a welcome; thus they do not convey the same warmth and community that appeals to us all.

This brand was built on a dream. In a final stroke of genius, Leo Burnett recognized that the cowboy image and what it symbolizes should never be physically demolished. After you smoke a pack, you crush it and throw it in the trash or on the car floor or some other place to be trampled. The cowboy should not be mangled and discarded; therefore, the cowboy has never appeared on a single pack of Marlboro cigarettes. Burnett felt the dream should never be destroyed and, amazingly, it never has been.

"The Pause That Refreshes"—Coca-Cola

Agency: D'Arcy Co., 1929

Since Coke came upon the scene in the late 1800s, the company has used over one hundred lines to impress the world with its worth in everyday life. The first known tagline for Coke in 1886 was simply "Drink Coca-Cola."

In 1917, one line in use was "Three million a day." Today, Coca-Cola sells somewhere north of one billion can equivalents per day and company officials insist that a million new customers are added daily. As successful as Coke has been, they make a mistake every time they try to stay in tune with the times by changing taglines. They have made a lot of mistakes. Of all the Coke taglines, the two best remembered are: "The pause that refreshes" (1929) and "It's the real thing," first introduced in 1942 and later reissued in 1971.

"The pause that refreshes" is what a Coke is all about. It is a singularly good feeling to grab a Coke and take a break. The experience can, in fact, be refreshing. Even back in the late 1920s, people complained about the hectic pace of life. A pause is something people like to take. The use of the word is unusual and has not been used in any other major tagline since.

Owning the "pause" was very valuable to Coke and served it well for many years. I bet it could still be used with better effect than almost all the lines that have been thought up since by legions of Coke marketers and their agencies. Do you have any idea what Coke stands for today? My bet is no.

Coca-Cola and its challenge to find the right powerline will be explored in more depth in Chapter 8.

"Think Small"—Volkswagen

Agency: Doyle Dane Bernbach, 1959

Bill Bernbach, one of the great admen, wrote this line for the Volkswagen Beetle in 1959. Marketers often ask how to create a great tagline: should they hold brainstorming sessions or get groups of people together in some other fashion to collectively create a powerful descriptor of the product or service? My answer is always the same: "Great lines are rarely, if ever, created by committee." Most powerlines are the work of one person who sees something in the product that is an everlasting hook, one that no other individual or group can grasp or articulate in just the right way.

For the Beetle, Bernbach created the perfect positioning with two simple words, "Think Small." In the 1950s and 60s, the Beetle, or "Bug" as it was affectionately nicknamed, was the antithesis of practically every other car in America. During that twenty-year period, all car manufacturers believed the bigger, the better. Cars were larger and longer than ever before. Ninety-eight percent of them had front-mounted engines and were loaded with horsepower. They were advertised as sleek and fast and roomy, with much copy devoted to the absence of outside noise and distraction.

Into this mine-is-bigger-than-yours environment entered the Beetle, a car originally designed by Adolf Hitler and Ferdinand Porsche in 1933 and used by the German Army in various forms throughout World War II. In its post-war production and assembly, it was created as Hitler had actually intended—very basic transportation for average people who could not afford expensive mega cars.

When Bernbach got his hands on the advertising account, he immediately saw the way to glory. Here was a car with no styling, a rear-mounted engine of limited horsepower, terrific gas mileage during a time when it hardly mattered, a manual floor-mounted shift that was anything but easy to manage, and a heating and cooling system that usually did the reverse of what the driver intended.

Bernbach's solution was to position the Bug as the anticar. At a time when concern for the environment was limited to Smokey the Bear and his cautions about using matches in the woods, Bill Bernbach saw the way to uniquely position what some would consider nothing more than a covered motorcycle. He decided to take the path not taken (see Chapter 5 discussion of Robert Frost) and highlight the Bug's weaknesses as strengths. Bernbach's two words stood for a longer message: "Yes, you should think small. Think about how cheap this car is and the money you will save to do other things, many other things. Think about how the design never changes so your Beetle is never out of date. Think about being able to park the Bug practically anywhere. Yes, even think about saving hundreds of dollars a year on gas. And think about being the one person on your block who is so comfortable in their own skin they can show off a car that's ugly and completely lacking in status. Fellow Bug owners, let everyone else think big and even bigger while you laugh all the way to the bank and glide into a parking space when others search in vain to find places for their football-field-size hunks of steel."

"Think Small" was code for "You are smarter than the rest of the pack." Millions of Americans agreed. The Beetle remains the single most successful car design ever produced and, to date, close to thirty million have been sold.

No small feat.

"Just Do It"—Nike

Agency: Wieden & Kennedy, 1988

The Nike company has come a long way from its humble beginnings in founder Phil Knight's kitchen in 1968. Nike reported fifteen billion dollars in revenue in 2006 and employed more than twenty-six thousand people worldwide. It also has the distinction of being the only Fortune 500 Company headquartered in the state of Oregon.

Twenty years after Nike launched its first shoe, it introduced the tagline that is now famous worldwide and instantly recognizable as Nike's philosophy: "Just Do It." Surprisingly, the Nike "swoosh," created by graphic design artist Carolyn Davidson, has appeared on every product from shoes to apparel to golf clubs and snowboards almost from the start in 1971.

Philosophy is the right word to describe Nike's lasting impression in the minds of millions of people worldwide. The company takes the position, expressed in the tagline, that the person, not the product, makes everything happen. In other words, "You are the star. Yes, we at Nike make great quality products for all manner of sports and leisure activity but, at the end of the day, you must be in control. You must act. You must do something to create your own well-being." Nike offers a universal challenge to "go make things happen." The only other official Nike tagline, created in 1977, was a less-direct expression of the same sentiment: "There Is No Finish Line."

If it's smart, Nike will keep "Just Do It" for the rest of its days. It perfectly places them above the fray and reflects their unique selling proposition: "It's all about you, not us." One can only think kindly of a company dedicated to helping people focus and apply themselves to the task at hand.

"You Deserve a Break Today"—McDonald's

Agency: Needham, Harper & Steers, 1971

It's hard to argue with the world's most successful fast-food empire. What McDonald's has done right and wrong in positioning itself over the years is instructive for marketers everywhere. Since the first Golden Arches appeared nationwide in the early 1960s, McDonald's has trotted out almost thirty different taglines. The vast majority has one jumping-off point in common: "you," just like Nike. Basically, McDonald's works to get millions of customers into their restaurants every day with the promise of a great eating experience—one that "you" clearly deserve.

By all accounts, McDonald's best-remembered powerline in over fifty years of selling burgers, shakes, and fries, is "You Deserve a Break Today," created by advertising agency Needham, Harper & Steers in 1971. It was put to music as part of a jingle that became the centerpiece of a multimillion-dollar television and print campaign. The television spot that launched this effort showed a McDonald's cleaning crew with mops in hand singing about everything but the food. The message was: "It's clean at McDonald's. You deserve a break today. So get up and get away to McDonald's. Yes, you. You work hard on the job, or take care of the kids (more hard work), or sit in class all day. Each and every one of you deserves a break. You deserve a place that's clean and bright, with food you can trust."

It's worth noting that every time McDonalds has revenue problems, they are either caused by a system-wide cleanliness issue or by too much advertising focusing on burgers as opposed to the McDonald's experience.

In the world of marketing, one or two taglines can really hit on all cylinders and make just the right impression. But instead of sticking with a great line, management often gets bored and/or the new head of marketing needs to show they can create a better one. If you have a great line like McDonald's, give your whole company a break and keep it.

"When It Absolutely, Positively Has to Be There Overnight"

—Federal Express

Agency: Ally & Gargano, 1982

There is a well-known tale about how Fred Smith, the founder of Federal Express, submitted his idea for overnight freight delivery in a term paper at Yale and got a C for his effort. Perhaps he would have improved his grade if he had just written the line above to explain his concept.

Starting with a fleet of fourteen Dassault Falcons and a central processing hub in Memphis, Tennessee, Smith built the largest package delivery carrier in the world. Prior to the launch of Federal Express, the concept of that kind of guarantee seemed absurd to others in the industry. Smith delivered on this promise right from the start, and two years after the first Falcon jets took off, the advertising agency Ally & Gargano created this perfect powerline—the ultimate customer promise of the brand.

FedEx used this line for fifteen years and also introduced lines like "Don't panic," "Whatever it takes," and "FedEx it." But none are as memorable or reinforce the fundamental reason for the company's existence.

A little-known fact, and perhaps the ultimate compliment: the U.S. Postal Service spends over $1 billion a year with FedEx to ship packages that must be delivered the next business day.

The power of a great line has rarely been as crystal clear as with the FedEx story. The goal of any company is first to guarantee customer satisfaction, and secondly to be known in a few words for the precise way that guarantee will happen. Until beaming people and objects from point to point becomes a reality, FedEx is absolutely, positively the gold standard in package delivery.

"When It Rains It Pours."—Morton Salt
Agency: N. W. Ayer & Son, 1912

This tagline for Morton Salt Company was created in 1912 and along with the Morton Umbrella Girl, who came along two years later, has represented the company ever since.

Salt has a fascinating history and there are many references to it in the Bible. One of the best known is the story of Lot's wife, who is turned into a pillar of salt when she disobeys several uptight angels and takes a peek at Sodom—the original Sin City, yes, long before Vegas. The phrase "he is not worth his salt" comes from ancient Greece, where salt was used as currency in payment for slaves. Even our work salaries have a salty origin. During the days of the Roman Empire, soldiers were often paid "salt money," or the Latin *salarium argentum*, which translates into the English word *salary*.

Back to the last one hundred fifty years … Morton Salt began as a growing concern in 1848. By 1910, the company had patented a round container with a spout for easy pouring. The Umbrella Girl and the tagline above were added to the container with its unique blue label in 1914. The only noticeable change since then has been to the girl who, from time to time, appears a bit more contemporary as she holds her umbrella under the rain. The idea for the tagline came to Morton's agency, N. W. Ayer & Son, who understood that the patented packaging ensured that salt would always pour freely even in damp weather. Ayer's original suggestion was to use the old English proverb, "It never rains, but it pours." The Morton team was concerned that this line was confusing and, with a bit of additional wordplay, the agency copywriter got it exactly right.

Remember, a great line never really needs to change. Morton Salt has never changed its Chicago headquarters, its packaging, or its basic logo and tagline. It keeps pouring and continues to be a "great old salt" of a company.

"M&M's, Melts in Your Mouth, Not in Your Hands"—Mars
Agency: Ted Bates & Co., 1954

When I was a young kid running amok through the house, often with some form of candy in one or both hands, my parents were thrilled when the candy in question was M&M's. These candies virtually guaranteed no messy transfer from hands to white walls, shirt, or pants. It was great that American kids in the 1950s helped save on their parents' laundry bills, but the M&M miracle was created long before as a result of far different circumstances.

The British came up with the original concept, a chocolate covered by a hard candy shell, for their soldiers in the field. It was a simple idea: provide quick energy in the form of a chocolate pellet with a sugar coating designed to prevent sticky fingers and inaccurate rifle shots. For sure, no one wants soldiers endangered because of messy trigger fingers. This candy, called *Smarties*, was used during the Spanish Civil War. Forrest Mars, Sr. took note of this battlefield invention and with his partner at the time, Bruce Murrie, bought the rights to the British confection in 1939, only to discover that in America there was another candy called *Smarties*. Being smart businessmen but no ad geniuses, the two partners decided to name the candy for their two last name initials—M&M.

From the beginning, M&M's were a hit in America and, in the early 1940s when air conditioning was nonexistent, they were the only reliable candy for ready distribution during the summer months. M&M's were first provided to American GIs at the beginning of World War II in 1941 for exactly the same reason the British invented Smarties. A few years later, M&M's were introduced to noncombatants and have remained at the top of our sweet-tooth list ever since.

It wasn't until 1954 that Mars's agency, Ted Bates, created the line "The milk chocolate melts in your mouth—not in your hand." Over time, this was shortened to "M&M's, melts in your mouth, not in your hands."

M&M's. M&M's "spokescandy" was introduced in an ad in 2000. "Sitting Pretty" ad © 2000 Mars, Incorporated. M&M's is a trademark of Mars, Incorporated.

Ninety million baby boomers grew up with this powerline, and while it has been out of use for several decades, the product promise of chocolate with no melt has remained etched in boomers' minds and has transferred to their kids and their kids.

When taglines get at the core benefit of a product, exactly and clearly, they tend to remain in our subconscious for the rest of our lives. If the benefit is real and everlasting, the line will come to mind whenever we happen to see, hear, or smell the product.

The M&M's ad above uses an M&M peanut candy as its spokes-person. This humanization of different-colored M&M's has been a popular campaign for the last several years and, true to the origin of the product, every promotional execution still reinforces the original tag. In this case, it is clear that Mr. Blue Peanut can lounge on his back on a mountain of M&M plain candies because they won't break and drown him in a sea of chocolate goo. Yep, the M&M will never melt in your hands and the powerline created fifty-four years ago this year will never melt away until the last M&M is eaten.

"You Don't Have to Be Jewish to Love Levy's Rye Bread"

—Levy's Baking

Agency: Doyle Dane Bernbach, 1949

So how do you sell a Jewish product to the 97 percent of Americans who are not Jewish? This was the assignment handed to Bill Bernbach, the brilliant and legendary ad man, who created this line for Levy's Baking Co. in 1949. Bernbach's genius was to not dance around the core of the product but, rather, to highlight it and make the product stand out by the very fact that it was built on a different premise than its competitors.

His work for Volkswagen Beetle was all about why this simple ugly car with a small engine and a shape that never changed was an inspired choice for basic transportation. And this was in a day when no one cared about fuel conservation and the rage among car buyers was to have the biggest, latest model with the newest shape in your driveway for all to see.

Well, it was pretty clear for all to see that Levy's Jewish Rye Bread was baked and packaged by a firm run by Jews. The challenges to make Levy's a preferred household staple were daunting:

- The general perception was that "Jewish food" was different and not at all tasty. Didn't rabbis have to bless it and didn't Jews eat that matzah bread, which wasn't really bread at all?
- In 1949 for sure, and still a bit today, associating with Jews too closely made non-Jews feel uncomfortable. The view back then was that Jews should stick to their business and non-Jews should stick to theirs.

Bernbach decided on a straightforward approach with a campaign that headlined the ethnicity of the product and made it okay for non-Jews to join in and enjoy the taste of really good rye bread. This was a bold move. Of course, it helped that Levy's was primarily distributed in the New York tristate area with the nation's largest concentration of Jews who lived and worked in close proximity to many millions of non-Jews. But Bernbach didn't stop with just the tagline "You don't have to be Jewish," and in another brilliant stroke, depicted other minorities and stereotypes enjoying the experience. Three of the better-known executions showed an American Indian, an Irish-looking New York City cop, and a black youngster, each with looks of satisfaction on their faces and a Levy's sandwich in hand.

The campaign was a hit from the start and Levy's biggest problem turned into keeping up with demand. Again, as in many cases when powerlines turn consumers into true believers, the Levy's tagline became the hero of all visuals. Unlike today, when so many slogans or taglines are impossible to see, positioned as an afterthought in the bottom corner of an ad or hidden within body copy, the great lines above were and still are front and center. You don't have to love large, bold type, but it sure helps if our fellow art directors do. Sadly most don't and, consequently, many of us never see what a product really stands for.

The Top Ten Worst Commercial Taglines. Ever.

This segment was actually hard to put together because there were so many lines to choose from. To narrow the field, I have selected lines that had major dollars invested in their creation and execution and, despite the money, did nothing to burnish the brand. All remain completely void of recognition by most consumers in the target audience. If my comments appear harsh, well, you be the judge. My intent is for you to learn what not to do if you are in a position to select a tagline for your company or product.

To review, powerlines become just that when they

- are memorable
- instantly recall the brand name
- often include a key benefit
- make the brand stand for something special in its category
- provide an original thought
- are totally believable

Nonpowerlines fail to engender brand loyalty or much of anything else when they

- share the same key words as many other lines in use
- are generic
- are pretentious
- are clearly forced
- are just plain false
- have no clear meaning whatsoever

The last ten years in particular have been marked by uninspired lines created by folks with no clue about how to capture the attention of the consumer. The lines listed below all have been launched with various degrees of numbness during this time period.

"Your World. Delivered."—AT&T

Okay, thanks, but what exactly is being delivered? I have no idea and no patience to wait to find out. Long ago when AT&T was a strong brand, it had a strong powerline: "Reach out and touch someone." I even gave our son the spokesperson's first name—it was Cliff Robertson. The people from phone land have been going downhill ever since. The good news is the tagline above is so poorly executed in advertising that most consumers never see it. My suggestion to AT&T: keep it that way.

"The Power to Make It Better"—AARP

The American Association of Retired Persons wisely shortened its name to AARP years ago. Baby boomers, its current primary audience, dislike the word retired and don't want to walk softly into retirement twilight.

Too bad they didn't think through their tagline as well. "The power to make it better" just doesn't work.

Usually the word *power* is an immediate tip-off that the tagline probably means nothing. This line is no exception. A few professional marketers will ask the obvious question: make what better? Everyone else will just ignore the line altogether.

AARP needs to "make it better" and come up with a line that is meaningful and defines what AARP can do for its millions of fifty-plus-year-old members.

I suppose a line like "Drop Dead or Join AARP" is a bit too out there, although it might have worked in the 1970s.

"The Coke Side of Life"—Coca-Cola

Launched with great fanfare a few years ago, this line is completely dead on arrival. I have lost count of the number of companies that use *life* in their taglines, but the list is long and undistinguished. Coke has totally dropped the bottle with this latest attention grab in the cola wars. The Pepsi executive team must be beside themselves with glee. "The Coke Side of Life" means absolutely nothing to anyone and presumes there is a coke life we care to live. When I ask friends and acquaintances to name Coke's current tagline, I get nothing but blank looks. Not even in Atlanta, Coke's long-time headquarters, do the locals have any idea what Coke stands for today. Amazing that so many smart people at a company devoted to marketing have such a disconnect in bringing the fizz back to Coke's marketing efforts.

This slogan is perhaps the flattest in the long lineup of Coke taglines. The company could probably bring back "Coke. It's the Real Thing" and generate Coke-grabbing excitement all over again.

"Life/*Changing*"—The State of Iowa

Perhaps picking on a state is unfair and I make fun of this line earlier in the book, but it's so bad it demands a spot on this list. Perhaps Samuel Butler was right when he wrote, "Man is the only animal that laughs and has a state legislature." All states compete for tourist dollars and some, like Iowa, with little to offer in the way of dramatic landscapes, seem keen to create slogans/taglines to entice potential visitors.

This line doesn't deliver on any promise to make Iowa a stop on the way from east coast to west. Since I went to college in Iowa and return on occasion, I can assure you that Iowa remains a nice place to launch a presidential bid, given the timing of its primary. Otherwise, life does go on there pretty much like everywhere else. Life changing? Not that much changes in Iowa. The corn grows. The people are friendly, generally well educated, and prosperous. But there is not a lot of drama that will change someone's life. The state is overwhelmingly Caucasian, culture tends to be found on several major college campuses, and the best restaurant in the state would hardly make the Top One Hundred list in any major city. So what's changing? If the current governor is smart, he'll start with the line above.

"Rising"—United Airlines

Well, I would hope so. Falling is clearly not the right image for an airline. But rising from what? It implies from somewhere lower, which would translate to what—rising prices? Certainly not rising service or convenience or even profits. The word is too hard to figure out and no one did. It comes across as another reminder that airlines never quite have their act together and can't even tell us what they are all about. "Fly the Friendly Skies of United" was a terrific tagline in use for many years prior to "Rising." Then United changed their long-time ad agency relationship and the strangeness started. Ever since, United hasn't had any advertising to make customers take notice or care what the airline is all about. It's about cramped seats and a small bag of pretzels in the minds of most of the flying public. Maybe no tagline is the best policy these days.

"Do More" and "My Life. My Card."—American Express

Look, two bad lines for the price of one. Here's a company that lives and breathes marketing. It's in the blood of all seventy-five thousand employees, and this is the best they can do? Who needs a credit card company telling me to do more? Do I want to do more? Of what?

Bad lines have no relationship to the core brand promise of the company. American Express is first and foremost about great service. Sure, spending limits tend to be larger than on bank-issued credit cards, or at least used to be. But the plain truth is no one believes Amex outdoes Visa or MasterCard in overall utility. What makes Amex stand out is prestige, service and, to some degree, special merchandise offers it makes with merchants that accept the card. Following "Do More" is "My Life. My Card." Yes, life again. This tag supposedly harkens back to the "Do You Know Me?" campaign of the 1970s, but a direct connection is not made and the line is further challenged by Visa's equally pretentious line, "Life Takes Visa." Are we tired of life yet? Well, not our lives, merely all these companies selling life as if it is something you buy.

There are two great lines from the past that use the word life. One was a tagline for *Life* magazine that appeared briefly in a promotional campaign in the late 1970s: "Life. Consider the Alternative." It made sense for a product called *Life*. All other firms should consider a much better alternative to how their products can help us cope with daily life. The other life powerline was for General Electric.

"Imagination at Work"—General Electric

For starters, never use a five-syllable word in a tagline. It's just too hard to say smoothly. In 2004, after twenty-five years of the well-known and respected powerline, "GE, we bring good things to life," a new chief marketing officer was hired and presto, the line was eliminated along with all the brand equity built up over the years. Despite plenty of money spent on the new tag, nary a consumer has a clue what it means. GE makes a lot of jet engines, power turbines, and locomotives, precision objects that are built with exacting detail. One could argue that imagination is the last thing needed when it comes to an assembly line.

GE will never get this line to settle in consumer's minds. Leave imagination to fiction writers and inventors like Thomas Edison who imagined GE in the first place.

"The Last Real Beer"—Coors

A stupid line if ever there was one. Let's see, all those great-tasting other beers from around the world are—unreal? Heck, there are probably a thousand beers made in Germany alone that, if ever exported to the United States, would wipe out most American brands. Whatever they are smoking in the rocky mountain highs of Golden, Colorado, they should change their agency.

"Higher Standards"—Bank of America

There is no shortage of bad taglines in financial services, and Bank of America wins the award for the most generic and least-cared-about line among the major banks. Higher standards than what? Outright crooks, or an airline, or perhaps some other bank whose standards are what, lower? By who's reckoning? A line like this implies the whole industry is suspect and Bank of America is just above it—and with no proof. Where's the beef? What the largest branch-banking outfit in the United States should say is exactly that—"The best branch banking in America." Or maybe "Bank Rising." Just kidding.

"Can You Hear Me Now?"—Verizon

Although this line is popular with some in the marketing world, I strongly disagree with their assessment of its worth. All the ad accomplishes is to set in stone the impression that cell phones drop too many calls or skip in and out of range.

Here's how it happens: Hand in hand with the question, "Can you hear me now?" goes the answer "Maybe you can't," an all-too-common complaint among U.S. cell-phone users. No one who sees the ad remembers which phone service the line represents, demeaning the whole industry. The television ads are annoying, but that has never stopped an ad's effectiveness before. This case is no exception. The bottom line: We love our cell phones and, in spite of ample evidence to the contrary, we don't want to be reminded they are far from reliable.

As you have undoubtedly noticed, few great lines remain in force today and even fewer were created in recent times. Chapter 9 will explore today's marketers' inability to create lines their target audience cares about or remembers. It will tackle why we fail to understand the need to define a product or service in a few words, make it timeless and instantly meaningful or clever or humorous, and still make a point that sparks a purchase decision instead of a yawn.

The twenty-first century is pretty much devoid of marketing excellence in the form of lines that make us think, smile, or are easy to remember. Perhaps this century needs a good tagline. The good news is there is still plenty of time.

The other void in marketing circles is a lack of appreciation for the power of music, and specifically jingles, which earlier generations of ad people understood instinctively. Jingles are simply not used now by most companies and yet are one of the easiest ways to get consumers to remember a specific marketing pitch. Small companies, especially with limited promotional dollars, really miss the boat by not insisting on a jingle. And there are many talented songwriters looking for commercial work today. As you jingle your way through the following pages, you may decide to hire one for your product or service. A smart decision in my book.

CHAPTER **8**

Jingles All the Way

Commanding Attention with Music and Jingles

To UNDERSTAND WHY jingles became such a strong marketing force, it's helpful to go back fifty thousand years. Initially, music was a way for men and women to choose partners. Later, it became a central part of religious experience. From religion, it morphed into a way to combat fear in battle, and today it is a form of entertainment as well as a powerful medium in which to target consumers with marketing messages.

Beginning with Darwin, many anthropologists agree that music most likely played a key role in mate selection among our ancestors. The basic premise suggests that females, in their search for a good provider of food, clothing, and potential offspring, looked for a male who was so confident of his vigor and position among other males that he had the time to hum a tune, chant, or dance to a rhythmic beat. These males went on long, organized animal hunts, chased their prey for hours, and brought them down with spears or rocks. Returning to the village with their spoils, males underlined their success with long and often-elaborate dances set to loud musical tones, an exhibition meant to show off their prowess to the females.

Then came religion and, with it, stirring hymns and chants that are an emotional highpoint for all denominations. Since at least the tenth century, churchgoers have been soothed by music and sing together as an organized expression of their faith. Who can resist the countless Christmas carols and their power to inspire belief in goodwill and cheer to all fellow men and women?

For centuries, armies have marched into battle with drums beating and bands playing. Music can alter mood, and in times of war, it almost acts like a drug to dull the mind to the potential horrors ahead. A similar musical strategy was put to use with the introduction of background music in elevators during the 1920s and 1930s. The fear of being stuck in a small steel box hurtling up and down a newly built skyscraper was assuaged with soothing musical sounds to accompany the ride.

We all know the phrase *silence is golden*, and many of us still cherish those quiet, uncluttered moments. But more often, we tune in, log on, plug in, and load more forms of sound than ever before. From the youngest child to the oldest adult, we spend a good part of our day under a musical spell. We wake up to it, listen to it on the way to school or work, and hear it throughout the day in stores and restaurants. In cars, we barely fasten the seat belt before hitting the play button to access CDs stored in the audio system. And if CDs weren't enough, in 2006 Volkswagen introduced a version of their GTI sedan with an electric guitar hookup. They sold every car in inventory in a matter of weeks.

Although music is often mass-produced, the experience it creates is highly personal. No two people listening to the same melody have exactly the same response. More than ever before, music has become a personal signature, like the selection of a particular ring tone or popular tune to announce an incoming cell-phone call.

In Japan, imaginative marketers continue to invent new ways to match music with a target audience. Now, a Japanese teenager can adapt a mobile phone to play background sounds of a party in progress or music in a shopping mall. Just as creative as those marketers, an enterprising teen can call home from her boyfriend's apartment to tell her mom that she's still at the mall or at her girlfriend's slumber party. Not to worry, she'll be home first thing in the morning.

What Is a Jingle and How Is It Used and Misused?

In a very real sense, jingles are commercial hymns. Done well, they are impossible to resist and remain in people's memories from the first few hearings through the rest of their lives.

The dictionary defines a jingle as a memorable advertising slogan set to a catchy melody. To be considered effective, a jingle should literally ring a bell in the brain that immediately registers the product or service the jingle represents.

Despite the power a jingle can wield in consumer purchase decisions, its usage has diminished significantly from the highpoint of its popularity in the 1950s. The following are several reasons why jingles today are viewed as an old-fashioned technique to get attention:

- Clients no longer demand jingles and rarely ever question why their ad agency never suggests one.
- For the most part, today's marketers have forgotten how powerful sound can be in musical form.
- Few products are marketed with original music and instead rely on popular tunes that don't speak uniquely for the product.
- Marketers don't give jingles enough time to become implanted in consumer's minds. If they use jingles at all, they change or drop them after just a few months, driven by the theory that consumers get bored with the same tune over and over again.

It's funny how we often refer to another person as moody or being in a bad mood. Truth be told, we all are "moody" every waking minute of every day. Our brain is hardwired to seek out signals as to how to behave. And the most powerful marker that guides us from mood to mood is music, or in a broader context, sound. It can switch us from one emotion to another with the greatest of ease. While the other senses play their role, they are not as dominant.

The greatest enemy to marketing success is silence. It is particularly true if the advertising effort is restricted to a print medium like newspaper, magazine, or even outdoor. Without the overriding power of music, the ability to evoke any kind of emotion is severely limited.

American business started to understand the role of music as a sales tool in the early nineteenth century. In 1830, an Illinois land developer created what may be the first known jingle, sung at town halls and other public events when Illinois was considered pretty far west.

Move your family westward,
Bring all your girls and boys,
And rise to wealth and honor
In the state of Illinois.

That same era saw the rise of enterprising "snake-oil salesmen," who conjured up and sold all manner of medical potions. With little or no basis for their claims, they peddled wares that would supposedly cure pretty much everything with one stout swallow on a regular basis. One of the most famous was Lydia Pinkham's Vegetable Compound, a medicine to help barren women become fertile.

> Sing, oh sing of Lydia Pinkham and her love for the human race,
> How she makes her vegetable compound and the papers they
> publish her face.
> Widow Brown, she had no children though she loved them very dear,
> So she took some vegetable compound and she had them twice a year.

Long before the Clydesdale horses pranced into Anheuser-Busch beer commercials, the Busch family produced songs to sell their product. This 1915 tune is a request for a beer and a woman's hand.

> Come, come, come and make eyes with me under the Anheuser
> Busch,
> Come, come, come drink some Budweiser with me under the
> Anheuser Busch.
> Hear the old German band! Ach du lieber Augustin
> Let me hold your hand, do, do, do
> Come and have a stein or two under the Anheuser Busch.

There is nothing very complicated about a jingle. It's basically an audio brand promise with a clear product or service benefit. The first radio jingle was produced for the breakfast cereal Wheaties in 1926, and aired in one form or another for over thirty years. In the early years, the radio show host would announce "Jack Armstrong, the All-American boy," while a live male quartet sang:

> Have you tried Wheaties? They're whole wheat with all of the bran.
> So just try Wheaties. For wheat is the best food of man.
> They're crispy; they're crunchy the whole year through.
> Jack Armstrong never tires of Wheaties and never will you.

When I was a kid growing up in the New York tristate area, like millions of others I heard countless renditions of a jingle for Robert Hall Clothiers. I still remember every word:

When the values go up, up, up,
And the prices go down, down, down,
Robert Hall is the reason
You are always in season.
Low overhead. Low overhead.

The Robert Hall jingle changed verses now and again to keep interest up and varied its sound with different recording artists including Arthur Fiedler and the Boston Pops. It ran for thirty years.

In 1939, Pepsi Cola and its advertising agency, Lord & Thomas, collaborated on a jingle that many ad historians tout as the most successful commercial song ever created. Launched on WOR radio in New York City between news announcements of Hitler's invasion of Poland, it was played hundreds of thousands of times and even became a best-selling hit on jukeboxes across America. As you can see, this catchy jingle packed a lot of product benefits into four little lines:

Pepsi-Cola hits the spot,
Twelve full ounces, that's a lot.
Twice as much for a nickel too,
Pepsi-Cola is the drink for you.

With the arrival of television in the 1950s, the jingle really hit its stride. The combination of visual motion and song was just too good for most major advertisers to pass up. My three favorites:

Chock Full o' Nuts is that heavenly coffee....
better coffee a millionaire's money can't buy.

N...E...S...T...L...É...S...Nestlés Makes the Very Best...Chocolate.

("sung" with great flair by a large dark brown dog named Farfale)

I'm Chiquita Banana, and I've come to say
Bananas have to ripen in a certain way.
When they are fleck'd and brown and have a golden hue,
Bananas taste best, and are best for you.

Chiquita-brand bananas started down the jingle route in 1944 and still use variations of the fast-paced calypso rhythm today.

The Love Affair Between Beer and Jingles

Men love beer. Without a ton of research, beer companies have always known their primary target audience is men between the ages of eighteen and thirty-five. Surprising, then, that the regional beer producers, and not the larger national breweries, were among the very first advertisers to commission jingles for radio and then television with high concentration on sports programming and, in particular, baseball. For sure, baseball is a perfect fit with beer drinking. With a game of little action that takes hours to play, a six-pack of beer is the perfect companion.

In 1951, Carling Black Label Beer was ranked as the twenty-eighth-largest beer company in the United States. In that same year, Carling produced television and radio spots that featured an appealing blonde bartender named Mabel. With heavy concentration on baseball programming and the strength of the fetching Mabel, their one-line jingle, "Hey Mabel, Black Label" helped move Carling up the ladder to sixth place just six years later.

In the 1940s and 1950s, three Northeast regional beer makers adopted baseball as their primary field in the bottle-share battle, and two of the three got millions of baseball fans singing or humming their jingles.

Rheingold's jingle was:

My beer is Rheingold the dry beer
Think of Rheingold whenever you buy beer.
It's not bitter, not sweet, it's the extra-dry treat
Won't you try extra-dry Rheingold beer?

Schaefer countered with:

Schaefer is the one beer to have when you're having more than one.
Schaefer pleasure doesn't fade even when your thirst is done.
The most rewarding flavor in this man's world
For people who are having fun.
Schaefer is the one beer to have when you're having more than one.

Schaefer keep their jingle top-of-mind from the early 1950s through 1971, when it became socially unacceptable to promote drinking more than one.

Seeing their "little brothers'" success finally sparked the larger breweries into action. They had the money to move beyond just baseball and became big advertisers for all major sports, including auto racing, a spectator sport that just cried out for a beer.

The first breakthrough ad campaign was the national launch of Miller Brewing Company's jingle in 1971: "If you've got the time, we've got the beer." Budweiser countered with "For all you do, this Bud's for you," and the major beer makers have tried to out-jingle each other ever since.

As Miller managed the success of its core brand, Miller High Life, it also tinkered with a whole new concept—a reduced-calorie beer eventually dubbed Lite Beer from Miller. Lite's marketing challenge was to avoid turning off customers who might be offended by a "sissy" beer.

The first Lite commercials appeared in 1973 with the theme "Everything you always wanted in a beer. And less." These commercials soon added a heated argument between two guys squaring off. One yelled repeatedly "Tastes Great" and the other answered, "Less Filling." This manly debate continued through more than ten years and eighty commercials and included more than forty celebrities such as Billy Martin, Dick Butkus, Mickey Mantle, John Madden, Mickey Spillane, and Rodney Dangerfield. "Tastes Great," "Less Filling" could be considered one of the most successful short jingles. It certainly sold billions of bottles of beer.

Can a Well-Known Song Define a Product?

Since the late 1980's, popular and mainstream music has been the overwhelming choice for songs that sell products. By the year 2000, original music, commissioned to sell a company or its wares, had become the rare exception to the rule. The benefit of the use of popular music is the instant recall among the millions who have enjoyed the tune. The downside is that these songs are not specifically tied to any one brand. For example, while in the kitchen on a quick snack break from your favorite television show, you hear a great pop song coming from your flat screen. Entertaining, but without direct vision, you don't have a clue about what's being sold.

When *Advertising Age* listed its picks for the top ten jingles over the past hundred years, it did not include any with popular tunes. Each of the top ten has its own original score.

Advertising Age Top Ten Jingles of the Twentieth Century

1. "You deserve a break today."—McDonald's
2. "Be all you can be."—U.S. Army
3. "Pepsi Cola hits the spot."—Pepsi
4. "M'm! M'm! Good."—Campbell's Soup
5. "See the U.S.A. in your Chevrolet."—Chevy Motors
6. "I wish I were an Oscar Mayer Wiener."—Oscar Mayer
7. "Double your pleasure, double your fun."—Wrigley's Doublemint Gum
8. "Winston tastes good like a cigarette should."—Winston Cigarettes
9. "It's the real thing."—Coca-Cola
10. "A little dab'll do ya."—Brylcreem

Although the application of well-known songs makes it much harder to distinguish a product, their use as background music for radio and television ads is at an all-time high. I don't really consider pop tune jingles legitimate because they are not a unique identifier of the product being sold. Many advertisers have created seemingly brilliant ads with well-known music only to see the ads pulled after a short time because of no discernable bump in product sales.

One example was the Nissan 1996 television spot with Ken and Barbie dolls in a break-up argument over a third cool guy in a Nissan sports car. The commercial cost well over a million dollars to produce and was set to Van Halen's "You Really Got Me." The only problem was that neither Nissan nor Van Halen inspired us to buy cars.

In 1999, Coke used the Platter's classic, "Only You" to little effect. Contrast that to thirty years earlier when Coke commissioned an original song, "I'd Like to Teach the World to Sing," which went on to be a Top 40 hit for many months. Every play reminded us that Coke was a part of life worth enjoying.

This print ad campaign for Diet Coke also utilized an original jingle on radio and television that reinforced the tagline, "Just for the taste of it." A very successful effort, it reminded consumers that a diet drink didn't mean a flat, blah taste, at least in the case of Diet Coke.

"Just for the Taste of It." Trademark of the Coca-Cola Company, 1983. Created by SSC&B-Lintas.

There are examples of songs by popular artists, some obscure and some quite mainstream, that have been effective as jingles, and in every case, the song has a direct link to the product being advertised. If you can make this kind of connection, then by all means do so. Otherwise, the use of popular songs as jingle background makes no sense. The following are five television spots that did a spot-on job of matching a song's lyrics to the core product:

1. ***Heinz Ketchup:*** The ad showed the wait time for thick Heinz Ketchup to finally exit the bottle onto a hamburger with Carly Simon's "Anticipation" in the background.
2. ***California Raisin Advisory Board:*** Claymation raisins danced to the Marvin Gaye 1968 hit song "I Heard It Through the Grapevine."
3. ***Mercedes-Benz:*** The 1999 campaign featured Janis Joplin's "Mercedes Benz" as she sang, "Lord, won't you buy me a Mercedes-Benz? My

friends all drive Porsches, I must make amends." Historic note: Janis owned a Porsche.

4. ***Chevy Pickup Trucks:*** The use of Bob Seeger's, "Like a Rock," has reinforced Chevy's tagline by the same name for the past thirteen years.
5. ***United Airlines:*** Noted for its use of well-known music for many decades, the airline made good use of John Denver's rendition of "Leaving on a Jet Plane."

Tingles

A jingle is generally defined as a catchy tune that elicits instant recall of a product and, in many cases, its core or most distinctive benefit. I have created an additional term: *tingles*. The dictionary describes tingle as a pinched nerve and perhaps that's just the right thought. To me, a tingle is a tagline that also serves as a jingle and is sometimes sung and other times spoken with great emphasis in a way that makes it memorable.

The John Houseman campaign for Smith Barney in the mid-1980s is one example. This campaign consisted of ten television commercials. There was no other media used, so that Houseman's signoff was only delivered in one way. The line was: "Smith Barney. They make money the old-fashioned way. They EARNNN it." His unique delivery of the word *earn* was a tingle. It hit you in just the right way so that you would never forget Smith Barney and its association with earning your business.

Karl Malden did a similar job for American Express Travelers Checks with his full, earnest delivery of the line: "American Express Travelers Checks. Don't leave home without them."

Other examples are: the State Farm Insurance tagline, "Like a good neighbor, State Farm is there"; GE's tagline for more than twenty-five years, "GE. We bring good things to life"; Marlboro Cigarettes' "Come to where the flavor is. Come to Marlboro Country"; "Pizza, Pizza" for Little Caesars; and "Zoom, Zoom, Zoom" for Mazda.

The combination of a tagline with a forceful and unique spoken or sung cadence is a concrete way to avoid the popular song trap: easy and enjoyable memory of the tune and no recall of your product.

Among states and countries competing for tourist dollars, there are only a few examples of tingles. You would think in this multibillion-dollar global battle for visitors, jingles and tingles would be a common way to get attention. And, you would be wrong. There is only one American state that sets its tagline to music, and that's New York State's, "I Love New York."

Among countries, you have to go back to the 1980s and a campaign for Spain where the tingle was a five-second singing of the word *Spain* at the end of each radio and television spot.

Today, practically every industry, from financial to drug to auto and packaged goods, has taglines that are rarely if ever spoken and, when they are, more often than not have no attitude or unique flair. On the Web, company taglines, for the most part, don't appear at all.

If nothing else, we have failed to remember how our minds are wired to seek out and retain interesting delivery of a commercial message in musical or lyrical form. In their effort to make an impact, advertisers have left the distinctive jingle and tingle behind and settled for the low-risk, low-return approach.

Songs of all descriptions are great background music for stores, restaurants, many workplaces, and even hospitals and prisons. The so-called Muzak industry is thriving as never before, as stores and businesses of all types have come to recognize the positive effect music has on shoppers to buy more and on workers to be more productive. Some songs have a huge following as background favorites. The Beatles' "Yesterday" is listed in the *Guinness Book of World Records* as the most frequently played Muzak selection, with over five hundred variations in circulation.

Background music does not make a brand stand out. It is mass audio branding and not product specific. If life were a salad, music would be the dressing. Without dressing, a salad is pretty much dead on arrival. The trick in marketing is to create a dressing for our "product salad" that is 100 percent unique to the sale.

We have lost our way. We have forgotten what works. We have cancelled out millions of years of evolution and billions of promotional dollars by failing to focus on the power of sound—unique sound—in the selling process. Businesses of all sizes need to think more carefully about the opportunity they are missing and start to use the unsung hero of the past: the product-specific jingle or tingle.

There's more ahead on what we're doing that is dead wrong and what we can do that is right on target to create powerlines that command a starring role in successful brand building.

CHAPTER 9

The Gun That Won the West

Transforming Ordinary Products into Extraordinary Brands

ACCORDING TO MANY advertising historians, the period from the 1950s through the 1980s was the Golden Age of Advertising. By that reckoning, the work that has come out of the ad industry from 1990 through today might be considered the Leaden Age of the business.

We have fallen so far that we no longer have the ability to create advertising and promotional campaigns that resonate with the consumer and have a hold on the collective imagination. What's wrong with political slogans and commercial taglines today? Pretty much everything.

We have more choice than ever before in the products and services we can buy. Yet few companies even attempt to distinguish their brand and compel the consumer to select it over its competitors. Never have companies paid less attention to the fundamental principle of marketing success: Create a powerline that everyone will remember and that truly separates a product from all others.

There was a time, way before advertising's Golden Age, when American ingenuity and instinct added up to first-rate marketing acumen.

Firearms and the right to carry them have always been part of the American heritage. Today, when much of our wilderness has been urbanized, the United States still issues twenty million hunting licenses each year for elk, moose, caribou, long-horned sheep, and bear. Even buffalo hunts are popular, though nowhere near the levels of 1850–1880 when over 100 million bison were hunted down by white settlers and the professional hunters who worked for the railroads. Through America's long history of hunting, one gun has stood out as a legend. It was famous for its reliability and endorsed by Jimmy Stewart and John Wayne in numerous Westerns, as well as by avid and high-profile sportsmen including President Teddy Roosevelt. That gun is the Winchester repeating rifle, specifically the 1873 lever action model.

Over a century ago, a clever person, whose name is no longer known, dubbed the Winchester, "The Gun That Won the West." The tagline lives on and any hunter or rifle owner knows its association with the Winchester brand.

It's a perfect powerline and Winchester used it at every opportunity to define their rifles and emphasize the history behind them, one that no other rifle manufacturer could claim. Fundamentally, what do people want in a firearm? That it works every time they pull the trigger. That it never jams or wears out or misfires or mechanically disappoints in any way. Well, if Winchesters won the West, they must be the best. This is a powerline that stands for something. It highlights the product and makes it the hero. It puts emotion into the selling equation with the reminder that America is what it is today partly because of this firearm. Very few companies know how to do today what someone did for Winchester so many years ago.

Get a Life!

A tagline must be a unique identifier and brand promise for a product or service. Alas, the ability to be original and create a distinct brand is practically a lost art today.

There is no better way to describe this lack of differentiation than to show a sampling of the latest trend: the inclusion of the word *life* or *living* in a tagline. If someone recommends one of those words to you, demand your money back.

The list:

"Live Your Life"—American Eagle
"My Life. My Card."—American Express
"Be Life Confident"—AXA
"Life May Appear Larger"—Blackberry

"The Coke Side of Life"—Coca-Cola
"Grab Life by the Horns"—Dodge Cars
"The Styles of Your Life"—Dillards
"When Life Feels Perfect"—Four Seasons
"Live by It"—Harley Davidson
"*Life*/Changing"—The State of Iowa
"Build Your Business. Love Your Life"—The State of Ohio
"Total Living"—Merrill
"Life Takes Visa"—Visa
"Volvo for Life"— Volvo

The net effect of all these "life lines" is that none stand out. It's particularly amazing that two direct competitors, American Express and Visa, use exactly the same message worded slightly differently, and both try to convince us that our entire lives revolve around a plastic credit card. I think not. Convenient? Absolutely. Fundamental to life on the planet? Hardly. Can't they give a core benefit? American Express used "Don't Leave Home Without It" to great success in decades past. It is still what consumers remember as the promise of the brand.

Iowa … "*Life*/Changing"? I have been there many times and I still feel pretty much the same. Then there's Ohio, which Easterners often confuse with Iowa. Ohio wants us to love our lives. And all along, I hated mine.… Thanks Ohio, wherever you are.

Powerlines: The Rules of the Road

It is not that difficult to understand what must occur so that a tagline has a chance to become a powerline—a line that lights up the target audience and makes them think of a brand every time they are in the mood to buy in that product category.

Marketing professionals complain that it is much tougher today to get a line to stick with consumers. There are too many media choices and too little attention paid to advertising. I don't buy this convenient excuse. The real answer is that it is easier to create a line with no real meaning than to devise one that is absolutely spot-on with its description of a brand promise.

Here are the simple rules that must be followed to create powerlines, not empty lines.

1. Remember: A brand is a promise that delivers an experience, hopefully a unique one. The line must describe that promise.
2. State the claim in an original way, one that has not been done by others. It must be specific, with a choice of words that makes sense for the category.
3. Avoid platitudes.
4. Make the line elicit emotion. Be sure employees and customers will nod their heads in recognition and agreement, and feel special for their effort.
5. No powerline ever came out of a focus group. Focus groups with random customers are a waste of money. To audition potential lines, create a focus group of employees who thoroughly understand the business.
6. Make sure the line can answer this question: what will the product or service specifically do for me?
7. To have a hope of catching on, a line must be large enough to be seen in advertising and spoken with a unique delivery on radio, television, and the Web.
8. The line should appear prominently everywhere: on all advertising, letterhead, brochures, websites, new employee materials, and communications in any form to customers. Practically every company breaks this rule. Taglines are generally not widely displayed, almost as if companies are ashamed to put them front and center on every touch point with customers, clients, and prospects. Perhaps because they know, more often than not, that the line is pretty lame.
9. Don't change a great line. People don't like change and don't trust it.
10. Don't be afraid to create a line with attitude or edge, particularly if it represents a destination, premium product, or a new product that is first in its category.

They're Kidding, Right?

The tagline examples in this section break many of the rules above, and in some cases, all of them. It is not for lack of big marketing budgets, but rather as a result of inattention to basic marketing principles.

AT&T

In 2006 and 2007, the new AT&T ran an ad announcing its merger with BellSouth and Cingular with the new AT&T (see page 128, Chapter 7). Given the power of the Cingular name, it was a curious rebranding strategy to drop it in favor of AT&T, a twentieth century brand that went awry. The headline makes absolutely no sense: "Yesterday you connected to the world. Today the world starts connecting to you." This is tech-speak with no conceivable logic to the reader. What's more, the tagline, "Your world. Delivered" is small and pretty much buried on the page. Why bother to create one at all?

Power is a word that is almost as overused in taglines as *life* and *living*. I discuss two ads below and refer to four other organizations that use the word to little effect and no power.

Honda

Honda wants you to know they stand for "The Power of Dreams." Therefore, they ran an ad depicting eight Honda models. Cars. Power. All those horses under the hood. Get it? Maybe their latest models put you in a dreamlike state? Not a good thing if you are taking a curve at forty-five miles an hour. In the ad I'm referring to, there is a competing line near the Honda name: "Safety for Everyone." Maybe that's the tagline. Who knows? The only thing worse than having one bad tagline is having two, even if one line, in this case the safety line, is better than the other.

Yet another auto manufacturer, Kia Motor Company, uses the line "The Power to Surprise." I hope they surprise me with something good like free service for life. I certainly don't want any mechanical surprises that lead to lots of visits to the service bay.

Even huge blue-chip companies pay big bucks for worthless lines that have no recall and no relationship to the product and service. Is there power in software? Well sure, as software giant SAS wants us to know with their line, "The Power to Know." Not to be outdone, Time

Warner Cable wants to remind you that you are, in fact, "you" with the line "The Power of You."

Then there is AARP, the American Association of Retired Persons, which made my top ten worst list in Chapter 7 with their tagline, "The power to make it better." The good news is that the line could mean anything—maybe reduce my electric bill or improve the relationship I have with a nasty uncle. This claim is so universal that it promises nothing.

Financial services is a category that needs to entertain and educate in order to get people to pay attention. A typical ad is filled with meaningless phrases and hackneyed images and there is virtually no company that stands out among the pack. Here are a few examples of the dead-on-arrival work that dulls our senses and leaves no impact on the prospect.

Deutsche Bank and Van Kampen Investments

Ads for both these companies have appeared regularly in major newspapers and magazines. Both feature lighthouses. Unfortunately, Van Kampen is stuck with the overused lighthouse as its logo. Not to be left in the dark, the big German bank wants you to know they can light up a stormy night as well. Then there are the taglines. If you can find it in the ad, Van Kampen's reads, "Look for the right lighthouse." Am I on a road trip up the Maine coastline? Deutsche Bank implores us to remember they are "Lighting the way to financial success." And they are vehement about this fact, as exhibited in their tagline, "A Passion to Perform." Lots of passion out there, but the reader is only eager to flip the page as quickly as possible.

The banality continues.

Royal Bank of Scotland (RBS)

Unlike in most of their competitors' ads, the RBS tagline is clearly visible. Alas, just like most of the competition, RBS's line means absolutely nothing. "Make it happen." And notice the visual. It appears they are celebrating a colleague who was able to hail a cab in New York City. It's not even raining, so what's the big accomplishment?

"Make It Happen." Trademark of the Royal Bank of Scotland Group.

"World Wise." © 2007 Morgan Stanley.

Morgan Stanley

Beam me up, Scotty. Or maybe the visual is supposed to depict a stalled conveyor belt for luggage at the Hong Kong airport? Who knows, as we are told, in type too faint to read, that Morgan Stanley is "World Wise." Spanning the globe looking for soulless pictures depicting am empty tunnel. If that's world wise, perhaps it would be wise to move on.

Several years back, UBS adopted "You and Us" as their tagline, a play on the letter *U*. Their attempt at cleverness falls short, as all investment banking and similar services are relationships between the firm and its clients.

Then there is the venerable British banking house, Barclays. They want us to know that they are "quietly conquering the world of finance." Hmmm ... Morgan Stanley is wise to the world while Barclays is quietly conquering it. What this all has to do with your money and investments is one of the great mysteries of the world.

Lots of other industries line up right behind financial services in their inability to create meaningful lines. Platitudes seem to be the order of the day.

Microsoft

For a company of such notable success, Microsoft has played around with taglines for years. "Your potential. Our passion." It's hard to believe that a company with zillions of customers cares about me and my potential.

Nortel Networks

Nortel simply wants you to know that they are some form of networking company with the philosophy, "Business made simple." I wonder if their highly paid technical staff slaving away hour after hour sees it that way. Just saying something doesn't make it true.

Hitachi

Just when you thought you had seen the worst tagline possible, another one pops up. Hitachi is going for the grand prize with "Inspire the Next."

Maybe it is a very, very short haiku.

HITACHI
Inspire the Next

"Inspire the Next." © Hitachi, Ltd. Created by Dentsu, Inc.

"*connectedthinking." Trademark of PricewaterhouseCoopers LLP.

PricewaterhouseCoopers

Although PwC's long-running campaign makes little sense, they continue to march on like the picture in this ad of a band walking through rows of yellow tulips. What on earth is this ad supposed to convey? The body copy is even more confusing and their tagline, "connectedthinking," with two words run together, is way short of clever. To continue the gimmickry, there is an asterisk at the beginning of the tagline just in case someone makes the connection with the asterisk at the end of the ad's headline. Since the entire pitch makes no sense, perhaps they could explain it with another asterisk.

Don't Confuse Motion with Emotion

One of the world's most competitive industries, automobile manufacturing spends billions of dollars a year to encourage us to buy a new shiny vehicle that matches the image of who we are or want others to think we are. The car you drive is a very visible declaration of your self-image. It's a personal badge of iron and rubber worn for the world to see. Curious, then, that so many models today fail to truly differentiate themselves and leave the consumer with no strong impression of one car versus another.

"Life. Liberty. And the Pursuit." Trademark of the GM Corp. © 2006 GM Corp. All Rights Reserved. Created by Modernista! Introduced August 2006.

Many car marketers seek to inject motion into their taglines, with no emotion and zero differentiation. The net result is a line that speaks to transportation and nothing else.

Note Cadillac's tagline "Life. Liberty. And the Pursuit." Who knew America's Declaration of Independence had such marketing get-up-and-go?

And notice the woman driver whose expression suggests she's fleeing a carjacker or perhaps driving the getaway car from a bank heist.

Plenty strange. Our friends at Lexus are also in the running with the tagline "The Pursuit of Perfection." And, since both Cadillac and Lexus are pursuing much the same customer, perhaps all this pursuing makes some sense to them.

Two other upscale names, Mercedes and Hummer, try to create emotion with their lines and manage to set themselves apart from the pack. In the end, they bump into each other with basically the same message. Hummer wants you to know it's "Like Nothing Else" and Mercedes tries to squeeze Hummer out of that parking spot with "Unlike Any Other." The good news is they could swap lines and no one would notice.

Powerlines That Almost Work

Not all is doom and gloom. The following taglines have potential but don't quite pull it off. They generally miss the mark because their theme is separate from the real focus of their core business. The connection is loose and/or very difficult to grasp.

There are very few original lines today. It's almost as if all ad agencies merged into one gigantic recycling firm that sprinkles similar words across different industries. Another word making the rounds is journey, as the two ads below show.

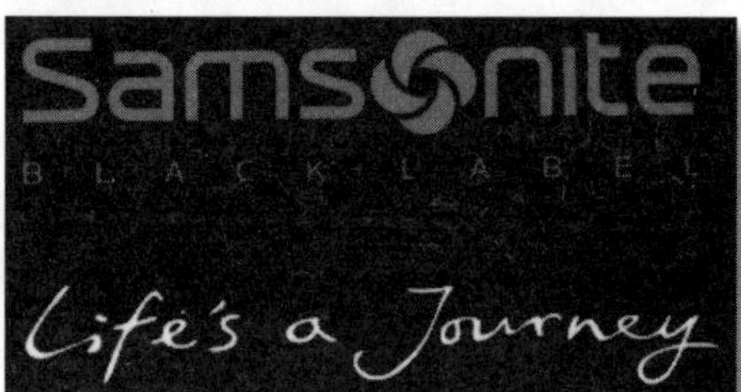

"Life's a Journey." Trademark of the Samsonite Corporation. Developed by TBWA\Worldwide (via TBWA\Brussels), 2005.

Samsonite

Samsonite reminds us that, "Life's a Journey." Now if only their luggage would fit in the overhead bin on a Boeing 737.

The Wall Street Journal

This ad is one of a series showing famous people like Sheryl Crow, and some not so famous, with glazed-over expressions while, nearby, an abbreviated version of their life stories snakes across the page. We might notice the tagline "Every journey needs a Journal," and we might wonder what that has to do with reading the *Wall Street Journal*. Last time I checked, it wasn't a diary. Does Sheryl even read the *Journal*? The visuals are striking and you want to

"*Every Journey Needs a Journal.*" © 2007 Dow Jones & Company. All Rights Reserved. Web and print campaign created by T3.

figure out what exactly is going on. But after trying for three seconds, you give up and journey on to other pages. As it turns out, the *Journal* is asking you to subscribe, but with no mention of what action they want you to take. Dare I say, a journey in search of an experienced marketing guide?

Lufthansa Airlines

Gee, a cute German blonde babe asleep in coach class, next to an empty seat. I am told below, "There is no better way to fly." Another line highlighted in the ad is "All for this one moment." The trouble with airline advertising is they overpromise and underdeliver every time. A line

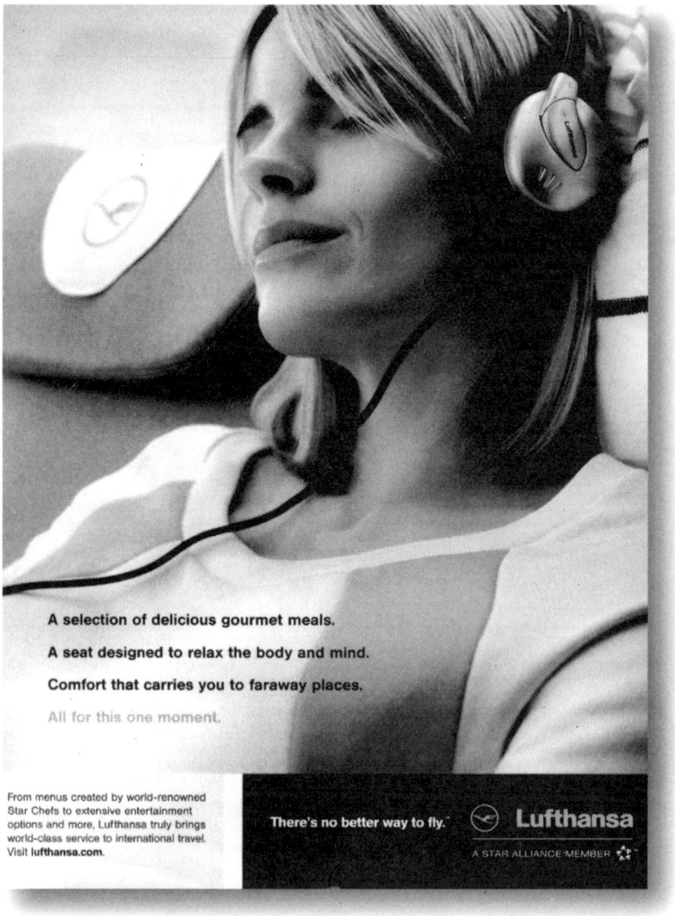

"There's No Better Way to Fly." Trademark of Deutsche Lufthansa AG.

needs to be believable to be a true powerline. Maybe Lufthansa is the best way to fly, but they would get more credibility if a real customer said so and the visuals weren't totally preposterous.

United Technologies (UT)

United Technologies is a manufacturing giant, and while rival General Electric gets all the attention, UT gets a much better stock multiple. UT's ad series shows various products, like the elevator seen here, dissected in great detail. It's probably a fascinating story if you are Superman and can read the tiny type. We mere mortals only see the words: *Capacity: One Billion*. But if we somehow found the tagline "You can see everything from here," we'd see a cute play on words. Unfortunately, the thought is way too generic and has no specificity to the company. Can they really see everything? What is everything? There is actually a better phrase for a tagline hidden in the body copy at

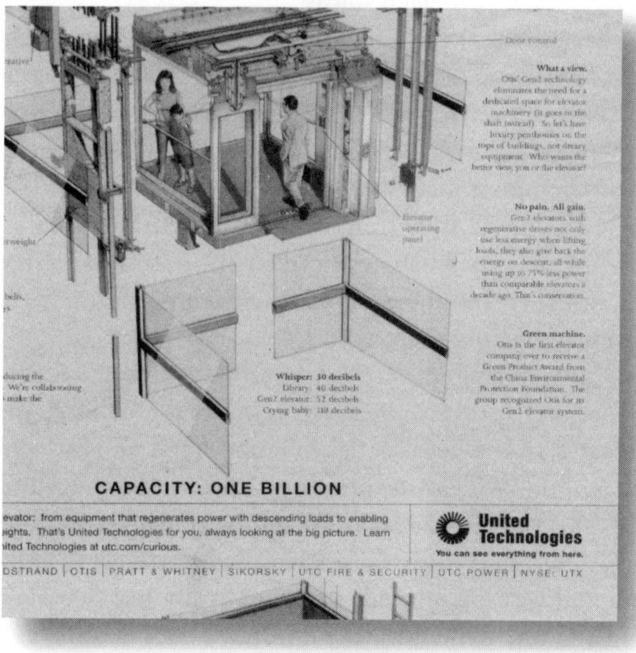

"You Can See Everything From Here." Trademark of United Technologies Corporation.

the bottom of the ad: "always looking at the big picture." That sounds closer to what UT really is all about.

Don't Be Afraid To Have Some Personality. In Fact, Be Afraid If You Don't.

Unique personalities are memorable. Rule No. 10 for creating a powerline suggests expressing an attitude that captures the soul of the destination, product, or service. In today's politically correct environment, where we are afraid to state anything that might offend any number of special interest groups, marketers who have the gumption to try are often rewarded for a little risk taking.

There is no better example of succeeding with attitude than the city of Las Vegas. This city comes clean with their primary selling proposition as a destination: you come to Las Vegas to have a really good time as an adult. That good time can include legalized prostitution, gambling, R-rated live entertainment, and nonstop gawking at babes and guys regardless of your sex or marital status.

A few years back, Vegas decided to promote itself as Disneyland in Nevada. This mistake reduced the numbers of visitors at an alarming rate. Then, the city council decided to promote Vegas as Vegas (also known as the original Sin City), and adopted the line: "Las Vegas. What happens here stays here." This admission of the real DNA of the place was an instant hit with potential visitors. The new tagline, supported in television and print, accompanied visuals of suggestive adult situations and quickly became familiar to millions of Americans and foreigners.

The curious aftereffect of this powerline is that most people think the line is "What happens in Vegas stays in Vegas." Whether intended or not, the creator of the Vegas official tagline came up with a mind trick that we all fall for. We hear the line but we hear it as we want to, and not as it is. This situation is rare and difficult to predict. In the case of Vegas, the payoff is huge and tourist visits have increased every year since the current tagline was introduced. A tagline really has two versions: one we are told and one we insist is the line, but isn't. For sure, Vegas hit the powerline jackpot.

Australia is another destination that has done a great job of marketing with attitude. After all, if a destination is really far from everyone, it needs to offer a good reason to rationalize the long plane ride there and back home. In the 1980s, Australia used Paul Hogan of *Crocodile Dundee* fame to sell tourist campaigns with cute local sayings like, "Put another shrimp on the barbie."

Lately, they have decided to just jar us with provocative lines minus a spokesperson. The most recent call to visit is, "Where the Bloody Hell Are You?" While offensive to some, this line is impossible to ignore. And it's targeted: if potential visitors lack a sense of humor, why would the Aussies want them anyway?

With a little bit of thought and the courage to get beyond soulless expressions, anyone can sell attitude. One organization that takes edginess to the limit is a group in New York City called the Freelancers Union, an organization of writers and artists for hire as independent jobbers. The Freelancers Union runs a series of ads seeking new members. Pointedly, the ads consist of just one long headline and no body copy. One long powerline, if you will. My favorite from their campaign: "Find an Insurance Plan. Find a Gig. Enjoy Not Giving a Crap About Office Politics." I hope the union member who created that one was well compensated.

Happily, a small but ever-growing number of groups take the plunge and create taglines with flair, vigor, and originality. Here are a few that make us smile or think or both.

New Orleans

Attitude and New Orleans have always gone hand in hand, particularly when it comes to the concept of a good time, rain or shine, all day and all night. These ads are part of a campaign to lure visitors back to a fabled city, which has suffered greatly as a top destination since Hurricane Katrina. The campaign theme "Forever New Orleans" puts visual emphasis on the word *New* and the copy reminds you to always expect the unexpected—a great new jazz spot, restaurant or antique shop, or nifty neighborhood. The headlines are clever and fun: "Shaken. And Stirred," "Open. To Just About Anything," and "Dry? We Were Never Dry."

"Forever New Orleans." Trademark of the New Orleans Metropolitan Convention & Visitors Bureau. Created by Pat McGuiness and Robbie Vitrano.

Tumi

If you visit New Orleans, perhaps you'll take along some new Tumi luggage. Their tagline, "Where Next?" has some spunk to it with the visual of an edgy young couple on a scooter. She drives in a provocative outfit that bares a little leg and he rides along in a pinstripe suit. How often do you see that type of transportation photo? Never, and

"Where Next?" Trademark of Tumi, Inc.

that's the point. It's hard to make luggage exciting, but this execution does an excellent job.

Kohler

Kohler makes fixtures for the bathroom—not the most glamorous room in the house, but certainly one of the most indispensable. They want us to know that bathrooms can have style as well as function, style with its own kind of sexy feeling created by the shapes and materials made by Kohler. To that end, their tagline "The Bold Look of Kohler" appears on all their promotional materials with the Kohler name in bold type to emphasis just that point. This long-running promotional campaign shows Kohler products in surreal surroundings

"The Bold Look of Kohler." Trademark of the Kohler Co. Number 1 from the "As I See It" series by Sanjay Kothari.

that have nothing to do with the bathroom. The message clearly comes through: Kohler can transform a bathroom into a desirable, attractive room. Kohler's campaign delivers on the promise.

Converse

The ad is about as edgy as any created today for mainstream magazines. With positive attitude, its tagline makes the point that we all wish to feel eternally young: "Clothes and Shoes for Guys and Girls." Clearly, this is apparel for people who want to feel young regardless of age. The headline "Get Chucked" is cheeky to the extreme and the implication is

"Get Chucked." Trademark of Converse Inc. Created by Yard, New York, for the John Varvatos line of Converse products, 2006.

reinforced by the visual of a "girl" with a nicely toned, Converse-clothed derriere enjoying a massage from a pair of male hands. The owner of the hands is out of the picture, but we assume it's the aforementioned Chuck. Aside from its questionable taste, the ad loses effectiveness because of the small size of the tagline. Most readers will just see "Get Chucked," smirk or quickly shake their heads, and move on.

Here are five other examples of mainstream businesses that permit attitude front and center in their ads.

IWC Schaffhausen

This high-end Swiss watchmaker states its mission plainly and without apology: "IWC. Engineered for men." Our watches are made for men. Period. Sure, women can wear them, but we really don't care. In fact, the line discourages the idea that any woman would. There is no other watch company with the nerve to eliminate half the population from its potential buyer pool. Even with a limited target audience, IWC has been around for one hundred and forty years and affluent men swear by the brand.

British Petroleum

British Petroleum shortened their official name to BP many years ago and, since the turn of the century, has tried to position itself as an oil company with a passion to protect the environment. Their tagline "Beyond Petroleum" was a gutsy move with its statement that the source of their livelihood is not their corporate focus. That's assuming one believes them. Many BP ads talk about their expansion efforts in solar and wind technology and cite $50 million for one initiative and $70 million for another. In the world of oil giants, those numbers are a rounding error and almost laughable. BP needs to be careful not to promise more than they seem to deliver … beyond petroleum.

Fox News Channel

The Fox tagline "We Report. You Decide." is a smart strategy. The network's news reports are often cited as being far to the right, a unique position for a television news channel. Fox seems to embrace the accusation and plays to it with its tagline challenge "You decide." Until the launch of this line, no news organization had asked its audience to judge the quality of its news content. After all, viewers are supposed to trust the deliverers of news and not question their point of view. Like it or not, Fox is in your face with the challenge to use your brain and decide if their programming is right for you. Very foxy.

The New York Times

"These Times Demand *The Times*." No apologies here either, but also no call for a vote on the quality of their news reporting. They are the venerable *New York Times* and you are lucky they are around to provide global news each morning offline and every second online.

About one hundred years ago, *The Times* was just one of many news dailies, and had a solid but not exceptional reputation. These days, it is the standard-bearer for all city newspapers across America and is the only one with a legitimate national and international reputation. This tagline clearly reinforces their position and is hard to argue with. There is nothing fundamentally wrong with a superior attitude if a product is top of the line.

Stella Artois Beer

I like the pride of Stella's "Perfection has its price." It's not about the consumer but instead focuses on Stella's beer-making skills as being worth the premium price of the product. Stella has made beer for over six hundred years and is one of the oldest continuously running businesses in the world. Close at its heel in terms of longevity is Beretta Firearms, another Italian company. For sure, Italians take their beer and firearms seriously, and so should you. A premium product with a storied history should never shy away from charging the consumer accordingly.

Fumbling on the One-Yard Line

The worst crime in advertising and promotion is creating a great line that nobody sees. Most art directors today insist that people can read taglines that are essentially hidden from view. Now, some lines are so lame that they are better left to obscurity. But when a company has a solid line that reinforces its brand promise, it's criminal to keep it concealed. Clients need to demand better from the people who create and deliver these ads at great cost. Alas, the price is even higher when the message can't be seen.

Advertisers have about one second to get someone's attention. Just one. Take a look, if you're able, at the following four examples of decent taglines that were fumbled within a yard of the goal.

A.G. Edwards

Tagline: "Fully Invested in Our Clients"

Don't let the capitalization fool you into believing you can read the tagline in the ad. You can't. A.G. Edwards has invested in the egg as their advertising icon and their ads are cleanly constructed. In each one, an egg represents a particular investment challenge. Too bad that a perfectly good tagline never gets the type size it deserves. Someone at A.G. Edwards should have egg on their face.

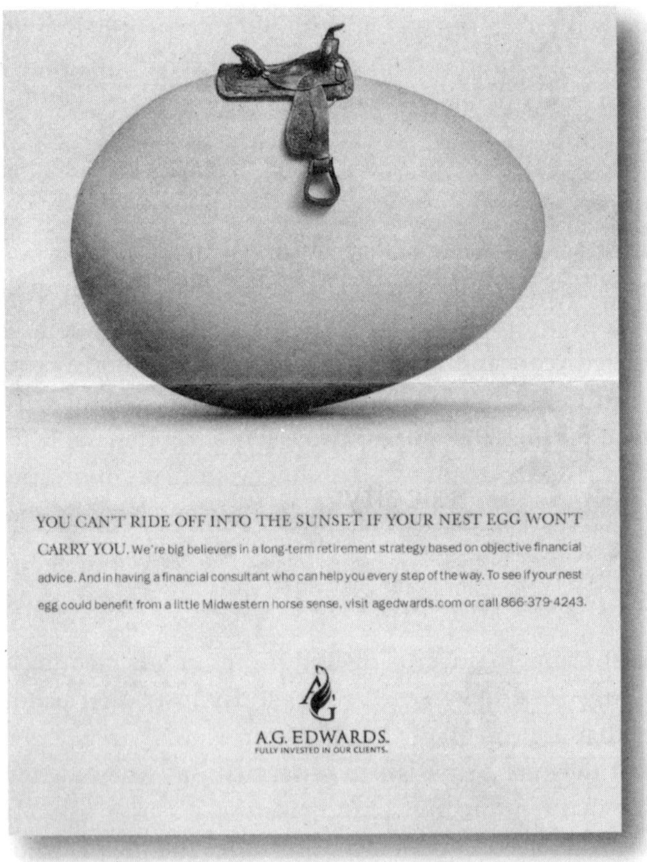

"Fully Invested in Our Clients." Trademark of A.G. Edwards & Sons, Inc. © 2007 A.G. Edwards & Sons, Inc. Created by Carmichael Lynch.

It is interesting how insurance, one of the most boring of industries, is filled with great taglines from Principal, Allstate, State Farm, MetLife, and others. All these firms have not changed their lines in years, while companies outside the insurance industry have increasingly traded old ones for new since the 1980s. Insurance is tough enough to get excited about. So a fully vested tagline that has decades of recognition is correctly viewed by this group as an asset not to be tinkered with.

Principal Financial Services

Tagline: "We'll Give You an Edge"

Principal has kept their line for years, as well as their three-sided logo and cartoon figure displaying the logo as a protection device. All the

"We'll Give You an Edge." Service mark of Principal Financial Services, Inc. © 2005 Principal Financial Services, Inc.

elements of this campaign fit together well. Yet, they fumbled the ball with a copy layout that looks like insurance-speak. A potential reader does a quick glance and never sees the tagline, which is the central point and a good one at that.

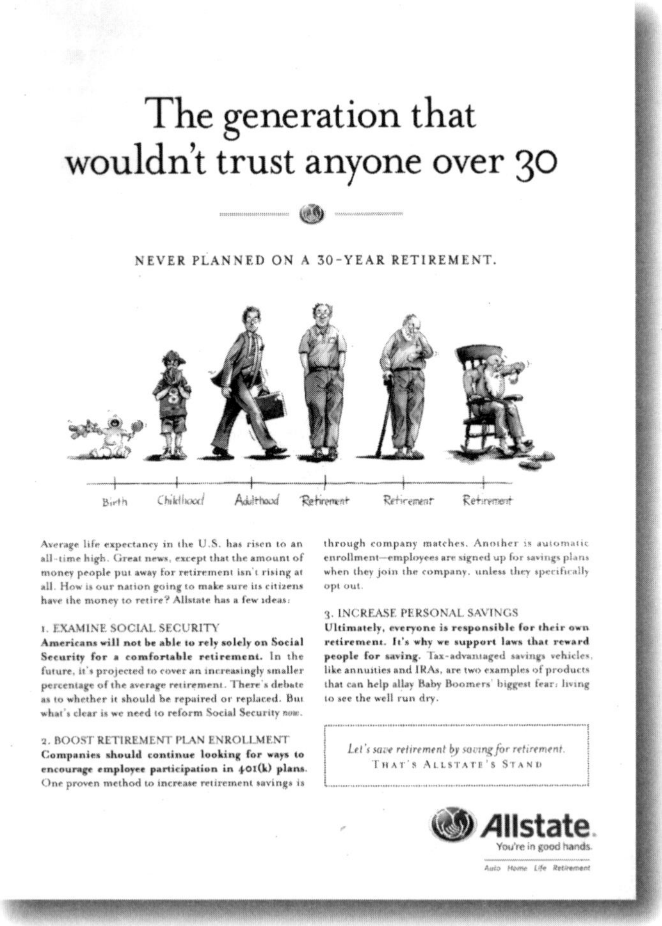

"You're in Good Hands with Allstate." Registered trademark of Allstate Insurance Company. This slogan was created half a century ago by Allstate general sales manager Davis W. Ellis to demonstrate Allstate's ongoing commitment to customers. The phrase came to him as the result of a reassuring remark made to his wife regarding their ailing child.

Allstate Insurance

Tagline: "You're in good hands."

Allstate is well known for the powerline that has appeared for over fifty years, "You're in good hands with Allstate." Recently, they have made visual modifications that change the emphasis. The line no longer is the "hero" of the ad, but rather an afterthought. Originally, this line got recognition because it appeared as the headline in every television and print execution. Now it has been shortened to "You're in good hands" and sits in very small type under the Allstate name. Even the symbol of two open hands has become so stylized that the hands are hard to make out. It looks as if Allstate is experimenting with other lines, such as "That's Allstate's Stand," which is highlighted in a white box above the Allstate name. Do too many lines dilute the takeaway message? Yes, they do.

Good Lines. Good Line of Sight.

The following seven ads all break the mold of "try to read me if you can" and position the taglines in easy-to-read type connected to the logo of the company or product.

U.S. Trust

No fuss, no muss. "The standard for wealth management since 1853." Nicely positioned next to the U.S. Trust standard.

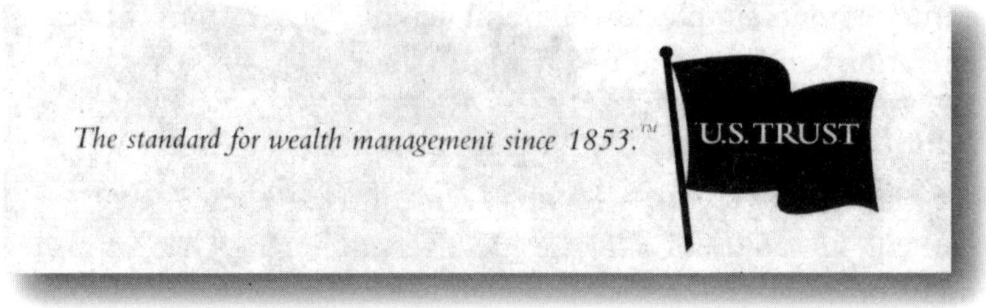

"The Standard for Wealth Management since 1853." Trademark of Bank of America Corporation.

"The Ultimate Driving Machine." Registered trademark of BMW AG. Created by Ammirati Puris AvRutick, 1975.

BMW

Everyone knows "The Ultimate Driving Machine" is a BMW. This line has remained highly visible for over three decades and is a major contributor to BMW's success.

Continental Airlines

Other airline campaigns come and go, but Continental sticks with this unique look using bold color and type with their tagline signoff in the lower right corner: "Work Hard. Fly Right." The two lines appear horizontally opposed in every ad.

Brooks Brothers

Their Golden Fleece logo has been around since the early nineteenth century with its simple, to-the-point tagline "Generations of Style." Any generation can also read it with no problem.

Cohiba Cigars

Made famous by Castro before he decided to live longer and ditch cigar smoking, this ad uses bold type effectively to portray the Cohiba brand and its promise.

Staples

Staples' goal as a business is to make your work life a whole lot easier. They even practice what they preach and make the tagline highly visible. Now wasn't that easy?

"Work Hard. Fly Right." Registered trademark of Continental Airlines, 1998.

"Generations of Style." Trademark of Brooks Brothers. In 2007 the venerable clothier updated this powerline for their high-end Black Fleece line of apparel: "Style For A New Generation."

"Extravagant Taste." Trademark of General Cigar Company Inc.

"That Was Easy." Service mark of Staples, Inc., 2003.

"Home Page for the World's Business Leaders." Trademark of Forbes.com.

Forbes.com

Malcolm Forbes always looked for ways to get reader's attention. His heirs continue the tradition with a strong, easy-to-read line reminding us of the value of their comprehensive news/business website.

Unusual and Perplexing Lines

You've got me. See if you can figure out the next three ads and determine what they try to convey. Maybe they are designed to confuse, or perhaps that would give more credit than is probably justified.

Transamerica

Tagline: "The Power of the Pyramid"

This is a very strange ad. Power is a completely overused word and does the top of the building in this ad look like a pyramid? Plus, how many people know the Transamerica headquarters building is shaped like an elongated pyramid? And what exactly is pyramid power anyway? As for this ad's headline "I Want Easy," when it comes to money, nothing is easy, especially for people who try to preserve and grow their investments at the same time.

And what's the Johnny Carson look-alike standing on that puts him high in the sky at building's top level? A very strange ad, indeed.

"The Power of the Pyramid." Registered trademark of the Transamerica Corporation.

PPL

Tagline: "61 Straight Years of Dividends."

Is that good? Sure, and here's a line that will seemingly advance the number to sixty-two next year and sixty-three the year after, and so on. All fine and good except that you and I have absolutely no idea what

"61 Straight Years of Dividends." Trademark of PPL Corporation.

this company is. I have combed every line of this ad and still don't have a clue. Perhaps it is Pacific Power & Light or Pittsburgh Power & Light. Or People Power Limited. Maybe the website will tell me, but no … it's in mice-sized type, which pays my eyes no dividend at all.

University of Chicago MBA Program

Tagline: "Triumph in your moment of truth"

And exactly what moment would that be and what is this ad trying to convey? If you actually read the body copy, it makes very little sense. Hmmm, maybe the copywriter skipped English comprehension in good old undergraduate school.

"Triumph in Your Moment of Truth." Trademark of the University of Chicago Graduate School of Business.

Type Hype, A Good Technique to Consider

Shangri-La Hotels and Resorts

Tagline: "Heaven on Earth"

Bold and to the point, a rare occurrence in advertising today, this oversized tagline becomes the whole focus of the campaign. The layout encourages the reader to believe Shangri-La's hotels and resorts are like heaven on earth. For sure, your eye cannot ignore this graphic treatment and the message is grasped immediately. What else can an ad hope to do? This hotel group gets high marks for being dramatically different. It clearly understands that a simple message conveyed in a unique way has real staying power.

Paul Smith Clothiers

Tagline: "Paul Smith"

In the world of luxury goods and high-end fashion, taglines can often seem quite beside the point. After all, if you charge three to ten times the price for clothing, as does Paul Smith, versus Target or JC Penney or Macy's, what can you possibly say without sounding ridiculous? Luxury brands like this one—Prada, Versace, Armani, and others—sell their brands by the name itself. Their whole proposition is their name. If you change, define, or explain the name,

"Where Will You Find Your Shangri-La?" Trademark of Shangri-La Hotels and Resorts.

the power of the brand is diminished. The sell here is all illusion; no words and prices are ever shown. If you have to ask about cost, you're not the target audience for these high-end clothes.

Paul Smith. © Paul Smith.

United Parcel Service (UPS)

Tagline: "What Can Brown Do For You?"

Does UPS use brown as its signature because the color has been rejected by everyone else? Has anyone, except possibly some UPS employees, ever referred to brown as their favorite color?

Surprisingly, UPS adopted brown as its official color in 1920, thirteen years after the company was founded. In the first half of the twentieth century, all railroad Pullman sleeping cars were decked out in different shades of brown. As a result, those who rode in luxury in these bedrooms on the rails viewed brown as an upscale and even elegant color. From 1920 to 1940, only well-heeled rail travelers could afford Pullman service and it was the equivalent of first-class air travel today. The founders of UPS decided that what was good enough for luxury rail service was good enough for their corporate color. It was also helpful that brown doesn't show dirt and grime as vividly as most other hues.

Brown has been synonymous with UPS for over eighty-five years and the company has made excellent use of this distinctive color in all of its advertising. "What Can Brown Do for You?" is immediately understood worldwide as a question only UPS can answer.

Thanks New York. We Can Use That.

While New Yorkers are often thought to be different from most Americans, their views on life are universal, especially when it comes to ad campaigns. Two notable examples are taglines that have been picked up by towns and cities across America as well as by other locales around the world.

Over forty years ago, a New York City television station, WNYW, began its nightly 10:00 p.m. local news recap with the words, "It's 10:00 p.m. Do you know where your children are?" In a city as mobile as New York, where kids can be on their own at all hours, this warning was not viewed as a strange question. WNYW, the local Fox affiliate, still begins each evening news show with the same query. Over the years, local advertisers have lined up to sponsor this nightly news opener and it brings a considerable amount of annual revenue to the station. WNYW also licenses the line to other news stations across the country. Leave it to New Yorkers to figure out how to provide a public service and get paid in the process.

They're baaaack. Government-generated taglines have made a comeback since World War II and have returned more recently with announcements to the public to stay alert. In the war years, these lines encouraged people to be on the lookout for foreign spies and warned them not to discuss troop or ship movements in public. Today, it's all about terrorism. We are all too familiar with airport security procedures, but what about other public transportation like subways, trains, and buses? Clearly the screening of individuals as they board is never going to be practical. The New York Transit Authority's answer is a highly visible campaign done much like it was in the 1940s—large posters throughout the transit system with the central theme and tagline: "If You See Something, Say Something." These posters tell a variety of quick stories, like how highly trained dogs can sniff a suspicious package or how transit riders can join transit workers and greatly enhance the sheer number of eyeballs in search of objects or people that just don't look right.

This campaign is front and center with its punchy line and high visibility, the essence of an ongoing awareness effort. Radio and television are being added to the mix and the immediate popularity of the line has spread far and wide. Since the campaign began in 2002, over forty other transit systems in America and other countries have asked for and received permission to use this line or a slight variation.

Do Powerlines Really Make a Difference?

Most companies that have been market leaders over long periods of time employed taglines that built their brand promise into a powerful motivator for consumers to react to and purchase their product. In each of my picks for the top ten commercial taglines mentioned in Chapter 7, the product and the line are one and the same in the mind of the consumer. Whether it is De Beers's "A Diamond Is Forever," Nike's "Just Do It," or FedEx's "When it absolutely, positively has to be there overnight," these powerlines clearly define the culture of the product.

True powerlines are promises that deliver and never change. They are the voice of the brand.

The ongoing fight for market share in the erectile dysfunction drug category is a perfect illustration of a powerline's value. As male baby boomers entered their fifties and sixties, they created a huge new market for a product to guarantee sexual performance. Pfizer was the first pharmaceutical company to capitalize on this need with the launch of Viagra, a purple miracle pill that would never let men down.

Viagra became an instant hit worldwide, quickly captured seventy-five percent of the market, and generated billions in annual sales. Products from rival companies soon appeared, but none were able to capture significant market share. Lilly Pharmaceuticals, the manufacturer of Cialis, was particularly vexed because they believed Cialis to be a superior picker upper. They ran a continuous series of ads for months, with little impact on the market.

Then, much like this miracle product, a marketing phenomenon occurred. Embedded in the fine print required by the FDA for any and all erectile dysfunction drugs was this line: "If an erection lasts more than four hours, you must seek immediate medical attention." Eureka. With this discovery by a clever copywriter, Cialis changed its television and print advertising and made this line the hero. In print, it was the headline copy you couldn't miss, and on television, the voice-over ended each spot with the line as it simultaneously appeared on the screen.

Within three months, Cialis gained over thirty percent of the market and climbed to parity in sales with Viagra. One line made the difference. Just one line.

Six Essentials for Perfect Powerlines

1. ***You are different. Say so.*** Don't use common words everyone uses. Particularly words like life, power, world, advance, performance, deliver, guarantee, etc.
2. ***Have real attitude.*** Bypass wishy-washy phrases that could apply to any business. FedEx did it right years ago when they avoided lines like "We deliver on time" or "We guarantee delivery." Instead, their agency created a line with attitude and swagger: "When it absolutely, positively has to be there overnight." And while you're at it, lose the word "we," a position that has no credibility with the consumer. Smith Barney recognized this fact when they launched their famous campaign in the mid-1980s with John Houseman as its believable spokesman: "Smith Barney. They make money the old-fashion way. They EARNNN it."
3. ***Be the headline.*** This is Marketing 101: Make your tagline large enough to be seen. Easily. In print, you must deal with the lack

of sound and its ability to build attention and emotion. The only marketing weapon at your disposal is large, easy-to-read type. Basic, basic, basic.

4. ***Be everywhere or you are nowhere.*** Ninety-nine percent of advertisers today, commercial, governmental, or nonprofit, make the same mistake. They put their tagline or slogan in a couple of ads and think their job is done: everyone now knows what they stand for. In fact, the opposite is true. For a line to make a lasting impression, it must appear in all touch points with employees, customers, and prospects.

   More than twenty-five years ago, Mary Wells Lawrence created the "I Love New York" campaign to encourage tourism to all parts of the state. It's a catchy line with attitude and even has an original musical theme on television and radio. Yet even with all these positive attributes, we rarely hum or think about it because we rarely see or hear it. Every spring, a few television spots and print ads appear in advance of summer vacation, only to disappear for 85 percent of the year. This great line should appear everywhere—in state buildings, on stationery, business cards, and even on tickets issued by the state police. It should remind people of New York's great activities, geography, art, culture, and ethnic diversity. All year round.

5. ***Change everything else but a great line.*** Changing an established line is like changing a brand name. It should rarely if ever be done. Yet, today it is done all the time. Car manufacturers who constantly change their brand promise complain about their inability to get new model cars noticed. A few smart companies avoid this trap, most notably BMW, which sticks with the oldest line in the industry, "The Ultimate Driving Machine."

   The financial services industry has the same affliction: creating new lines all the time, to little effect. Most of these firms simply forget how they were noticed in the first place, with great lines like: "The Thundering Herd," "Do You Know Me?," "The Citi Never Sleeps," and "Have You MetLife Today?" People in all cultures fear change and especially dislike it in the products and services they consume, even if the newer version is better. One way to smooth the path to consumer acceptance is to maintain the basic selling proposition: We still do what we always did even as we make things better for you. A well-written powerline never has to be altered. It can be a constant promise in an ever-changing world, making a company a safe haven—one consumers always know they can count on.

6. ***Yes, it's an art.*** The best slogans and taglines come from individual flashes of inspiration. A small number of people just know how to create great taglines, slogans, and jingles. They don't sit in brainstorming meetings with thirty other creatives, and they often aren't experts in the specific product category. They are just people who love to write advertising copy. There are no hard statistics to back up this view other than what I have seen throughout thirty-five years in the business. In every case, a terrific individual writer just sat down and took the time to develop a winning line.

Stay True and Prosper

I recently saw an amusing line for Boulder, Colorado. Some call it the Cambridge, Massachusetts of the West. Others think of it as the Rocky Mountain capitol of illegal drugs. And some remember it best for the still unsolved murder of Jon Benet Ramsey. What makes Boulder unique is that it's just that: offbeat, to many off-putting, and often off current trends and on to new ones before the rest of us have caught on.

"Keep Boulder Weird" is a brand promise that reflects the uniqueness of the town. It's part of what makes Boulder special. There is nothing ever wrong with truth in advertising. And once articulated, in a few perfect words, there is never any reason to change.

Human Nature

The final element that marketers can bring to bear to create powerlines is using a spokesperson or spokescharacter to deliver the tagline and/or assume the visual brand identity associated with the tagline. There is no technique more powerful than finding or creating a compelling spokesperson who can readily be identified with your product or service.

It is basic human nature that we pay more attention to each other than to anything else such as inanimate objects or stand-alone symbols. A vivid example is the Christian cross, which would never have made the huge leap from a criminal execution platform to a holy icon for billions of followers without Jesus literally tied to it. With any product or service, a personality can make all the difference between no discernable impact and a tremendous lasting impression. Chapter 10 will show exactly how success works and failure lurks for those who don't pay attention to this critical topic.

CHAPTER **10**

Character Building

Speaking in a Distinctive Voice: The Persuasive Power of Characters from Pitchmen to Spokescharacters to Spokespeople

In the world of advertising, people identify a slogan or tagline better and remember it longer when it comes out of the mouth of a specific individual, an animal that appears human, or a custom-made character, that is, a spokescharacter. This is not surprising, given fundamental human traits. For millions of years, animals have looked to each other for behavioral guidance. Translated to marketing terms, human beings are conditioned to buy products that other people, or figures that act like people, are selling.

The history and use of characters in advertising and promotion is also a straight-line history of social change in America that begins with the onset of the Civil War and its accompanying influx of immigrants and others to industrial cities. The factories in those growing urban areas soon became mass producers of clothing, household items, and foodstuffs, which were then distributed by railroad to the growing American population.

Before 1860, not much of anything was mass-produced; a family either made whatever it needed in the way of food, clothing, and shelter, or acquired the stuff of life from neighbors or a general store within a radius of a few miles. America was about to tear itself apart in a war that was fueled in part by the shift from rural to industrial production; simultaneously, it was also about to enter a new age of consumerism. For the first time, makers of everything from furniture to firearms to handbags to beer faced direct competition on a national scale. A whole

Characters and Spokespeople Defined

SPOKESCHARACTER
A fictional object or human figure or a representation of a human by an animal or animated character. Prior to the advent of radio and television, these characters had no speaking roles. In modern times, most do.

SPOKESPERSON
A real person who either plays a role invented for promotional purposes or uses their own celebrity to endorse a product or service.

new way of selling was about to begin, one in which products needed to be distinguished from one another and remembered by brand name.

From Pitchmen to Puppets: One Hundred Fifty Years of Spokespeople

Before 1850

There were two basic forms of character endorsement prior to the Civil War: wandering minstrels selling their brand of eternal salvation for a price and pitchmen who traveled across the land peddling medical cure-alls at town gatherings. More often than not, these potions were bogus and, in some cases, caused drastic intestinal distress and even death. Nevertheless, pitchmen roamed America's villages and towns for close to a century and were popular attractions from the "outside world."

1870 Through 1900

The Quaker Oats Man is the oldest human-like advertising character and is still in use today. In 1877, several small cereal manufacturers banded together to form a larger, single company and introduced a character to reinforce the benefits of cereal and become a familiar face to consumers. Since the above-mentioned snake oil salesmen and their quack concoctions, advertising has always had a bit of a credibility issue, and sometimes with good reason. In this case, the company that became known as Quaker Oats had not a single Quaker on the payroll. Quakers are known to be people of outstanding moral fiber, obsessed with healthy living and the best sanitary conditions that ingenuity can provide. The Quaker Oats Man implied that all the sect's benefits could be had in the big tubular cereal box. Known as the Society of Friends, the Quakers objected to this wholesale image and, for years, petitioned the courts to remove their name from this commercial application. All court pleas continue to be turned down and the Quaker Oats Man, an enduring face in the world of cereal, carries on.

Although the Quaker Oats Man was relatively harmless and actually reflected well on the Quaker movement, another packaging trend at the time was much less positive and reinforced the image of blacks as servants, complete with smiling faces and perpetual grins. The Pearl Milling Company, the first company to develop packaged pancake batter, opted for the image of a plump, older black woman and named her Aunt Jemima. Her name came from a popular minstrel song, and she began to appear on pancake boxes in the early 1880s.

Though slavery had been outlawed for many years, as recently as in 1940–50, black women were often referred to as "girls" and, when older, as "aunts," just as young black men were called "boys," and then "uncles" in adulthood. This form of address was a direct throwback to slavery, when white masters refused to address blacks as Mr. or Mrs., titles that were reserved exclusively for whites. Another recognizable character, created by the Cream of Wheat Company, was a smiling black waiter with a steaming bowl of porridge. This character was named Rastus, an extreme racial slur but perfectly acceptable at the time.

Aunt Jemima and the smiling Rastus survive to this day, though both have been stylized to look less like servants and more like good neighbors.

1900 Through the 1920s

By the beginning of the twentieth century, mass consumption had reached a fever pitch. Companies in large numbers required their ad agencies to develop characters that could attract attention, create amusement, and win affection. In other words, characters as brands.

The big rage during these decades was the art nouveau movement, which was all about the use of symbolism, mystical and mythical creatures, and the celebration of asymmetric forms and shapes in fashion and jewelry. Not surprising that people dealing with the ever-quickening pace of invention, with its mechanical applications like cars, phones, and appliances, would be attracted to evocations of the complete opposite. Fairies, pixies, and nymphs became very popular product mascots. After all, they represented the fresh spirit of a new century and served to remind the populace that despite major upheavals, packaged products could bring cheer and good spirits—literally—to American households.

The first "spirit" to engage consumers, a character dubbed Psyche, appeared on White Rock Soda bottles in the 1890s. She was a nymph made famous by a German artist, Paul Thurman, who had painted *Psyche at Nature's Mirror*. Psyche still stares at herself on White Rock bottles and is the grand dame of fairy characters in advertising. Many followed in her path and in 1915, Wrigley Gum introduced a pixie named Spearman. The company published children's booklets of rhymes illustrated with the Spearman character. Over the years, Spearman changed shape and eventually morphed into a walking, talking piece of gum. He was honorably retired to gum heaven in 1969.

A gang of three who are still in use today got their start as elves in 1928: Kellogg's Snap, Crackle, and Pop. In later years, a long line of elves and related characters followed, including the Jolly Green Giant, Little Sprout, the Keebler Elves, and the Lucky Charms cereal leprechaun known as Lucky. All are still alive and well today.

Other characters born in this era were more literal figures, devoid of pixie or fairy charm. Notable among them were Buster Brown and his dog Tige (1904), Dutch Paint Boy (1907), Morton Salt Girl (1911) (see Chapter 7), Mr. Peanut (1917), Betty Crocker (1921), and the Gerber Baby (1927). Other than Buster and Tige, the rest of the crew are very much still in use with billions of impressions to their credit.

The 1930s Through the 1950s

Many promotional characters made their appearance during this thirty-year period. Much to the chagrin of social commentators, stereotypes that reinforced common prejudices made a comeback. Uncle Ben's rice,

Chef Boyardee Italian food products, and the Juan Valdez figure that was used to represent the National Federation of Coffee Growers all made their debuts in this period, as did Miss Chiquita Banana, who appeared as a South American fieldworker with little more to offer than a friendly smile and a voluptuous figure. She eventually went on to further fame with a popular jingle she sang in the fifties and sixties and still appears in label form on every Chiquita brand banana.

Other characters with broad appeal made the products they endorsed instant hits: Peter Pan for peanut butter with the same name, Elsie the Cow for Borden's milk, the Coppertone Girl, and the Campbell's Soup Kids.

In 1954, America and the world met the Marlboro Man cowboy who, by most accounts, is the single most recognizable product figure ever created (see Chapter 7). Just as he appeared to join the large stable of promotional characters that, for the most part, carried out their roles in silence, television had begun rising as the major national pastime.

In the 1950s, television changed from a luxury for a privileged few to a household necessity for every American family who could afford one. On television, characters could act exactly like us. They could move and turn and smirk and laugh. They could whisper or shout and jump all about. They were now transformed from static, staring images to active companions and eternal friends. They were not just characters anymore—they were real personalities.

These personalities became better known and loved than most stage and screen idols. Through the power of television, they could deliver a punch line that turbocharged the product name into our minds and made room for the character to "move in" as well.

Kids were targeted first with Tony the Tiger proclaiming that Frosted Flakes were "G-r-r-reat!" Then Trix the Rabbit came on the scene to remind us that Trix were for kids and *not* for rabbits. Viewers, including adults, became familiar and thoroughly amused with these adorable characters' tales of woe. And no character had a harder time than Charlie the Tuna. Poor Charlie—his singular passion and goal was to some day, somehow be good enough to get caught and then processed as canned tuna. But Starkist Tuna had high standards and always rejected Charlie's pleas. Fifty years later, Charlie still hopes for acceptance.

Attitude with a capital *A* became a mainstay of the characters who achieved mindshare in television land. Marky Maypo refused to eat his

Maypo oatmeal until other family members tried to grab it from him. Kellogg's introduced Sugar Pops Pete, who forever blasted perfectly fine puffed wheat with endless streams of sugar. The cheerful and practical Speedy Alka-Seltzer reminded us to plop him in a glass of water to instantly dissolve him and indigestion as well.

Mr. Clean came on the scene in 1958 and turned an entire category upside down. Prior to this genie-like cartoon character, who whirled around the house and spiffed up everything in his path, the liquid cleaning category was dominated by a product called Lestoil. Just a few months after Mr. Clean made his debut, complete with singing theme "Mr. Clean, Mr. Clean, Mr. Clean," Lestoil was literally knocked off supermarket shelves to make room for Mr. Clean. Lestoil never held first place in the category again. In fact, the only real competition Mr. Clean encountered was from the White Knight, another animated character introduced a few years later by Ajax.

Who would have guessed that more than one hundred characters would bombard us with sales pitches during the first ten years of television's dominance as the central source of family entertainment. Characters sold everything and anything from gasoline to aluminum to all kinds of food items, cigarettes, lumber, and even adding machines.

These characters would do anything to get our attention as they ran and flew and walked and talked and squawked through the post–World War II era. Companies quickly realized that with a surplus of goods for consumers to now choose from, the race for market share was often won by the most creative use of a character as spokesperson.

Mainstream media got into the act in 1957 as the mighty NBC network introduced a colored animated peacock logo to remind viewers that it led the charge for "programming in living color." No matter that in the fifties, it took an electrical engineer to figure out how to make the color on the screen something other than a bad shade of green. NBC made its impression first as the technology leader in television land and continues to use the peacock a half century later.

In 1954, *Mad* magazine hit the newsstands to the delight of many teenagers, particularly boys, who were bored by squeaky-clean publications like *Boys' Life*, produced by the Boy Scouts of America. *Mad* was filled with irreverent humor and mercilessly satirized the world of adults, jobs, education, dating, and even nuclear war. Its spokescharacter,

Alfred E. Neuman, was a teenage nerd complete with missing teeth, big ears, and a tilted head. His philosophy to one and all was, "What—me worry?" For awkward teenage boys, Alfred was a reassuring reminder that there really wasn't much to do about the state of the world other than to laugh and hope the adults had half the sense that *Mad* magazine had. Although Alfred was a silent character, his consistent proximity to his one-line philosophy made it one of the best-known phrases of the baby boomer teenage years.

The 1960s Through the 1990s

This forty-year period brought every conceivable type of character to America and the world. The use of animals, some silent and some very talkative, came into fashion, as did characters with real attitude. Even sex made its way into character development, most notably in a series of commercials for Taster's Choice Coffee. This instant coffee company introduced us to two appealing male and female apartment neighbors, who began a serious flirtation over borrowing each other's Taster's Choice. Cleverly produced, the thirty-second commercials were set up like a mini soap opera, with the viewer held in suspense until the next episode. Would these two become a couple? Would one move in with the other? Many thousands of viewers wrote Taster's Choice to suggest plot lines or to encourage the relationship in one way or another. Not surprisingly, Taster's Choice saw a dramatic uptick in sales throughout this campaign.

During this era, many animals became commercial stars, including Morris the Cat, the AFLAC Duck, the Esso—then Exxon—Tiger, Spuds MacKenzie for Bud Light beer, and the Talking Frogs for regular Budweiser. An inspired choice for America's favorite beer, the Talking Frogs still appear as a threesome with their spiel, one after the other, "Bud" "weis" "er." Amazingly, characters can be made to effectively tout a brand's name in ways that would sound silly or insincere from a human—AFLAC Insurance's silly duck continues to gain new customers by waddling around yelling "A-F-L-A-C."

Several animals performed as endorsers by just being themselves. Two notable favorites were the Exxon Tiger, which gracefully moved about the terrain as an announcer extolling the virtues of a tiger in your tank. Another popular animal was a large male gorilla, which attempted to smash a piece of American Tourister luggage. One figured if this gorilla couldn't tear apart the luggage, then maybe, just maybe, the airline baggage-handling "gorillas" wouldn't be able to either.

A strange but successful matchup of animal to company is The Hartford Insurance Elk, which began in 1974 and continues today. Clearly, elk do not roam the hills of Connecticut where the company is based. Yet, the elk stands guard as the symbol of strength and service for The Hartford. A particularly odd symbol, the elk is not especially noteworthy in the animal kingdom and is known primarily as an excellent source of low-fat protein. Why then does this work? Sometimes just being different in the category does the trick.

Attitude, a highly effective way to deliver a line, was in full force when Punchy took the stage. Created by Hawaiian Punch in 1961, Punchy was always ready, willing, and able to punch some unfortunate drinker as he rhetorically asked, "How about a nice Hawaiian punch?" Little Caesars Pizza's hyperactive and aggressive animated Caesar ended each commercial with "pizza, pizza," said as fast as he could get the words out. And in the eighties, the popular Peanuts cartoon-strip characters brought a little life to the insurance category as they debated the reasons why MetLife was the right insurance company. At first, each ad finished up with, "Have you met life today?" and then later, "Get Met, it pays."

Born in the 1970s, Pillsbury's classic character Poppin' Fresh, the Dough Boy, was a rather shy little creature who always blushed at the end of each commercial. The Dough Boy was originally conceived to create awareness for Pillsbury's refrigerated dough, pastries, and biscuits in tubular packages which, when opened correctly, literally popped out.

An extremely skilled team from the Leo Burnett agency, which also invented many of the other popular characters used in advertising, created Poppin' Fresh. This brilliant campaign actually instilled anticipation in the viewer as soon as the Dough Boy appeared on the screen. In a matter of seconds, a human finger would appear and gently poke Dough Boy in the belly. Dough Boy then made an adorable sound of pleasure in response. This campaign is the only one of its kind where a human body part directly touches and elicits response from a make-believe character. This animated powerline has remained Pillsbury's signoff for decades.

Another character from this era was not treated as gently as Dough Boy. Poor Mr. Bill, an animated clay character who appeared on *Saturday Night Live*, suffered continual harm at the hands of humans. Though never actually touched by human hands, Mr. Bill was squashed, flattened, cut, and otherwise mangled by a barrage of mishandled objects. The popular punch line delivered by the clumsy humans was "Oh no, Mr. Bill!"—a fitting prediction of the decreased usage of these characters in the years to come.

2000 to Present Day

Although less prevalent on television, many of the characters mentioned above and a host of others are still around. Some have lost their "voices" and are relegated to appearances on packaging or as toys or plastic models.

Various analysts who study trends like these chalk this change up to the more serious times of our day. One could argue if things are so serious, why not ask our always friendly character pals to spend more time cheering us up. A few still do.

Ronald McDonald continues in McDonald's promotions after almost fifty years. The Fandango Puppets sing and dance and remind us to fandango our movie tickets online. Mars Incorporated's M&M's characters have made a strong comeback in recent years. With cutting-edge graphics, they are more delightful to watch than ever. Kermit the Frog pops up now and again, most recently reminding us that it's good to be green in a 2006 ad for Ford's hybrid car line.

How to Use Spokescharacters and Spokespeople

The trend so far in this new century is to rely on spokespeople more, and characters less. Maybe we are more serious than ever before. Responding to this cue, advertisers have tried to establish a more realistic human bond between their products and the potential buyer. Given that humans look to each other for continual guidance, the use of spokespeople as guides can heighten brand awareness far beyond what would occur without their presence.

But whether a company chooses to create a make-believe endorser or use a human in a spokesperson role, the character and the lines they deliver, with proper marketing strategy and execution, become one strong consumer memory. Not surprisingly, there are similarities and differences between the proper use of make-believe characters and human spokespeople.

What Spokescharacters and Spokespeople Have in Common

- ***Exclusivity.*** They should be exclusive to the product or service. If marketers cannot secure exclusive rights to a character or group of characters, they should not use them. Likewise, if a spokesperson merely *adds* a product to their long list of product endorsements, the ability to use them to their maximum potential is severely diminished.
- ***Fit.*** They should be a natural fit with the product or service. Tiger Woods is clearly the best person to endorse golf equipment and apparel. A cat selling cat food makes an obvious connection. The Doughboy, the Jolly Green Giant, Elsie the Cow, Charlie the Tuna, Peter Pan for peanut butter with the same name—these are character fits that make perfect sense. And spokespeople, with appropriate wardrobe and props, can be made to look as if they fit with the product. If a nonhuman character is not an extension of the actual product, it can be made to fit with a tie back to the product name, like Sugar Pops Pete.
- ***Integration.*** They should be used at every touch point to deliver maximum impact. A character or spokesperson should appear everywhere the product appears—it's that simple. Everywhere means just that: all media online and off, company presentations, annual reports, posters in stores or branches, even as the phone voice on a customer service number. Today, only a handful of companies do this integration successfully. A spokesperson/character will always be remembered better and longer if they are associated with a particular line that they deliver in a certain cadence, tone, and manner. This character/line association is the most powerful element in consumer recall and lasting impression of the brand.
- ***Stability.*** They should rarely, if ever, change. The Quaker Oats Man is one hundred thirty years old, still has all his teeth, and appears on every cereal box produced by the company. The Morton Salt Girl

was "born" in the same year the *Titanic* sunk, 1912, but she remains steadfast and unsinkable. The Marlboro Man still saddles up and the Maytag Repairman continues to slouch idly next to a washer/dryer. When an identifiable person or celebrity associated with a product dies, tough decisions must be made. When Frank Purdue died, his son immediately took over spokesman duties. Colonel Sanders, for Kentucky Fried Chicken, died a decade ago, but his image lives on as the company logo and in animated form in commercials. It makes no sense to change an instantly recognizable spokescharacter unless there is absolutely no choice. The associated tagline can live on indefinitely and, nine times out of ten, should. Sure, products improve over time, but that doesn't mean the basic pitch should. Humans are not big on change and hate it when products they have come to love and trust alter their look and basic selling proposition. The only people who seem vague on this concept are chief marketing officers who land in a new company and immediately make changes just to show how valuable they are. These types can destroy a brand in short order.

How Spokescharacters and Spokespeople Differ

- ***Mortality.*** Made-up characters never age, never die, never act irresponsibly, or demand a star trailer on a commercial shoot. A human spokesperson does all of the above and more. There is no question that characters are a lot easier for companies to manage. Characters are eternal friends. They live on from generation to generation. They are immortal.
- ***Morphing capabilities.*** Make-believe is just that. Nonhuman forms can appear in any shape and size and change both without appearing ridiculous or strange. A miniature collection of the Campbell's Soup Kids is a cool collectible. A miniature collection of real children would be just plain creepy. Make-believe characters can get away with whatever the animator's mind can think up. Human's are much more limited to human expressions and accepted social settings. There's just no way around this fact.
- ***Public appearances.*** By and large, spokespeople are excellent representatives at shareholder meetings, press briefings, and any event where their presence is required for extended periods of time.

Stand-in make-believe characters, that is, people in the character's costume, can make appearances and delight the crowd, although their presence often wears thin after a short time. A spokesperson can have a powerful impact during an evening event with customers or as a visible presence at a tradeshow or employee meeting. They shake hands, look people in the eye, and discuss current events and common interests.

- ***Spokespeople can be company employees.*** Clearly Mr. Clean, Mr. Peanut, or Comet's Josephine the Plumber are never going to be in the running for CEO of the companies they represent. On the other hand, company founders, CEOs, or other senior officers can be incredibly powerful representatives and salespeople for their products. Dave Thomas, Frank Purdue, Orville Redenbacher, and Victor Kiam for Remington Shavers are a few examples of bosses who can serve as credible and powerful preachers for products.

How Spokespeople Deliver Powerlines Effectively

Who can forget Karl Malden, who implored people to not leave home without their American Express Cards or Travelers Checks? Or John Houseman for Smith Barney, Brooke Shields and her Calvin Klein Jeans, Mr. Whipple's demands not to squeeze the Charmin bathroom tissue, or Dunkin' Donuts' Fred the baker mumbling to himself, "Time to make the donuts."

The affection and affiliation people feel for a perfect fit between spokesperson and the company they represent is completely natural behavior. It's a fact of human nature that people pay more attention to a product pitch if they identify with the pitch person. Throughout world history, all the great religions were launched, in a marketing sense, by a spokesperson. To a large degree, the power of religion and its effect on the flock is based on the speaking ability of its founder and followers.

Many fundamentalist preachers have swayed millions of people to their brand of Christianity through their verbal skills. Men like Oral Roberts, Billy Graham, Jerry Falwell, Robert Shuler, Pat Robertson, and Jimmy Swaggart had the ability to deliver spellbinding stories in front of large audiences of the faithful. They also sold millions of bibles, books they authored, and tapes of their speeches, and raised vast amounts of money to support buildings for their ministry, learning centers, and churches. They were masters of the appeal for ongoing financial support through relentless television and radio broadcasts. Their collective success is based on the most important element in the selection of spokespeople: They must be, or at least appear to be, passionate about the product or service they represent.

Rules of the Road

A spokesperson can effectively deliver brand awareness far and above any other marketing method. But there are specific rules of the road that must be followed to effectively call attention to a product or service. A good spokesperson must be:

1. ***Exclusive.*** Never hire anyone unless they are willing to be solely focused on the business.
2. ***Committed.*** Not the same as exclusive, this means they are true believers in what they pitch to the public. It also means they are willing to speak publicly, and not just in advertisements, about why they represent the company and love the product or service they endorse.
3. ***Broadly appealing.*** They are popular with both sexes and all age groups. Even if they sell power tools primarily targeted to men aged thirty to fifty, it is important that kids and girlfriends and wives can relate and help reinforce the purchase decision.
4. ***In all media.*** So many spokespeople today put restrictions on where they won't appear. For instance, they will do television and print, but not billboards, Internet, or phone. Great, let them have their specific demands met by someone else. Like a great preacher or politician, a spokesperson and/or image should appear everywhere a consumer is likely to interact with the brand.
5. ***In all countries.*** Make sure the pitch people are okay with their international exposure and with having remarks translated into other languages. For those only operating in the United States, this proviso is not as important, but increasingly more companies than ever before operate in multiple countries.

The Four Categories of Spokespeople

1. ***Company employees.*** Extremely credible if they are naturally articulate, have a strong sense of ego, and want clients and prospects to love them and their message.

2. ***Paid actors playing a character.*** Generally, the actor is unknown and the character is the sole focus for consumers. Who played the Marlboro Cowboy or Maytag Repairman, or Frank Bartles and Ed Jaymes for Bartles & Jaymes Wine Coolers? Nobody has a clue and only three people care: the actor, the agent, and the company marketing chief.
3. ***Paid actors or well-known personalities playing themselves.*** These stars are most effective when they pitch products they are identified with, and less effective when the connection seems forced or just plain laughable. Michael Jordan selling basketball shoes—slam dunk. Michael Jordan selling a particular watch or clothing line—maybe. Michael Jordan selling a management consulting company—missing the jump shot completely.
4. ***Deceased.*** Occasionally, the now departed can be effective and sometimes attention-getting. Generally, this is not a good idea. Clearly they can't attend company functions or give press interviews. And, there is often the accurate feeling among consumers that the deceased had no say in the decision to be walking and talking among the living.

Successful Spokespeople, Great Lines

With careful thought, casting, and creativity, a spokesperson can catapult a brand to a position of prominence in short order. The result can be dramatic and, if nurtured correctly, can endure over time. There are many examples of companies that successfully solved this equation and alas, many that missed the mark.

In every case cited below, product sales or service expanded dramatically after the spokesperson or people first appeared in promotional executions. In many cases, category dominance remains even long after their last appearance. In alphabetical order:

Bartles & Jaymes Wine Coolers

The genius adman Hal Riney created two rural ah-shucks, down-home characters, Frank Bartles and Ed Jaymes, who coined the term *wine cooler* and made millions rush to buy this product from 1985 to 1991. At the end of every television ad, Frank would look right at the viewer and say, "And thank you for your support." He got that right. People bought and the actors were handsomely compensated.

Brooke Shields for Calvin Klein Jeans

How to get consumers to pay a lot more for the same old jeans? Calvin Klein pumped new energy into a literally fading product with the introduction of a young Brooke Shields as primary spokesperson for the first widely advertised line of what came to be known as designer jeans. The year was 1980, and this fifteen-year-old darling of the fashion camera sold her kittenish passion far and wide.

Brother Dominick for Xerox

The 1970s had many clever and humorous ad campaigns and this effort for Xerox copiers was one of the best. The interesting twist here is that the spokesperson is silent and his "boss" does all the talking. The television spot opens with a battery of monks at labor over their desks with quill pens in hands, copying elaborate manuscripts. All of a sudden Brother Dominick has a revelation and sneaks off to copy his assignment on a Xerox 9200 Copier. He then appears at the Abbot's office with a shy grin and five hundred perfectly reproduced copies of his assignment—one that should have taken years or even a lifetime to complete. The abbot immediately looks skyward and says, "It's a miracle." Technology does create what earlier times would clearly consider miracles. Monk, copier, proclamation of miracle. A perfect match of old and new held together by a timeless line.

Clara Peller for Wendy's Hamburgers

The unassuming Clara Peller achieved instant stardom and a cult following from 1984 to 1986 when she peered at a large hamburger bun and asked, "Where's the beef?" Where indeed? These ads reminded people that Wendy's didn't skimp on the meat and this simple question sent their competitors into a frenzy to show they too could provide supersize burgers. So much for the last skinny American … no one was safe from overeating anymore.

Crazy Eddie

Who can forget television's Crazy Eddie during the 1970s, with his bulging eyes, flailing arms, and desperate pleading to get to his electronic stores immediately where, "Prices are Insaaaaane!" The real Eddie (Antar) was a shy and diminutive self-made millionaire who built his chain of stores on a loudmouthed barker played to perfection by Jerry Carroll. Business went insanely well for years until the Internal Revenue Service noticed Crazy Eddie was also crazy about not paying taxes. Liquidation and jail time followed, but while it lasted, the campaign was right on the money.

Dinah Shore for Chevrolet

Dinah Shore was Miss Chevrolet for millions of viewers who watched her variety show sponsored by Chevy from 1956 through 1963. She performed in many Chevy ads during this time and always reminded us to "See the U.S.A. in a Chevrolet." Back then, vacation by car was about it for the average American family. Trains were not what they used to be and air travel was still considered exotic and financially out of reach. Dinah and Chevy were the perfect promotional pair. Men thought she was kind of sexy and so did women, but not in a threatening way. She was like a very pretty, wholesome neighbor. At the time, the public had no clue if she was married, single, gay, or divorced, and instead focused on her great smile and love for her Chevrolet. How could the public not enjoy this entertaining hostess?

"Do You Know Me?" for American Express

Beginning in 1975, and running off and on for twenty-five years, a variety of actors, sports figures, and small-business owners would begin each commercial for the American Express Card by asking, "Do you know me?" Most of the time people didn't, until the end of the spot when their name would appear on an American Express Card and the voiceover would proclaim, "Don't leave home without it." American Express relentlessly focused on brand building before other credit card providers had a clue. From the beginning, American Express realized that a higher monthly fee than their competitors, MasterCard and Visa, implied a higher-status card. "Do you know me?" No, so please tell me about the many successful people who have an American Express Card. These ads used viewers' natural curiosity to their advantage and made the American Express Card the one to carry.

Fred the Baker for Dunkin' Donuts

Who makes all those donuts anyway? Dunkin's answer for fifteen years was good old Fred the baker, played by Michael Vale. Fred always dragged himself out of bed at 4:00 a.m. to get to the store pronto, because it was "time to make the donuts." And Fred made a ton of donuts in a total of one hundred television spots. The campaign reminded consumers that some storeowner or employee did indeed lose sleep each night in order to get fresh donuts in the racks every few hours. Nothing fancy or flashy was required. All people needed was Fred's assurance that, through thick and thin, the donuts would be there. On the day Michael Vale retired as Fred, September 27, 1997, Dunkin' offered a free donut nationwide to anyone who came into a store—a fitting tribute to a loveable character who created donut mania and brand dominance for the company.

Joe Isuzu

With Isuzu Motors' introduction of Joe Isuzu in 1986, many Americans thought: Finally, a car company comes clean. Joe, of course was a pathological liar, the quintessential sales guy played wonderfully by David Leisure. With total sincerity, Joe would make all sorts of outrageous claims about performance, handling, and price, while superimposed comments like "he's lying" or "oh, no, not again" flashed across the screen. Joe finished off each spot with "You have my word on it." No car company had ever dealt with the deeply held consumer belief that car salespeople are generally dishonest and will say anything to get a sale. Overnight, Lying Joe became immensely popular, gained wide awareness for the little known Isuzu, and charmed us with his lies again and again for the next five years.

John Houseman for Smith Barney

Made famous as the gruff yet fair Harvard Law professor in the movie and subsequent television series *The Paper Chase*, Houseman stayed in character to pitch Smith Barney brokerage in the mid-1980s. In total, he starred in ten television commercials; no print ads were ever created. After discussion of a particular investment challenge and the need for the experience and expertise of a Smith Barney broker, Houseman would treat viewers to a very professorial verbal thrashing with his closing statement: "Smith Barney, they make money the old-fashioned way. They EARNNNN it." The implication was that other brokers don't work their hardest on a client's behalf. A great delivery by a wise and experienced "professor" is one of the best-remembered taglines.

Over twenty-three years after the last spot, if you say Smith Barney and John Houseman to practically any adult, they will repeat this tagline word for word except for the substitution of *we* instead of *they*. This curious word shift occurs 100 percent of the time, even among long-time employees of Smith Barney. The mind wants to remember John Houseman as one of the Smith Barney guys, and thus the word we. Occasionally, a powerline can make us turn a phrase the way we expected it to be delivered.

John Cameron Swayze for Timex Watches

Swayze was not only a highly respected newscaster prior to his affiliation with Timex but, in 1949, he was also the first TV anchor for what became known as NBC's Nightly News. In 1956, he began a twenty-year stint with Timex and their indestructible watches. In newscast style, Swayze demonstrated every conceivable calamity that could happen to a Timex and showed that the watch continued to work. "It takes a licking and keeps on ticking." Some ad observers ridiculed the campaign, Swayze, and the indefatigable slogan, while millions bought the product. The line has stood the test of time just fine.

Karl Malden for American Express

Like John Houseman and his law professor character, Karl Malden represented American Express in the role that made him a household name: the wise and worldly street cop in the television series *The Streets of San Francisco*. For twenty-five years—a spokesperson record—Malden reminded people to always carry American Express Travelers Checks and Cards with the words, "Don't leave home without them" (or it). This is the American Express tagline that has stuck in consumers' minds. None of the many new taglines introduced over the years has gained any traction and none is remembered.

Mr. Whipple for Charmin Bathroom Tissue

An unlikely candidate for the world's record for one spokesperson in the most number of television commercials, Mr. Whipple, played by Dick

Wilson, was the firm but friendly shopkeeper who caught the gals at it again and again: "Ladies, please don't squeeze the Charmin!" In an incredible five hundred four separate television spots from 1965 through 1989, the ladies never learned. Part of the charm in these Charmin commercials was that Mr. Whipple didn't practice what he preached. After each of his reprimands to stop squeezing the Charmin, Mr. Whipple would sneak off and do exactly that. Nice touch.

Honorable Mention: Johnny Carson and Ed McMahon

During the first decades of *The Tonight Show*, Johnny Carson and sidekick Ed McMahon often did paid pitches for sponsor's products during commercial breaks. Hint to advertisers and television channels today—viewers loved Johnny and Ed's lame attempts to look serious as they peddled garden weed killer, cereal, or Alpo dog food. No one broke away to raid the fridge or refill a scotch glass. Instead, viewers looked forward to seeing how Johnny and/or Ed would flub their lines and often break out laughing. One memorable moment occurred during an Alpo commercial, when a cute puppy refused to eat the product. Johnny tried to coach the pup with "Yum, yum, good doggie." The more he tried, the funnier it became. The puppy never budged, but the laughs were loud and Alpo received a ton of good-natured publicity.

Spokespeople We Could Have Done Without

Here are a few examples of spokespeople who couldn't get traction despite large sums of advertising dollars spent. It's interesting to note that in every case, there is an absence of a strong line to carry the campaign.

Whoopie Goldberg for MCI

And the connection is … ? Precisely. Throughout this short-lived campaign, Whoopie looked as if she was having trouble reading the teleprompter and didn't much care. Nor did anyone else.

Catherine Zeta-Jones for T-Mobile

Same teleprompter problem as above? In this case, here was a gorgeous woman selling cell-phone service. Who would have the nerve to call her?

Actually, the real problem is people just don't believe a model and actress best known for marrying Michael Douglas is really interested in T-Mobile's forty-five-dollar-a-month unlimited call plan. Turns out she isn't, and the camera makes that abundantly clear.

Sam Waterston for TD Waterhouse

A decent actor who has spent twelve seasons as the slightly too intense and prone-to-drink assistant DA on NBC's *Law & Order* has also served a five-year "sentence" hawking TD Waterhouse online brokerage. Waterston tries to act natural as a brokerage spokesman and never pulls it off. It looks like he believes "I am being paid to do this gig so I should try and look convincing." He doesn't, and this association is like a flimsy case built on circumstantial evidence that has no hope of a conviction.

Herb the Nerd for Burger King

So let's take a perfectly fine actor, John Merrick, dress him up to look like a goofball, and call him Herb. Then, we will tell the world that Herb needs to see the promised land, a.k.a. Burger King (BK) land, because he has never had the pleasure of eating a tasty BK burger. Still with me? Problem is, Herb is too odd and weirds viewers out over and over again during the course of one year, 1985. BK's business drops, maybe because people are afraid they might encounter Herb at a Burger King outlet. Certainly one of the biggest flops in ad history—poor Herb really fizzled on the grill.

Mr. Six for Six Flags Theme Parks

Mr. Six reminds me of the serial killer John Wayne Gacy Jr., who performed circus acts for young boys before he chopped them up. Do parents want their kids to head over to Six Flags and meet some strange older dude who looks like Mr. Magoo, is odd beyond measure, and wants to greet the children? No, thanks; better to stick with Mickey Mouse or a couple of beers at Busch Gardens.

Why Spokespeople Today Are a Snore

Roughly 85 percent of promotions today fall flat for the same reason. Companies use models and actors who are never identified to play characters who are not named, have no unique personality, and deliver no lines worth remembering. I call these campaigns homogenized Kodak moments. They all look the same, sound the same, and as Macbeth said, "signify nothing."

The promotional industry has reached a low point in the creation of unique, memorable, and loveable characters or compelling spokespeople who grab attention and respect for the brand they represent.

Let's hope these last few chapters help some readers in the marketing profession understand what they are missing. Better still, perhaps they will think differently about how to create strong taglines, match them up with a believable or loveable character, and make marketing magic come alive once again for people to enjoy.

Everlasting

There is no good reason for so many marketing programs to be "dead on arrival" other than lack of knowledge about the essential ingredients for success. This book provides those ingredients. Use them. After all, life is too short for boring product pitches that no one cares about, remembers, or acts on. Do we marketers want to make an everlasting impression on consumers or just fade into oblivion wasting billions of dollars in the process? In a real sense, taglines that make the jump to powerline status are epitaphs of the marketers who create them. Famous commercial lines are just like famous last lines—they live on long after we exit the stage. Countless impressions come and go in a lifetime. Only a few really stick, often for decades or centuries. What a thrill to be a creator of those lines that conquer time.

Revelations

TIME NOW FOR A FEW WORDS on how marketers can maximize their media investments regardless of size and scope.

Start by appreciating the power of a few well-chosen words.

Slogans, taglines, jingles, and rhymes are a part of people's life experience and, in a very real sense, they can be surprisingly protective of them. Whether a nursery rhyme memorized in childhood or a line that defined the times in adulthood, powerlines have a special place in people's hearts and minds.

While researching this book, I asked hundreds of friends, colleagues, family, and random individuals about the slogans and taglines they remembered. The universal reaction was always an immediate "Steve, let me tell you ...." followed by an enthusiastic recitation of favorite beer or soda jingles, movie lines, political slogans, or lines from poetry and literature.

Clearly, a few well-chosen words can leave a lasting impression. Most marketers have forgotten how to create powerlines and build marketing programs around them.

To fill in the blanks, I offer seven revelations. Any business that follows this advice has a good chance of getting its message under the skin of the right consumers so that it remains there, causing them to take notice and place orders.

1. ***The more things change, the more taglines should not.*** Lines that connect with employees and consumers are priceless. Their power builds over time and is impervious to the whims of fashion.

A great line that sets a company or product apart from the competition should be kept and nurtured. Changing a tagline every few months means a failure to communicate the core brand promise. If that promise remains year after year, so too should the few best words that describe it.

Nevertheless, at many companies, a revolving door of marketing executives, marketing programs, CEOs, and CFOs guarantees a steady supply of executives longing to prove themselves by reinventing the wheel. In such circumstances, marketers find themselves on a short leash facing even shorter deadlines, answering to people who become impatient if the desired impact is not delivered within three to six months. This is very shortsighted behavior, with potentially dire consequences.

2. ***Creating a powerline is not difficult for people who understand how phrases become powerful in the first place.*** You can become one of those people by asking five questions about every tagline and slogan you consider.

1. Is the line clearly descriptive, and specific to nothing else in the category?
2. Is the line 100 percent true with no room for doubt? Do employees agree?
3. Is the line enjoyable, not bland or humorless?
4. Is the line the campaign's headline or head sound, depending on the media channel?
5. Is the line present in every communication to every constituency year after year after year?

When yes is the answer to all these questions, you have a powerline and will shortly find people adding your brand promise phrase to their top-of-mind instead of their never-mind.

These rules apply for any company or politician, country tourism board, nonprofit organization, new technogadget, fast-food item or, at a personal level, a new boyfriend or girlfriend.

Amazingly, most companies, politicians, and so on not only break one of these five rules, but break them all.

3. ***"Words calculated to catch everyone may catch no one."*** So said Adlai Stevenson, two-time unsuccessful presidential candidate. It is superb advice. Unfortunately, he didn't take it to heart when he ran against Dwight Eisenhower in 1952 and 1956. Stevenson's point seems lost on today's marketing wordsmiths, who continue to tout lines that are so general in meaning, they have no meaning. The in-vogue approach to creating slogans and taglines is this: agree on a generality, put it in small, hard-to-read type, never speak it out loud, and then change it every few months and see if another generality might work better. In the United States, where only 64 percent of people eligible to vote did so in the last presidential election, and where there are over five hundred thousand worthy causes to choose from, it is essential to present lines that set you far and apart from the competition.

Here's an example of what *not* to do. A few years back, the United Way of America paid good money to some consulting firm to coin the tagline: "What Matters." This has zero chance of making an impact on anyone and is best described by the line from *Macbeth* mentioned in Chapter 5: "signifying nothing."

What to do? Simply put, tell a unique story that no one else has ever said before, and do it with wordplay whenever possible. Also, try to inject emotion, attitude, or both.

4. ***Hollywood produces great lines because it is forced to.*** The film industry does a better-than-average job creating lines that sell. There's no room for error because a movie must grab attention in the marketplace quickly, and keep it for four to eight weeks prior to its release. By its very nature, a movie is a customized form of entertainment with a major story line or angle that strives to be different than previous movies. Other industries can learn from Hollywood and force themselves to think about an expensive marketing launch that must build

and maintain excitement in order to pay back the investment. The good news for Hollywood outsiders is the shelf life of products and services is often years and decades, not weeks and months.

5. ***A line delivered by a person or made-up character will gain more attention than a line delivered in any other way.*** Can you imagine a movie with no characters? Even most documentaries focus on individuals and tell a human-interest story. Key words: *human interest*. First and foremost, humans are most fascinated with other humans. Personality is everything. We look up to religious leaders, and have great passion for political front-runners, military heads, business icons, actors, chefs, fashion models, and occasionally … authors. Personality is everything. Even while asleep, we dream about people real and imagined. Thus, it is strange that the marketing profession and the business world in general think they can sell without the aid of a spokesperson or an endearing humanlike character. Yes it can be done, but it is much more difficult and dramatically reduces the odds of success. But be sure that the use of a character or spokesperson fits your selling premise and does not appear false or forced.

6. ***Sound off or risk consumer silence.*** Sound grabs attention and the mind is wired to accept and remember sound much more than the other dominant sense, sight. While smell, taste, and touch are very powerful, they are not part of the media mix from TV to radio to Internet, and are of limited use in print. If the receptivity to remember an advertising message equals 100 percent, 75 percent of that opportunity can be assigned to sound with the remaining 25 percent to the other senses combined. A line can become a powerline without the use of sound, but it takes far longer.

7. ***Marketing campaigns should be built around powerlines … not the other way around.*** It is clear from how slogans and taglines are used today that most marketers plug them into an overall theme or a communications plan merely as an afterthought. That is why most of these lines are invisible to the eye and make no impact with internal or external customers. A few companies do it right, like BMW who, for over three decades, has centered every ad on "The Ultimate Driving Machine."

There are other examples, such as De Beers with "A Diamond Is Forever," and The United Negro College Fund with "A Mind Is a Terrible Thing to Waste." None of these examples tries to force a line into a campaign theme. Companies large and small that make sure all their marketing efforts revolve around a great line are much more likely to steal mind-share and business from their competitors. The grand slam occurs when your slogan or tagline is also your unique selling proposition, that is, those few words that precisely define your core brand promise.

FINALLY, BEN FRANKLIN ONCE REMARKED, "either write something worth reading or do something worth writing." I sincerely hope you have enjoyed the subject of powerlines, which I believe if applied correctly can transform any company's marketing from ho-hum to wow in relatively short order. If you read this book and take my advice, chances are your marketing efforts will indeed be worth writing about. It all boils down to the way human behavior accounts for about two million years of evolution. You've got to hear it, and also see it, to believe it. And, with the billions of impressions that assault our eyes and ears during a lifetime, the ones that achieve real power are personality driven and exceed our expectations of normal everyday language. Think of a powerline as a Special Delivery message, one that continues to sell your product or service or candidate or experience—much to the delight and amazement of all.

NOTES

Introduction

viii *Words are loaded* Quoting French existentialist philosopher and writer Jean-Paul Sartre, from the essay "What Is Literature?"

xvi *There's a holdup* Television theme song, words and music by Nat Hiken and John Strauss (1960).

xvii *See the U.S.A.* "See the U.S.A. in Your Chevrolet," © 1950 by Chevrolet Division of General Motors Corp. Lyrics and music by Leo Corday and Leon Carr.

PART ONE: POWERLINES

Chapter 1 Powerlines Defined

3 *When it rains* "When it rains it pours®" Trademarked slogan of Morton Salt. Morton Salt tagline in 1912, created by N. W. Ayer & Son.

3 *You Deserve a* McDonald's tagline, introduced in 1971, created by Needham, Harper & Steers, words and music by Kevin Gavin and Sid Woloshin. © 1971 by G & W Publishing Corp.

3 *A Diamond Is* De Beers slogan coined in 1948 by N. W. Ayer & Son.

5 *A 1982 study* Ronald E. Millman, "The Infiuence of Background Music on the Behaviour of Restaurant Patrons," *Journal of Consumer Research*, 13 (1982).

6 *Many a page* Marshall McLuhan, *Understanding Media: The Extensions of Man*, Part II: "The Spoken Word" (Trussville, AL: Allied Publications, 1964).

8 *Rain, rain* Nursery Rhymes Origins and Lyrics (http://www.rhymes.org.uk/rain_rain_go_away.htm).

9 *Humpty Dumpty* Wikipedia (http://en.wikipedia.org/wiki/Humpty-Dumpty).

9 *Three blind mice* Nursery Rhymes Origins and Lyrics (http://www.rhymes.org.uk/three_blind_mice.htm).

10 *Jack and Jill* Nursery Rhymes Origins and Lyrics (http://www.rhymes.org.uk/jack_and_jill.htm).

10 *Ring Around the* Nursery Rhymes Origins and Lyrics (http://www.rhymes.org.uk/ring_around_the_rosy.htm).

Chapter 2 Powerlines Take to the Air

16 *a date that* Franklin Delano Roosevelt, National Archives, Washington, D.C.

16 *Yesterday, December 7,* "Yesterday, December 7, 1941 a date which will live in world history." Original draft of President Franklin Delano Roosevelt's congressional address (December 8, 1941) following the attack on Pearl Harbor. National Archives, Washington, D.C.

PART TWO: THE POWERLINE PERSPECTIVE

Chapter 3 Uncle Sam Wants You, Your Mind, Your Money

34 *We can do* World War II poster by J. Howard Miller urging women to enter the war effort by joining the work force.

34 *United We Win* A World War II poster (1943) depicting an African American participating in the war effort.

34 *Man the Guns* World War II Navy recruiting poster encouraging Americans to join the war.

34 *Loose Lips Sink* Slogan for the World War II information drive that warned Americans to limit talk about the war for reasons of security.

38, 39 *Live free or* Offlcial motto of New Hampshire, adopted by the General Court in 1945 from a toast written by General John Stark on July 31, 1809.

38, 39, 41 *I Love New* I♥NewYork—offlcial rebus motto of New York, created by Mary Wells Lawrence. In 1977, William S. Doyle, Deputy Commissioner of the New York State Department of Commerce hired the advertising agency Wells Rich Greene to develop a marketing campaign for New York State. Doyle also recruited Milton Glaser, a productive graphic designer to work on the campaign, and he created the design based on Wells Rich Greene's advertising campaign.

38 *Life Takes Visa* Visa credit card slogan introduced in 2006, during the Olympic Winter Games, created by BBDO.

38, 40 *Life/Changing* Business promotion slogan of Iowa, created by Write Solution Group.

38 *The Garden State* According to Alfred Heston's 1926 two-volume book, *Jersey Waggon Jaunts*, Browning called New Jersey the Garden State while speaking at the Philadelphia Centennial exhibition on New Jersey Day (August 24, 1876).

39 *Most of our* As reported in the *New York Times* article, "New Jersey Picks a Slogan: Come Read It for Yourself" (January 13, 2006).

39 *Unbridled Spirit* Brand of state of Kentucky, chosen by popular vote in the fall of 2004.

40 *The South's Warmest* The full slogan for Mississippi is "Feels Like Coming Home; The South's Warmest Welcome."

40 *The Green Mountain* Nickname for Vermont, in reference to the Green Mountains named by Samuel de Champlain in 1647.

40 *Beyond Your Dreams* "Beyond Your Dreams, Within Your Reach," © 2001–2007 Alaska Travel Industry Association. "Alaska (logotype) & Beyond Your Dreams" and "Within Your Reach" are registered marks of the Alaska Travel Industry Association.

40 *Georgia on My* Hit song, lyrics by Stuart Gorrell, music by Hoagy Carmichel, 1930.

41 *Right Here. Right* Illinois state slogan launched on April 25, 2000, created by BBDO Chicago.

43 *JAMAICA [logo]* Registered trademark of the Jamaica Tourist Board.

Chapter 4 You Can't Put the Toothpaste Back in the Tube

53 *Filthy Story Teller* *Harper's Magazine* (September 24, 1864).

58, 64 *Happy Days Are* "Happy Days Are Here Again," a song copyrighted in 1929 by Milton Ager (music) and Jack Yellen (lyrics); became closely associated with the 1932 campaign of Franklin Delano Roosevelt for the U.S. presidency and was prominent at the Democratic Party Convention of that year.

59 *Sunflowers die in* Kathleen Hall Jamieson, *Packaging The Presidency: A History and Criticism of Presidential Campaign Advertising* (New York: Oxford University Press, 1996).

60 *I'm Just Wild* A 1921 song written by Noble Sissle and Eubie Blake.

62 *Are You Better* Question posed by Ronald Reagan to President Jimmy Carter in the October 1980 presidential debate (In His Own Words, http://www.pbs.org/newshour/bb/remember/jan-june04/words_06-07.html).

63 *It's Morning Again* "Morning in America" is the common name of Ronald Reagan's 1984 political campaign television commercial, formally titled "Prouder, Stronger, Better" and featuring the opening line "It's morning again in America."

75 *Where have you* Lyrics of the song "Mrs. Robinson," written by Paul Simon and Art Garfunkel in 1968.

77 *Kinder, Gentler Nation* Promise by President George Herbert Walker Bush, In his inaugural address, of a more sensitive and caring policy toward the poor and disadvantaged.

77 *Read My Lips* A phrase used by George H. W. Bush on August 18, 1988 at the Republican National Convention as he accepted the nomination for the presidency in a speech written by Peggy Noonan.

77 *Building a Bridge* Campaign slogan and phrase of President Bill Clinton in his presidential inaugural speech in January 1977 (http://www.presidentsusa.net/campaignslogans.html).

77 *The Better Man* 1996 presidential campaign slogan of Bob Dole; television commercial aired on September 8, 1996 (http://www.presidentsusa.net/campaignslogans.html).

78 *Let America Be* A slogan used by John Kerry during his 2004 campaign (http://www.presidents usa.net/campaignslogans.html) and a phrase by the American poet, Langston Hughes.

Chapter 5 Shots Heard Round the World

81 *The shot heard* The phrase from the opening stanza of Ralph Waldo Emerson's "Concord Hymn" (1837), describing the impact of the battle at Old North Bridge in Concord, Massachusetts, on April 19, 1775.

82 *The die is* *De Vita Caesarum* ("Lives of the Caesers," best known in English as *The Twelve Caesers)* by Suetonius.

82 *I came, I* Plutarch and Suetonius (Plut. Caes. 50, Suet. Iul. 37).

83 *Put your trust* Actual quotation is, "Put your trust in God, my boys, and keep your powder dry!" This line is from the poem "Oliver's Advice" by Valentine Blacker, published in Edward Hayes, ed., *Ballads of Ireland* (originally published in 1856, currently published by Kessinger Pub Co.).

83 *I wish to* From John Paul's Jones' letter to Le Ray de Chaumont (November 16, 1778).

83 *Praise the Lord* Chaplain Howell Forgy, aboard the USS *New Orleans*, during the Japanese attack on Pearl Harbor on December 7, 1941 (http://www.history.navy.mil/photos/pers-us/uspers-f/h-forgy.htm).

87 *My fellow Americans* Phrase from John F. Kennedy's inaugural address on January 20, 1961 (http://www.bartleby.com/124/pres56.html).

87 *When we allow* From Martin Luther King's "I Have a Dream" speech on August 28, 1963, from the steps of the Lincoln Memorial during the March on Washington for Jobs and Freedom (http://www.usconstitution.net/dream.html).

87 *Mr. Gorbachev, open* Words of President Reagan at the Brandenburg Gate of the Berlin wall in West Berlin, Germany (June 12, 1987).

88 *Had we but* Andrew Marvell's "To His Coy Mistress" in Margaret Ferguson, Jon Stallworthy, and Mary Jo Salter, eds., *The Norton Anthology of Poetry* (New York: W. W. Norton, 2005).

89 *I will not* William Blake's "Jerusalem" in Margaret Ferguson, Jon Stallworthy, and Mary Jo Salter, eds., *The Norton Anthology of Poetry* (New York: W. W. Norton, 2005).

89 *How dull it* "Ulysses" in Margaret Ferguson, Jon Stallworthy, and Mary Jo Salter, eds., *The Norton Anthology of Poetry* (New York: W. W. Norton, 2005).

90 *Ah, love, let* "Dover Beach" in Margaret Ferguson, Jon Stallworthy, and Mary Jo Salter, eds., *The Norton Anthology of Poetry* (New York: W. W. Norton, 2005).

90 *Smart lad, to* "To an Athlete Dying Young" in Margaret Ferguson, Jon Stallworthy, and Mary Jo Salter, eds., *The Norton Anthology of Poetry* (New York: W. W. Norton, 2005).

91 *Stars, I have* "Stars, I Have Seen Them Fall" in Margaret Ferguson, Jon Stallworthy, and Mary Jo Salter, eds., *The Norton Anthology of Poetry* (New York: W. W. Norton, 2005).

92 *Turning and turning* "The Second Coming" in Margaret Ferguson, Jon Stallworthy, and Mary Jo Salter, eds., *The Norton Anthology of Poetry* (New York: W. W. Norton, 2005).

92 *Something there is* "Mending Wall" in Margaret Ferguson, Jon Stallworthy, and Mary Jo Salter, eds., *The Norton Anthology of Poetry* (New York: W. W. Norton, 2005).

93 *There where it* From Edward Connery, *The Poetry of Robert Frost* (Connery Lathem, 1915).

93 *Two roads diverged* "The Road Not Taken" in Margaret Ferguson, Jon Stallworthy, and Mary Jo Salter, eds., *The Norton Anthology of Poetry* (New York: W. W. Norton, 2005).

93 *Then took the* "Stopping By Woods on a Snowy Evening" in Margaret Ferguson, Jon Stallworthy, and Mary Jo Salter, eds., *The Norton Anthology of Poetry* (New York: W. W. Norton, 2005).

94 *Gentleman, I have seen* "Gentleman, I have seen hell. Hell, is a half-full auditorium." An interview with Robert Frost when he was asked if he thought that hell existed.

94 *In the room* "The Love Song of J. Alfred Prufrock" in Margaret Ferguson, Jon Stallworthy, and Mary Jo Salter, eds., *The Norton Anthology of Poetry* (New York: W. W. Norton, 2005).

95 *I am moved* "Preludes" in Margaret Ferguson, Jon Stallworthy, and Mary Jo Salter, eds., *The Norton Anthology of Poetry* (New York: W. W. Norton, 2005).

96 *This is the* "The Hollow Man" in Margaret Ferguson, Jon Stallworthy, and Mary Jo Salter, eds., *The Norton Anthology of Poetry* (New York: W. W. Norton, 2005).

96 *By the time* "Unfortunate Coincidence" in Margaret Ferguson, Jon Stallworthy, and Mary Jo Salter, eds., *The Norton Anthology of Poetry* (New York: W. W. Norton, 2005).

96 *Razors pain you* "Resume" in Margaret Ferguson, Jon Stallworthy, and Mary Jo Salter, eds., *The Norton Anthology of Poetry* (New York: W. W. Norton, 2005).

97 *it's / spring / and* "in just" in Margaret Ferguson, Jon Stallworthy, and Mary Jo Salter, eds., *The Norton Anthology of Poetry* (New York: W. W. Norton, 2005).

97 *I will not* "I sing of Olaf glad and big" in Margaret Ferguson, Jon Stallworthy, and Mary Jo Salter, eds., *The Norton Anthology of Poetry* (New York: W. W. Norton, 2005).

98 *To be or not to be* William Shakespeare's *The Tragedy of Hamlet, Prince of Denmark* (Act 3, Scene 1).

98 *Thus conscience does* William Shakespeare's *The Tragedy of Hamlet, Prince of Denmark* (Act 3, Scene 1).

98 *Get thee to* William Shakespeare's *The Tragedy of Hamlet, Prince of Denmark* (Act 3, Scene 1).

99 *The lady doth* William Shakespeare's *The Tragedy of Hamlet, Prince of Denmark* (Act 3, Scene 2).

99 *Why, then the* William Shakespeare's *Merry Wives of Windsor* (Act 2, Scene 2).

99 *All the world's* William Shakespeare's *As You Like It (*Act 2, Scene 7).

99 *Good night, good* William Shakespeare's *Romeo and Juliet* (Act 2, Scene 2).

100 *Now is the* William Shakespeare's feelings about the state of the English nation during the Wars of the Roses and put it into print in *Richard III* (Act 1, scene 1).

100 *Off with his* William Shakespeare's *Richard III* (Act 3, scene 4).

100 *A horse! A* William *Shakespeare's Richard III* (Act 5, scene 4).

101 *Et tu* William Shakespeare's *Julius Ceasar* (Act 3, Scene 1).

101 *way to* Part of Macbeth's soliloquy in William Shakespeare's *Macbeth* (Act 5, Scene 5).

Chapter 6 There Is Nothing Wrong with Your Television Set

105 *Frankly my dear* Rhett Butler delivers to Scarlett O'Hara in the movie *Gone With The Wind* based on the novel written by Margaret Mitchell.

105 *There's no place* The closing line in the story *The Wizard of OZ*, written by Lyman Frank Baum in 1898.

105 *Here's looking at* From the movie *Casablanca* (1942).

106 *Bond, James Bond* How the fictional British agent, created in 1952 by writer Ian Fleming, introduces himself in the novels and movies.

106 *Do you have* A line from *Dr. No* a 1962 spy film, the first film in the James Bond series written by Ian Fleming.

106 *I want to say* Quote from the movie *The Graduate* (1967), directed by Mike Nichols, based on the novel of the same name by Charles Webb.

106 *We older folks* Line from the 1967 comedy-drama-romance, *The Graduate* directed by Mike Nichols, based on the novel of the same name by Charles Webb.

106 *I know what* From the 1971 crime film *Dirty Harry*, directed by Don Siegel, the first of the series.

107 *Crime is out* Line from *Dirty Harry*, starring Clint Eastwood.

107 *I'm gonna make* From the movie *The Godfather* (1972), spoken by Don Corleone.

107 *In Sicily, women* From the movie *The Godfather* (1972), spoken by Calo to Sonny.

107 *My father made* From the movie *The Godfather* (1972), spoken by Michael Corleone.

108 *Leave the* From the movie *The Godfather* (1972), spoken by Clemenza.

108 *I'm mad as* From the 1976 satirical film *Network* written by Paddy Chayefsky and directed by Sidney Lumet.

108 *Going to hell* From the movie *Network* spoken by Howard Beale.

108 *I'll have what* From the movie *When Harry Met Sally* (1989).

110 *In space no* Part of the title of the movie *Alien* (1979).

110 *Don't go* From the movie *Jaws* (1975), written by Steven Spielberg, taken from the novel by Peter Benchley.

110 *Size does matter* Part of the movie title, *Godzilla—Size Does Matter* (1998), starring Matthew Broderick, directed by Roland Emmerich.

111 *A long time* Line from the opening crawl at the beginning of each *Star Wars* film, written and directed by George Lucas.

111 *Just when you* The publicity slogan for the film *Jaws 2* (1978).

111 *A lot can* The tagline of the movie *Fargo* (1996), starring Frances McDormand and William H. Macy and directed by Joel Coen.

111 *Earth. It was* Slogan of the movie *Independence Day* (1996), directed by Roland Emmerich and written by Dean Devlin and Roland Emmerich.

111 *He is afraid* Line from *ET, the Extra-Terrestrial* (1982), coproduced and directed by Steven Spielberg, written by Melissa Mathison and starring Henry Thomas, Robert MacNaughton, Drew Barrymore, Dee Wallace, and Peter Coyote.

111 *Look closer* Tagline for the 1999 comedy/drama film *American Beauty*, written by Alan Ball and directed by Sam Mendes.

112 *Love means never* Tagline of the movie *Love Story* (1970), written by Erich Segal and directed by Arthur Hiller.

112 *Die Harder* Tagline for the movie *Die Hard 2* (1990), written by Walter Wager and Steven de Souza and directed by Renny Harlin.

117 *Faster than a* Opening line of the TV series *Superman,* starring George Reeves in 1952, directed by Howard Bretherton and Thomas Carr, written by Dick Hamilton and Roy Hamilton.

118 *Man, woman, birth* Opening line of the *Ben Casey* show, spoken by Sam Jaffe (Dr. David Zorba), also starring Vince Edwards.

119 *The thrill of* Description of the catastrophic wipeout of Slovene ski jumper Vinko Bogataj at the World Ski Flying Championships in 1970.

119 *There is nothing* Opening line of *Outer Limits* which ran from 1963 to 1965 in black and white and from 1995 to 2002 in color.

120 *To boldly go* Part of the opening lines spoken at the beginning of the *Star Trek* television episodes and fllms, from 1966 onward.

121 *Space the nal* Phrase used in the title sequence of most episodes of the *Star Trek* series.

121 *Yada Yada* On the *Sein eld* television series, the phrase used by George's girlfriend.

PART THREE: PUT A POWERLINE IN YOUR TANK

Chapter 7 When It Rains It Pours

127 *M&M's, melts in* Developed from the original M&M's tagline, "The milk chocolate melts in your mouth, not in your hand" in 1954, created by Ted Bates & Co.

127 *When it rains* "When it rains it pours®" Trademarked slogan of Morton Salt, created by N. W. Ayer & Son.

127 *When it absolutely* Federal Express tagline, created by Ally & Gargano, 1982.

127 *The pause that* Slogan used by Coca-Cola in 1929, created by D'Arcy Co.

128 *Your World, Delivered* Trademark of AT&T, created by GSD&M Advertising in 2005.

129 *Children Cry for* Available at http://www.waltergrutchfleld.net/castoria.htm.

129 *A Diamond Is* De Beers slogan coined in 1948 by N. W. Ayer & Son.

130 *Come to Marlboro* Tagline created in 1965 by Leo Burnett; also "Marlboro—Come to where the fiavor is" (1964, Leo Burnett).

130 *Before you scold* Ad headline in *The Saturday Evening Post* 1950. Agency unknown.

131 *The Marlboro Man* Trademark of Philip Morris, Inc., created by the Leo Burnett Co., 1955.

132 *Come to Marlboro* Come to Marlboro Country (1965, Leo Burnett).

133 *The pause that* Slogan used by Coca-Cola in 1929, created by D'Arcy Co.

133 *Drink Coca-Cola* Slogan used by Coca-Cola in 1986 (http://members.aol.com/CColaRulez/index.html).

133 *It's the real* Coca-Cola jingle in 1971, ending the popular "Things Go Better With Coke" campaign.

133 *Think Small* Tagline for Volkswagen in 1959, created by Doyle Dane Bernbach.

135 *Just Do It* Nike slogan, created in 1988 by Wieden and Kennedy.

135 *There is no* Nike slogan, created in 1977 by Wieden and Kennedy.

135 *You deserve a* McDonald's tagline, introduced in 1971, created by Needham, Harper & Steers. Words and music by Kevin Gavin and Sid Woloshin, © 1971 by G & W Publishing Corp.

136 *When It Absolutely* Federal Express tagline, created by Ally & Gargano, 1982.

137 *When It Rains* "When it rains it pours®" Trademarked slogan of Morton Salt. Morton Salt tagline in 1912, created by N. W. Ayer & Son.

138 *M&M's Melts in* Developed from the original M&M's tagline, "The milk chocolate melts in your mouth, not in your hand" in 1954, created by Ted Bates & Co.

140 *You Don't Have* Levy's Baking tagline in 1949, created by Doyle Dane Bernbach, specifically Bill Bernbach.

142 *Your World, Delivered* Trademark of AT&T, created by GSD&M Advertising in 2005.

143 *Life/Changing* Business promotion slogan of Iowa, created by Write Solution Group.

144 *Rising* United Airlines tagline that, in 1997 for the flrst time since 1965, departed from the familiar "friendly skies."

146 *Life Takes Visa* Visa credit card slogan introduced in 2006, during the Olympic Winter Games, created by BBDO.

146 *The Last Real* Coors tagline, all but dropped by 1998, created by Foote, Cone & Belding.

146 *Higher Standards* Bank of America tagline, created by Catherine P. Bessant, Bank of America's chief marketing offlcer.

Chapter 8 Jingles All the Way

151 *Move your family* Early 1800s jingle by unknown artist (http://www.lyrics007.com/Unknown% 20Lyrics/Elanoy%20Lyrics.html).

152 *Sing, oh, sing* http://www.csufresno.edu/folklore/drinkingsongs/mp3s/field-work/other-collections/ed-cray-collection/american/lydia083.txt.

152 *Come, come, come* A 1903 Busch advertisement song, "Under the Anheuser Bush" (words by Andrew Sterling and music by Henry von Tilzer).

152 *Have you tried* First ever singing radio commercial in 1926, written by M. K. Jerome and Blanche Merrill, sung to the tune of "Jazz Baby," © 1929 by General Mills, Inc.

153 *When the values* Robert Hall Clothing Stores jingle, music by Leon Mitchell, words by Charles A. Gaston. Original version © 1946 copyright by Charles A. Gaston and Leon Mitchell.

153 *Chock Full o'* Chock Full o' Nuts jingle, "That Heavenly Feeling," written by Wayne and Bruce Silbert, frequently played over the radio airwaves in the 1950s and 1960s, sung by the boss's wife, singer Page Morton Black.

153 *N E S T L É S Nestlés Makes* Words and music © 1952 by Nestlé's Chocolate Company, Inc.

154 *My beer is* Reingold Beer jingle of the 1950s. Creator unknown.

154 *Schaefer is the* Schaefer Beer jingle, one of New York's most famous jingles, put to music and used as a jingle from the 1950s to the 1970s. The music was written by Jim Jordan of BBDO, on his son's xylophone.

155 *If you've got* Miller High Life Beer Jingle written by Bill Backer.

156 *You deserve a* McDonald's tagline, introduced in 1971, created by Needham, Harper & Steers, words and music by Kevin Gavin and Sid Woloshin. © 1971 by G & W Publishing Corp.

156 *Be all that* Army tagline, created by N. W. Ayer in 1981.

156 *M'm! M'm! Good!* Campbell Soup jingle, created by BBDO in 1935.

156 *See the U.S.A.* Chevrolet jingle, words and music by Leon Carr and Leo Corday. © 1950 by Leo Corday and Leon Carr and © 1950 by General Motors Corporation (Chevrolet Motor Division).

156 *I wish I* "The Wiener Song," written by Richard D. Trentlage (ASCAP) and Arthur L. Zapel, Jr. (ASCAP). © 1965 by Oscar Meyer Foods.

156 *Double your pleasure* "Double Your Pleasure," music by Richard Robinson ("Dick") Cunliffe, words and music by Myron Edward ("Mike") Chon. © 1959 copyright by William Wrigley Jr. [Chewing Gum] Company.

156 *Winston tastes good* Jingle for Winston cigarettes from 1954 to 1972, created by Reynolds president Bowman Gray Jr. and the William Esty Company, flrst aired in 1955.

156 *A little dab'll* Brylcreem Hair Cream jingle, music by John P. Atherton, words by Hanley Norins. © 1946 by Brylcreem Hair Cream.

156 *I'd Like to* Coca-Cola jingle, words and music by Roger F. Cook, Roquel B. Davis, William M. ("Bill") Backer, and Roger John Reginald Greenaway. © 1971 by Coca-Cola.

157 *Just for the* Trademark of the Coca-Cola Company in 1983, created by SSC&B-Lintas.

157 *Anticipation* Song, written by Carly Simon, made famous by a Heinz ketchup commer cial in the late 1970s.

157 *I Heard It* Composed by Barrett Strong and Norman Whitfleld in 1967.

157 *Lord, won't you* An a cappella song sung by Janis Joplin and cowritten with the poet Michael McClure and Bob Neuwirth, used by Mercedes flrst in 1995 and again in 2007.

157 *Like a Rock* Title song written by Bob Seger and used in Chevy pickup truck ads.

158 *Leaving on a* Song written by John Denver in 1967; a version of the song by Sophie Barker was also used in advertisements for British Airways.

158 *American Express Travelers* Tagline created in 1975 by David Ogilvy of Ogilvy & Mather, as part of an ad campaign featuring actor Karl Malden.

158 *Like a good* "Like a Good Neighbor" jingle, words by Jerry Gavin and Keith Reinhard, music by Barry Manilow. © 1976 by G & W Publishing Co.

158 *GE. We bring* "We Bring Good Things To Life" jingle by Thomas G. McFaul and David Lucas. © 1979 by General Electric.

158 *Come to where* Tagline created in 1965 by Leo Burnett.

158 *Zoom, Zoom, Zoom* Title of the song performed by Serapis Bey, recorded long before it became the offlcial song for Mazda, for the movie *Only The Strong* (1993).

159 *I Love New* I♥NewYork—offlcial rebus motto of New York, created by Mary Wells Lawrence. In 1977, William S. Doyle, Deputy Commissioner of the New York State Department of Commerce hired the advertising agency Wells Rich Greene to develop a marketing campaign for New York State. Doyle also recruited Milton Glaser, a productive graphic designer to work on the campaign, and he created the design based on Wells Rich Greene's advertising campaign.

Chapter 9 The Gun That Won the West

163 *Don't leave home* Tagline created in 1975 by David Ogilvy of Ogilvy & Mather, as part of an ad campaign featuring actor Karl Malden.

163 *Life/Changing* Business promotion slogan of Iowa, created by Write Solution Group.

163 *Total Living* *Total Living* is a service mark of Merrill Lynch & Co., Inc. © 2007 Merrill Lynch, Pierce, Fenner & Smith Incorporated.

163 *Life Takes Visa* Visa credit card slogan introduced in 2006, during the Olympic Winter Games, created by BBDO.

165 *Your World. Delivered.* Trademark of AT&T, created by GSD&M Advertising in 2005.

166, 167 *Make it happen.* "Make it happen.™" is a trademark of Royal Bank of Scotland Group.

168 *World Wise.* Slogan © 2007 by Morgan Stanley.

169 *Inspire the Next* Hitachi slogan, created by Dentsu, Inc.

170 *connectedthinking* Trademark of PricewaterhouseCoopers LLP.

171 *Life. Liberty. And* Trademarked slogan of GM Corp., created by Modernista, Boston, MA, and introduced August 2006.

172, 173 *Life's a Journey* Samsonite slogan, trademark of the Samsonite Corporation, developed by TBWA\Worldwide (via TBWA\Brussels) in 2005.

172, 173 *Every journey needs* Tagline of the *Wall Street Journal* © 2007 Dow Jones & Company. Web and print campaign designed by T3.

174 *There is no* Trademark of Deutsche Lufthansa AG.

175 *You can see* Trademark of United Technologies Corporation.

177 *Put another shrimp* Phrase that originated in a series of television advertisements by the Australian Tourism Commission starring Paul Hogan from 1984 through to 1990. The actual quote is, "I'll slip an extra shrimp on the barbie for you." The actual ad slogan was, "Come and say G'day." Ads were developed by the Australian agency Mojo in conjunction with N. W. Ayer.

178 *Where the Bloody* An AU$180 million advertising campaign launched in 2006 by Tourism Australia and created by the Sydney office of the London advertising agency M&C Saatchi.

177, 178 *Forever New Orleans* Trademark of the New Orleans Metropolitan Convention & Visitors Bureau. Created by Pat McGuinness and Robbie Vitrano.

178 *Where Next?* Trademark of Tumi, Inc.

178, 179 *The Bold Look* Trademark of the Kohler Co.

180, 181 *Get Chucked.* Trademark of Converse Inc. Created by YARD, New York, for the John Varvatos line of Converse products, 2006.

184 *Fully invested in* Trademark of A.G. Edwards & Sons, Inc. © 2007 A.G. Edwards & Sons, Inc. Created by Carmichael Lynch.

185 *We'll give you* Service mark of Principal Financial Services, Inc. © 2005 Principal Financial Services, Inc.

186, 187 *You're in good* Registered trademark of Allstate Insurance Company. Created by Allstate general sales manager Davis W. Ellis.

187 *The standard for* Trademark of U.S. Trust Corporation.

188 *The Ultimate Driving* Registered trademark of BMW AG. Created by Ammirati Puris AvRutick in 1975.

188, 189 *Work Hard. Fly* Registered trademark of Continental Airlines (1998).

188, 189 *Generations of Style* Trademark of Brooks Brothers.

190 *Extravagant Taste.* Trademark of General Cigar Company, Inc.

190 *That Was Easy.* Service mark of Staples, Inc. (2003).

191 *Home Page for* Trademark of Forbes.com.

191, 192 *The Power of* Registered trademark of the Transamerica Corporation.

192, 193 *61 straight years* Trademark of PPL Corporation.

193, 194 *Triumph in your* Trademark of the University of Chicago Graduate School of Business.

194 *Heaven on Earth* Trademark of Shangri-La Hotels and Resorts.

195 *Where will you* Trademark of Shangri-La Hotels and Resorts.

194–196 *Paul Smith* Slogan of Paul Smith Clothiers. © Paul Smith.

198 *A Diamond is* De Beers slogan coined in 1948 by N. W. Ayer & Son.

198 *Just Do It* Nike slogan, created in 1988 by Wieden and Kennedy.

198 *When it absolutely* Federal Express tagline, created by Ally & Gargano, 1982.

200 *I Love New York* I♥NewYork—offlcial rebus motto of New York, created by Mary Wells Lawrence. In 1977, William S. Doyle, Deputy Commissioner of the New York State Department of Commerce hired the advertising agency Wells Rich Greene to develop a marketing campaign for New York State. Doyle also recruited Milton Glaser, a productive graphic designer to work on the campaign, and he created the design based on Wells Rich Greene's advertising campaign.

201 *Keep Boulder Weird* A slogan and campaign begun by a local small-business owner.

Chapter 10 Character Building

208 *Mr. Clean, Mr.* Trademark of Procter & Gamble, created by Tatham-Laird & Kudner in 1958. Jingle was written in 1958 by Thomas Scott Cadden.

211 *Oh no, Mr.* "Mr. Bill" created, written, and produced by Walter Williams in 1974, flrst aired on *Saturday Night Live* on May 29, 1976.

216 *And thank you* Tagline for Bartles & Jaymes television commercials, created by Hal Riney (1985–1991). Two elderly gentlemen characters, Frank Bartles and Ed Jaymes (played by David Joseph Rufkahr and Dick Maugg, respectively), spoken by Bartles.

217 *It's a miracle.* Tagline spoken by Brother Dominick in 1977 Xerox Copiers television commercial.

217 *Where's the beef?* Tagline for a Wendy's television commercial, created by Joe Sedelmaier and delivered by actress Clara Peller, that first aired on January 10, 1984.

217 *Prices are Insaaaaane!* Tagline for Crazy Eddie stores, first delivered in 1972 by late-night disc jockey Jerry ("Dr. Jerry") Carroll.

218 *See the U.S.A.* Chevrolet jingle, words and music by Leon Carr and Leo Corday. © 1950 by Leo Corday and Leon Carr and © 1950 by General Motors Corporation (Chevrolet Motor Division).

220 *Smith Barney. They* Theme made famous by actor John Houseman from 1979 to 1986, later by Leo McKern in 1987 and 1988.

220 *Don't leave home* Tagline created in 1975 by David Ogilvy of Ogilvy & Mather, as part of an ad campaign featuring actor Karl Malden.

Revelations

227 *Words calculated to* Quote from Adlai Stevenson's speech to the Democratic National Convention, 1952.

228 *A Diamond Is* De Beers slogan coined in 1948 by N. W. Ayer & Son.

BIBLIOGRAPHY

Bisbort, Alan. *Famous Last Words*. Petaluma, CA: Pomegranate Communications, 2001.

Boller Jr., Paul F. *Presidential Campaigns*. Oxford: Oxford University Press, 1984.

Dotz, Warren, and Jim Morton, *What a Character! 20th Century American Advertising Icons*. San Francisco: Chronicle Books, 1996.

Ferguson, Margaret, Mary Jo Salter, and Jon Stallworthy, eds. *The Norton Anthology of Poetry*. New York: W.W. Norton & Company, Inc., 1996.

Foreman, Jonathan. *The Pocketbook of Patriotism*. New York: Sterling Publishing Co., Inc., 2005.

Hawkins, Jeff. *On Intelligence*. New York: Henry Holt, 2004.

Levitin, Daniel J. *This is Your Brain on Music: The Science of a Human Obsession*. New York: Penguin, 2006.

Lindstrom, Martin. *Brand Sense: Build Powerful Brands through Touch, Taste, Smell, Sight, and Sound*. New York: Free Press, 2005.

McDonough, John, and Karen Egolf, eds. *The Advertising Age Encyclopedia of Advertising*. New York: Fitzroy Dearborn, 2003.

McLuhan, Marshall. *Understanding Media: The Extensions of Man*. Cambridge, MA: MIT Press, 1964.

INDEX

W

X

Y

Z

ABOUT THE AUTHOR

Steve Cone is chief marketing officer for Epsilon, a leading provider of data-driven marketing technologies and services. With more than thirty-five years at the top of the marketing profession, Cone has worked with a wide array of major clients and companies, including Apple, AARP, Citigroup, American Express, and United Airlines, as well as global media companies, environmental groups, and presidential campaigns for both major parties. He lectures worldwide at leading universities and business groups on the proven marketing principles laid out in his first book, *Steal These Ideas!* (Bloomberg Press, 2005).